W9-APZ-505

Presented to the

Ironside Memorial Library

by

Daniel Rosenberger

 PRINTED IN U.S.A.

LIBRARY
BRYAN COLLEGE
DAYTON, TN. 37321

# THE WELFARE STATE AND THE NATIONAL WELFARE ❧ ❧ ❧ ❧

*A Symposium on some of the threatening tendencies of our times*

"The third and most cogent reason for restricting the interference of government is the great evil of adding unnecessarily to its power. Every function superadded to those already exercised by the government causes its influence over hopes and fears to be more widely diffused, and converts, more and more, the active and ambitious part of the public into hangers-on of the government, or of some party which aims at becoming the government."—John Stuart Mill, *On Liberty*.

ह**

"Those who won our independence believed that the final end of the State was to make men free to develop their faculties. . . . They valued liberty both as an end and as a means. They believed liberty to be the secret of happiness and courage to be the secret of liberty."—Justice Louis D. Brandeis, concurring in *Whitney v. California*, 274 U. S. 357, 375 (1927).

ह**

"Experience should teach us to be most on our guard to protect liberty when the Government's purposes are beneficent. Men born to freedom are naturally alert to repel invasion of their liberty by evil-minded rulers. The greatest dangers to liberty lurk in insidious encroachment by men of zeal, well-meaning but without understanding."—Brandeis, J., dissenting in *Olmstead v. United States*, 277 U. S. 438, 479 (1927).

ह**

"It is the duty of those serving the people in public place to closely limit public expenditures to the actual needs of the Government economically administered, because this bounds the right of the Government to exact tribute from the earnings of labor or the property of the citizen, and because public extravagance begets extravagance among the people. . . . A due regard for the interests and prosperity of all the people demands that our finances shall be established upon such a sound and sensible basis as shall secure the safety and confidence of business interests and make the wage of labor sure and steady, and that our system of revenue shall be so adjusted as to relieve the people of unnecessary taxation, having a due regard to the interests of capital invested and workingmen employed in American industries and preventing the accumulation of a surplus in the Treasury to tempt extravagance and waste."—Grover Cleveland, *First Inaugural Address*, March 4, 1885.

ह**

"He has erected a multitude of New Offices, and sent hither swarms of Officers to harass our people, and eat out their substance . . . for altering fundamentally the Forms of our Governments."—*Declaration of Independence*.

ह**

". . . Politics is a business of interpretation, and no men are fit for it who do not see and seek more than their own advantage and interest." —Woodrow Wilson, *Address on Occasion of the Rededication and Restoration of Congress Hall*, Philadelphia, October 25, 1913.

# THE WELFARE STATE AND THE NATIONAL WELFARE ❧ ❧ *A Symposium*

*on some of the threatening tendencies of our times*

❧ ❧ ❧ Edited, with an *Introduction,* by

SHELDON GLUECK

Roscoe Pound Professor of Law
Harvard Law School

1952

ADDISON-WESLEY PRESS, INC.
CAMBRIDGE 42, MASSACHUSETTS

*Copyright 1952*

**ADDISON-WESLEY PRESS, INC.**

*Printed in the United States of America*

ALL RIGHTS RESERVED. THIS BOOK, OR PARTS THEREOF, MAY NOT BE REPRODUCED IN ANY FORM WITHOUT WRITTEN PERMISSION OF THE PUBLISHERS.

# Contents

30218

*Preface*

THIS VOLUME is a symposium of addresses and articles dealing with some of the more questionable politico-economic improvisations of the past decade.

In November, 1949, at the invitation of the Faculty of the New York School of Social Work of Columbia University, I delivered an address at the installation of its new Dean, Kenneth D. Johnson. At the close of the exercises, in a conversation with General Dwight D. Eisenhower, then the active President of Columbia University, I remarked that it might be helpful to the perplexed citizen at the present juncture in American public affairs if he, President Eisenhower, were to bring out a collection of articles expressing the views of those who are as earnestly concerned with the dangers inherent in the political and economic drifts of the times as he so obviously is.

He suggested that I do so. Hence this book.

Preoccupation with other projects has prevented my getting at this one until recently; but I wish to point out that the idea of the book and most of its preparation occurred long before the historic announcement that General Eisenhower would be a candidate.

This symposium is, frankly, one-sided, although it is many-faceted. It presents some of the views of those who have doubt and concern about what has been happening in Washington, and thence in other parts of the country, on the socio-economic front. The materials brought together here are not designed to advance any new, earth-shaking economic theory. The contributors have attempted no more than the modest job of frankly setting down their views and apprehensions. It is perhaps not too great an exaggeration to say that their misgivings might well be mirrored in the quotations on the first page of this book.

Because of the distinction of the contributors in their various professions, it is hoped that their views may win a much wider audience than the limited, special groups before which they were originally presented.

While this collection emphasizes domestic socio-economic policies, no student of the vast issues involved can avoid noting their close relationship to foreign affairs.   But to keep the problem in focus, I have included here only statements regarding domestic policy, with an occasional exception such as notable passages in Mr. Baruch's testimony before the Senate Foreign Relations Committee in January, 1948, on his "Peace Waging Program."

As the one responsible for bringing these contributors together between the covers of this book, I may be permitted to introduce them; not, of course, as individuals, for they are obviously too well known for that, but as a group.

This company of protesters includes Democrats and Republicans and New Dealers (and, perhaps, a somewhat disillusioned Fair Dealer or two).   It embraces statesmen, educators, lawyers, engineers, economists, journalists.

Despite this variety of politics and professional interests, these men have a few striking characteristics in common:

They are wholesomely patriotic men—not in any cheap chauvinistic sense and not to the exclusion of a realistic recognition of the relationship of American problems to world affairs. Their patriotism consists simply of a justifiable appreciation of the American dream and the American achievement.   They would like our country to develop much farther its enormous potentialities, as an ever more striking demonstration and symbol of what free men of energy, vision, and devotion to ideals of the worth of man and the value of fair play can accomplish.

They are independent and courageous men, who feel it their

responsibility to raise their voices in protest or at least in warning against governmental policies that seem to them to be contrary to the best interests of the country as a whole.     This obligation, they feel, transcends any blind loyalties to political party.

They are men who, apart from the evidence of their conspicuous achievements in the various professions, possess a great deal of old-fashioned common sense, not easily deflected or duped by shibboleths or slogans.

I verily believe, therefore, that it will well repay the reader's time not merely to read but to reflect upon what these men have to say.

ॐ

I am very grateful to the contributors for their cooperation.

Earnest thanks are due the following for permission to reproduce some of the materials in this book: The Board of Trustees of the Leland Stanford Junior University, the New Jersey Bar Association, the Editors of the *Journal of the American Bar Association,* the Editors of the *Harvard Business Review,* the Editors of *Life* magazine, the Editors of *Newsweek,* and the Editors of *Vital Speeches.*

I regret very much that an article by Senator Wayne Morse reached me too late for inclusion in this volume.

As usual, I am indebted to the wisdom and encouragement of my wife, Eleanor Touroff Glueck.

My secretary, Esther C. Ghostlaw, deserves my sincere thanks for her careful and patient typing of the manuscript.

*Harvard Law School,*                        SHELDON GLUECK
*February 9, 1952.*

# Introduction

🙠 🙠 🙠 LIBERALISM AND THE
MANAGEMENT OF WELFARE

BY SHELDON GLUECK

## I

EVEN the most optimistic among us must now concede that the times are sorely out of joint, and that men stand fearfully in the presence of forces which threaten the downfall of values it has taken thousands of years to achieve.

We shall be reminded that on many previous occasions—at different crucial stages in the history of the Ancients, of Feudalism, of the Dark Ages—pessimism ultimately proved unwarranted. But in the total sum and substance of the threatening clouds, the drama of history has rarely before shown such potential for blood and destruction and the very quashing of civilization itself.

Is it necessary to catalogue the symptoms of society's malaise? Here are a few.

Abroad, among peoples of the Western democratic and humanitarian tradition, a darkening scene of profound economic weakness and physical and moral fatigue: Terrific destruction, in two brief wars, of goods, houses, instruments of production, and other wealth it has taken ages to accumulate. Continuous and health-threatening reduction of the standard of living. Cumulative physical, mental, and spiritual illness. A mass psychosis of hopelessness and cynicism engendered by first-hand acquaintance with terrifying danger and repeated

1

disillusionment in the power of man to govern his fellowmen efficiently, honestly, and justly. Governments established in the democratic tradition, but often woefully weak because pasted together of elements more interested in divergencies than in areas of agreement. A Stalin curtain relentlessly pushing forward to embrace peoples which, only when not watched by the ubiquitous political police, are still permitted to weep when they remember the Zion of freedom. A self-chosen camarilla of cynical and ruthless leaders who have committed the supreme crime of turning the first principles of elementary morality upside down by calling a slave camp a "people's democracy" and justifying the torture and slaying of millions of political, economic, or religious dissidents because, forsooth, the noble hearts of these self-chosen prophets of a new heaven on earth bleed for the common working man who has nothing to lose but his capitalistic chains!

The Marshall Plan and the galvanizing and inspiriting leadership of SHAPE have let rays of hopeful sunshine through the encircling gloom of hopeless despair. But while the weather has improved, the climate is still very unhealthy.

And at home?

Ever more colossal public expenditures. An ever-rising public debt, despite increasingly high taxation; and, striking at the very jugular vein of morale, an ever-growng alarm about the future, in respect to both internal affairs and foreign threats.

In such a condition of seething crisis, the quality most needed is stability—social and individual. Yet the trend in our country is in the opposite direction.

A very serious dilemma is presented by the dizzy dynamics of modern social change: the old agencies of social control are weakening; the new have not yet been sufficiently developed, some in fact must still be designed. Control and guidance and value-defining and standard-setting there must be, for the alternative is a progressively disintegrating society, an increasing conflict between customs and moral standards, a rising sense of

2

emotional and spiritual insecurity, an increase in crime, public corruption, child delinquency, mental illness, and, worst of all, a "flight from freedom." [1] * One major reason why men have permitted themselves to be enslaved by the totalitarian monster-state is the fact that the other instruments of social control had weakened to the point of impotence. Unless those other means are strengthened, or new ways are discovered for extending and deepening the channels of social understanding, mutual assistance, and mutual forbearance, our own country will also be in grave danger of succumbing to the siren song of the modern Lorelei.

Not only social, but individual stability, is a crucial necessity in times of crisis. But in this respect, too, conditions are not encouraging. While the effect of the machine age on mental health is difficult to gauge, there is a steadily mounting toll of emotional illness. Even a decade and a half ago it was authoritatively estimated that "approximately a million of the boys and girls now in our public schools will break down mentally at some time in their lives." [2] And that was before the Second World War and the atom bomb!

Today, people feel a new kind of insecurity—not merely economic but emotional; not merely emotional but spiritual. They have experienced the bloody events and earth-shaking aftermaths of two colossal wars. They have seen familiar economic and governmental systems go down in ruin. They have seen political juggernauts ride roughshod over powerful and erstwhile sacred institutions of religion. They have witnessed the rise of merciless political tyrannies and the apparent acquiescence of millions of ordinary folk, like themselves, in political systems in which the masses are helots and the masters fanatical slavedrivers. They stand in helpless fear before man's latest toys plucked from the Pandora's box of nature, the devastating atomic weapons. They are becoming less and less self-reliant and more dependent. In a desperate quest for peace

---

* Footnotes, p. 32 ff.

and security, they eagerly grope for some governmental shell into which they can crawl. A schizoid mental state on the part of millions makes more attractive and seductive the narcotic appeals of an Alice-in-Wonderland economic policy. It makes people far less alert to such twin dangers of the times as an unbridled inflation and an over-powerful and still burgeoning central government, the traditional threat to human freedom.

## II

How is our society attempting to cure these illnesses?

First, during this century there has been an ever-growing reliance upon the patent medicine of legislation. To an unprecedented degree our legislative mills are grinding out new laws to regulate an ever more complex social organization and disorganization.[3] Many of these statutes are passed in complete disregard of the fact that there are limits to effective action through *law;* that in many fields of human activity, the sum-total of legislative intervention in the private affairs of men may do much more social harm than good; that no law will function adequately unless nourished by the life-juices of morality and custom; that the law cannot take over the full burden heretofore carried by the home, the church, the shop, the neighborhood circles, and other agencies of individual guidance and social control, because the load is much too heavy and the relatively crude instrumentalities of the law are unsuited to many of the economic, cultural, psychologic, and ethical problems that have to be solved.

Secondly, there is an ever-growing reliance upon the *central government* to cope with problems that in our system more properly belong at the state or local governmental level. This is illustrated particularly by the ever-increasing resort to Federal tax money to subsidize needs, services, and obligations that should properly be financed by local government or voluntary contributions. A movement which was started to help out the needier and more backward states in respect to a few basic abuses and services has developed into a chronic stretching out of the hand to Washington.

Back in the seventeenth century the individualism of the English common law saw dangers in a continuous resort to central authority for every need and every problem. Lord Coke translated the well-known initials, *S.P.Q.R.*, not as the Latin abbreviation for the "Senate and People of Rome," but as *Stultus populus quaerit Romam*, "a foolish people runneth to Rome." [4] Similar dangers exist today. Too great reliance upon the distant and unwieldy central government dries up the springs of initiative and interest in local government upon which the life of a democratic and free people depends. It stimulates greedy requests for needless appropriations to serve local political promises regardless of the general economic welfare of the country. Moreover, it makes for inefficiency and waste. No President, however competent and conscientious he may be, can possibly give adequate thought to the vast quantity of complex issues entrusted nowadays to the chief executive. No Congress, however hard-working, can possibly give thorough consideration to the huge stream of bills poured into the governmental hopper in Washington, or to the astronomical appropriations which the present overgrown central government is making and ever enlarging.

But still more dangerous nostrums for our ills are increasingly being peddled by modern social medicine men, either deceptively or openly. Impatient with piecemeal legislation or, in some instances, moved by a more sinister spring of action, they insist that all our ills are economic, that man is essentially a stomach, and that the "common people" under their inspired leadership should take hold all along the line and without too much debate or delay establish the modern Utopia. Some see in Sovietized Communism the inside corridor to a gentle as well as abundant heaven on earth; and, to hustle people to those green pastures, these nimble enthusiasts are willing—quite incidentally, of course—to enslave and destroy the few million slow-

5

pokes on the highway of human progress. Others would solve all our problems by State Socialism, not bothering much about its relationship to precious political liberties. Still others are not averse to some form of Fascism. The theory of social ethics and social action being boldly pressed was exposed in a Commencement address at Columbia University in 1949:

> False teachers, [warned President Eisenhower] who magnify acknowledged errors in the practice of democracy, attempt to destroy our faith in man's right to self-government. As we seek to conserve what is good and sound even while we boldly explore and test new ways, we are belabored by the demagogues of right and left; both of whom would turn back the clock of history to the days of regimented humanity . . .
>
> Millions of us, today, seem to fear that . . . we have reached the point where the individual is far too small to cope with his circumstances; that his lifelong security against every risk is all that matters. More than this, we hear that such security must be attained by surrendering to centralized control the management of our society . . . To these fearful men, the free human individual is a social anachronism.[5]

Those who warn of the dangerous trend are condemned as "alarmists" or "reactionaries," while those who preach bigger and more powerful and more centralized and more subsidizing government bask in the self-applied sobriquet of "liberal." But it is no accident that within recent times a number of our most respected citizens, regardless of political party, who are not so chained down by the restraints of public office or party policy as not to be able to call their souls their own, have spoken out in accents of alarm against the recent trend in politico-economic affairs in the United States.

The views of some of these modern Minutemen are assembled in this symposium.

It presents one answer, in varying emphases and illustrations, to a vitally serious and increasingly pressing question: *Where are we heading under the "Fair Deal"?* The other answer to this crucial query has been abundantly put forward, in presidential messages, legislation, and executive and administrative action during the regime in question. Whichever political party the reader belongs to, it is hoped that he will give consideration to what the distinguished and thoughtful men whose views have here been assembled have to say. But if he happens to be a devoted Democrat, it will do no harm to remind him of the very relevant political philosophy of another faithful Democrat, President Grover Cleveland, who, in his *Inaugural Address* of May 4, 1893, warned prophetically:

> The lessons of paternalism ought to be unlearned and the better lesson taught that while the people should patriotically and cheerfully support their Government, its functions do not include the support of the people . . . The unwholesome progeny of paternalism . . . is the bane of republican institutions and the constant peril of our government by the people. It degrades to the purposes of wily craft the plan of rule our fathers established and bequeathed to us as an object of our love and veneration. It perverts the patriotic sentiments of our countrymen and tempts them to pitiful calculation of the sordid gain to be derived from their Government's maintenance. It undermines the self-reliance of our people and substitutes in its place dependence upon governmental favoritism. It stifles the spirit of true Americanism and stupefies every ennobling trait of American citizenship.[6]

To which warning may be appended a bit of sage advice from the Apocrypha: "Miss not the discourse of the elders."

### III

Differing in respect to detail and emphasis, the contributors to this book have at least two basic misgivings in common:

*First, they are convinced that a government's house, no less than an individual's, cannot long remain in order if it continues to spend far and away beyond its means; hence they are especially concerned about the dangers of Gargantuan budgets and an unbridled inflation brought about by unwise governmental economic and political policies.*

7

*Secondly, they believe that excessive and manifold subsidization of special classes, entailing the serious danger of seducing the ballot, and involving an ever-burgeoning bureaucracy, governmental centralization, and excessive political power of dictation, is bound to bring a host of major evils in its train.*

## IV

So much partisan political propaganda has been poured out to bedevil the true issues that it is necessary to clear the atmosphere:

*The line of cleavage in this matter is not between those who are humanitarian and those who are uncharitable. It is not between the benevolent and the malevolent.* Nobody could legitimately accuse the contributors to this volume of insensitivity to human need and suffering. Nor do they believe that in this land of rich natural resources the vast majority of the people should be content with the crumbs from America's table.

The potential riches of America—in human and natural resources—are tremendous. There should come a time when poverty—by any reasonable definition of that term—can be well nigh abolished; provided, always, that the motivating psychologic forces which bring about ample production are not too greatly stifled. Leaping ahead half a century, the President, in 1950, painted a pretty picture of Elysian comfort in the year 2000. But in envisaging a hypothetically roseate tomorrow on the basis of our prosperous past, we must not forget that an indispensable prerequisite to that prosperity has been a dynamic, enterprising economic system wherein the attraction of substantial private profits has played the propulsive role. It is a psychologic fact that if the mainspring of incentive be seriously crippled, the prediction of a fulsome future must, under our economic and cultural system, be revised. On the other hand, if it be retained, with adequate restraints upon excesses of greed, self-interest and unfair practices, the benefits which will accrue

8

to society and the individual through ever-mounting productivity and standards of living can be rich and varied.

The contributors to this volume differ from the cheerful governmental spenders, not in the degree or quality of their concern for the people's material welfare, but rather in urging, first, that the state, like the individual, should postpone the purchase of even good things until it can reasonably afford them without seriously crippling the very economic process that has produced the goods and the purchasing power and, secondly, that there be always kept in mind the threat to virile concern about freedom which is involved in an over-centralized, too big and too powerful government, especially if it has become so largely through the people's surrender to the glittering allurements of the politicians' deceptive generosity.

Let the reader consider some of the implications of these cautions:

Can there be any doubt that there is an obligation upon the central government, even more than on the individual or on local governments, not to become a shortsighted, debt-encumbered spendthrift; to live well within its means? Whether it be in the form of taxes or other types of wealth, it all comes out of the same bag—the industrial capacity of the nation. But it has been acutely pointed out that a major weakness of recent governmental economic practices is that they have brought about a "redistribution of wealth in the sense that . . . seed money which should be plowed back into the economy" is increasingly being "used up in present consumption." [7]

Moreover, granting that there are other motives, as well as desire for financial gain, involved in the willingness to work, does not continually rising taxation ultimately stifle a chief incentive of our economic order—the desire to make a substantial profit or to start a little business of one's own? If we want to retain the capitalistic system rather than to fly to others whose evils we know of only too well, are we not approaching a point where the geese which lay the golden eggs of tax money will be

9

reduced to very anaemic birds? For the paralyzing effect of excessive taxation is being demonstrated in England among all classes of society, including ordinary working men:

> The psychological effect of the feeling that "the government takes more than half of what I earn" cannot be ignored . . . We must never forget that for most people there are more pleasant ways of spending one's time than earning or risk-taking. Nor must we assume that this attitude is confined only to the very wealthy. I have heard plenty of professional people today raise doubts as to the desirability of additional hard work when the financial reward, *after tax*, is so relatively small. And England, which has been forced to dip into the incomes of workers to finance its public commitments for social welfare and other purposes, has found the same attitude expressed by workers who doubt the financial worthwhileness of working overtime.[8]

Further, a basic prerequisite to a progressively higher standard of living for all without succumbing to a dangerous statism is that the economy be fundamentally sound, instead of pseudo-sound. When the President begins his message on the economic status of the country in 1952 with the assurance that "The past year has been marked by great gains in our basic economic strength," which "have enabled us to move forward," he blandly overlooks the fact that our crisis prosperity is dancing on an uneasy volcano of a not so "cold war," and ignores what will happen if and when this atypical spur to excessive production and widespread employment runs out.

There can be no guaranty that we will not then run into another period of serious unemployment. If that should occur and, instead of having a backlog of public resources, we labor under an immense burden of national debt with a crushing interest obligation, how can we cope with a crisis of slowed down machines and workless people? Will any country in the world then be in a position to present *us* with a Marshall Plan? And what will happen to the remaining countries still within the

10

ambit of the free world whose economic health is sensitive to our own?

If our government is to play its important role of increasing public expenditures in times of abnormal unemployment by activating previously prepared plans for public works, then it must continue to be in a position to have an emergency surplus or at least an approach to a balanced budget, rather than crushing deficits. But since the government's policy is reaching a point where taxation is excessively burdensome and must be crippling to the expansion of enterprise as soon as cold-war atypical industrial activities begin to let up, how can it expect to balance the budget within any time in the foreseeable future?

On the inflationary stimulation of governmental leadership, let a distinguished expert, Dr. Edwin G. Nourse, the former Chairman of the crucially important Council of Economic Advisers, testify:

> On the last council assignment in which I took part—a memorandum on the economic impact of budget ceilings proposed for 1951—differences of view were so basic that I submitted a separate analysis. In handing these memoranda to the President, I suggested that the majority view be stated first. I then commented that I felt that that memorandum gave an unduly complacent view of moderate deficits, soon to be followed by comfortable surplus.
>
> I said I could not derive any such easy confidence from a reading of the discernible facts and foreseeable trends. I thought the President was being encouraged into taking inflationary short-cuts, which give us a superficial short-term prosperity but which seemed to me to carry unwarranted risks for the longer, but not very distant, future.
>
> The President said he would read both memoranda with care. But we never heard anything further from him. However, when I read his Pittsburgh address of last September 5th, it seemed to me a very clear reply not alone on the fiscal issue but on almost the whole of national economic policy. Deficit spending was depicted as only a "scare word" to "turn the American people against the programs which the people want and need." I quote:
>
> "The selfish interests [a phrase repeated 22 times in the speech]

11

say we can't afford these programs during a boom because that would
be inflationary. They say we can't afford them during a recession because that would be deflationary. They say we can't afford them
during a war because we are too busy with defense, and we can't afford
them in time of peace because that would discourage business. So
according to the selfish interests, we never can afford them. But the
truth is—we can't afford *not* to put these programs into effect. We
can afford them, we ought to have them, and we will have them!"

It seemed to be a casting to the winds of any economic analysis
of the intricate process by which the several segments of a total economy can be helped into workable balance and sustained high production. In its place I seemed to discern a highly political and dangerously inflationary economic program.

I view this as a menace to our American hope of making free competitive enterprise produce continuing abundance within a framework
of free government. [9]

Events are tending to prove Dr. Nourse to be a reliable prophet;
and nobody has as yet charged that he represents "the selfish
interests" or is any less humane or sensitive to the needs or the
prosperity, health, and welfare of his fellow men than the lusty
spenders in Washington.

It is simply irrelevant to close one's eyes to the questions being asked by dubbing those who demand a *pause for reflection*
as inhumane, blind to the welfare of the common man, and
otherwise villainous. The questions raised remain to plague
us no matter what labels are pinned on. It is beside the point
to resort to name-calling in considering the seriously threatening inflationary movement. Generous or stingy, humane or
brutal, *all* must pay the piper of shortsighted economic planning
in terms of reduced purchasing power of the money they saved,
paid into insurance policies, built into pension plans.

But beside the basic economic danger, there is the *moral* one.
It expresses itself largely in a growing popular attitude of dependency, of getting something for nothing from "the Government" or "the Relief," with the danger of an attendant creeping
paralysis not merely of the spirit of enterprise but, ultimately,

of the will to freedom on the part of the people. The all too human psychology of bread and circuses was not lost with the fall of Imperial Rome! Needs met by the citizen's own effort and saving add to his moral stature and self-respect. Doles tend to bring about the unwholesome attitude of which the following illustration is not atypical, as witness the widespread fraudulent "chiselings" into jobless, sickness, and other public funds:

> Battle Creek, Mich., Feb. 4, 1950 (U.P.)
> County Welfare Director William Morgan had to draw the line for a youthful applicant.
> A young man walked into Morgan's office and asked for relief.
> "Have you got a family?" the Director asked.
> "Not yet," the young man said. "But I'm getting married Sunday. I can furnish the groceries. All I want you people to do is pay the rent."

It is this sort of attitude—something so clearly to be expected by anyone with a realistic view of how human nature tends to work—that has brought about a growing clamor for legislation compelling the publication of names on welfare lists to purge them of thousands of chiselers.

That the tendency in question is not limited to a few is suggested in The Brookings Institution's analysis, *Cost and Financing of Social Security,* which points to an unwholesome change in the very concept of public assistance:

> In the past, legislators, administrators, and perhaps most voters agreed to the theory that public assistance allowances should be less than working persons or familes of comparable status were earning in the community. Assistance allowances, according to the view then prevailing, should offer no inducements to the recipients to prefer assistance to self-support. Today federal public assistance administrators and some legislators put the emphasis on adequacy . . . In Puerto Rico, the Virgin Islands, and certain areas of the South where a living is gained from subsistence farming, it would probably be found in many cases involving large families that maximum allowances would exceed normal earnings. Being on public assistance might be-

come economically a preferred status. The marginal worker who has a large family might be acutely aware of the fact that his family would be better off if he should desert them or be so far disabled that he and they could get an allowance on that score. In fact, in Oklahoma it was found that aid to dependent children in some cases had apparently led the father to desert in order to make the family eligible.[10]

But it is not alone the dangers to the basic economic foundations and the moral fibre of the traditionally self-reliant American people that is involved in wasteful, colossal budgets. Apart from these, there is the closely related unwholesome trend toward *excessive governmental centralization.* Taken individually, certain of the excursions of the central government into fields in which the more backward states have too long delayed elementary reforms (*e.g.,* child labor and child care) are justifiable. Taken *en masse,* the movement for federal control through subsidization in fields involving problems that should more properly be solved and financed by local government or voluntary philanthropy has reached dangerous proportions. In a trend of this kind, the whole is greater than the sum of its parts; for to the various individual "welfare" enactments must be added the dynamic of increasing momentum. Sir Stafford Cripps has benignly assured us that "all these things are matters of degree, . . . once it has been decided as it has in both England and the United States . . . that some degree of state interference in economic matters is necessary." [11] But a physician does not dismiss a temperature of even 100 degrees with the statement that the difference between 98.6 and 100 is a mere matter of degree; neither can the socio-economic doctor afford to overlook the possibility that in the matter of centralized governmental power a difference in degree can metamorphose into one of *kind.*

Once society is headed too rapidly in the direction of prospecting for the fool's gold of Utopia (that is, without objective and honest exploration of the economic, psychologic, moral, and governmental implications of prospective legislation), it is very difficult to call a halt.[12]   A stoppage of drug addiction brings painful "withdrawal symptoms"; and a cutting of subsidizing appropriations will bring social withdrawal symptoms without the patient realizing that in the long run the drastic action may be for the best health of himself and society.

When, therefore, the leading question is asked, *Which existing pieces of welfare legislation would you abolish?*, the answer must be that the symptoms of undesirable governmental planning are obvious; but a doctor cannot prescribe specific remedies without intensive examination of the patient.   Without a careful, unbiased, *nonpartisan* examination into the results—good and bad—of existing legislation, it is impossible to say.   One *a priori* line of cleavage is, however, discernible immediately: the distinction, on the one hand, between forms of social *insurance,* in which beneficiaries are not mere passive recipients of doles but self-respecting participants, through steady personal self-denial, in schemes of mutual protection against unavoidable hazards and, on the other, those provisions which deal with public assistance, subsidies, subventions, price supports, and the like.   The latter should then be subjected to careful scrutiny to determine, by unbiased follow-up investigations, whether or not, economically and morally, they do more harm than good to the body politic as a whole.

## V

*The line of cleavage is also not between the "liberal" and the "reactionary."*   In his address before the American Bar Association (p. 141), General Eisenhower warned of the mind-drugging effect of abuse of language: "You can [he advised the lawyers] clean out the ambush of catchwords, tags, and labels in which the plain citizen, including the old soldier, is trapped every time he considers today's problems.   How can we appraise a proposal if the terms hurled at our ears can mean anything or nothing, and change their significance with the

15

inflection of the voice? 'Welfare state,' 'national socialism,' 'radical,' 'liberal,' 'conservative,' 'reactionary' and a regiment of others—these terms, in today's usage, are generally compounds of confusion and prejudice. If our attitudes are muddled, our language is often to blame. A good tonic for clear thinking is a dose of precise, legal definition."

Not the least of the imps of evil let loose by twentieth century totalitarian tyrannies has been a rabble of kidnaped words which outwardly still wear familiar trappings but inwardly have been transformed to represent values diametrically opposite to those for which they formerly stood. How mischievously far from the realities and ideals as we have always known them is such a counterfeit Soviet coin as "People's Democracy!" The distortion of language is, of course, contrived to break down emotional resistances by making the victim believe he is welcoming well-tried semantic friends, when they are really enemies disguised in garb formerly associated with better times and more decent values.

Yet this process of distortion of words is not confined to representatives of totalitarian tyrannies; the movement has spread to those who ought to know better. Speaking of "liberalism," for example, the views of a leader who was fully aware of the weaknesses of the capitalistic system but eager to improve it might today be called "reactionary."

> Refuse to accept as inevitable any evil in business (*e.g.*, irregularity of employment). Refuse to tolerate any immoral practice (*e.g.*, espionage). But do not believe that you can find a universal remedy for evil conditions or immoral practices in effecting a fundamental change in society (as by State Socialism). And, do not pin too much faith on legislation. Remedial institutions are apt to fall under the control of the enemy and to become instruments of oppression.[13]

Are these the prejudiced words of some flint-hearted prophet of reaction, who detests the common people and mocks at the injustices done the exploited working man? Assuredly not. They happen to express the credo of one of the wisest, most humane, and most courageous liberals of the twentieth century, the late Justice Louis D. Brandeis, in a famous letter he wrote in 1922 to Mr. Robert W. Bruère. Yet not a few modern self-styled liberals would dismiss the social philosophy he expressed in that historic letter as hopelessly nonliberal, outmoded, inadequate.

The truth of the matter is that a great many modern liberals need to rediscover the spirit and essence of liberalism.

Of course, the passage of time, in itself, brings gradual changes in connotation of words so deeply charged with emotional history. The meaning and content of both political and economic liberalism have undergone many changes during the past two centuries and, more dynamically, within our own era. But its mental and spiritual *core* is such that "as an obvious corollary in the grammar of liberalism . . . any attempt on the part of the constituted authorities to exert artificial pressure or regulation on the individual, in his inner and outer adjustments, is an unjustifiable interference, a stultification of his personality and initiative. Against such coercive interference, whether in the moral, the religious, the intellectual, the social, the economic, or the political sphere, liberalism has consistently arrayed its forces." [14] An old definition of *liberal* is: "Free from restraint; uncontrolled; unchecked; hence, regardless of legal or moral restraints," as in Shakespeare's "most like a liberal villain." A later definition is: "One who favors greater freedom in political or religious matters." But the meaning which ought to be emphasized in our day and age is this: "Befitting, or worthy of, a man of free birth; *free, not servile.*"

And it is this definition which most nearly reflects the root concern of the contributors to this book. They see man's supreme value—freedom of mind and spirit—under real threat by the unbridled politico-economic improvisations and the saccharine seductions of the times. They insist that *governmental economic libertinism and traditional political liberalism cannot survive together*. They cannot escape the haunting fear that

17

an overly centralized, overly strong, heavily financed government tends, degree by degree, to emerge finally as an authoritarian state. They cannot overlook the dangers inherent in the permanent entrenchment of *any* single political party—Democrat, Republican, Socialist, or Communist—through a situation in which, to an ever-growing extent, voters can be enticed by means of lavish expenditure of public funds under the influence of special pressure groups. They cannot escape the feeling that government is becoming a nasty busybody, poking its long nose into most of the people's affairs and its long arm deep into their pockets. They sense the Washington trend as part of a larger and deeper sweep toward a frightful abyss:

> For at least twenty-five years before the specter of totalitarianism became a real threat, we had progressively been moving away from the basic ideas on which Western civilization has been built. That this movement on which we have entered with such high hopes and ambitions should have brought us face to face with the totalitarian horror has come as a profound shock to this generation, which still refuses to connect the two facts. Yet this development merely confirms the warnings of the fathers of the liberal philosophy which we still profess. We have progressively abandoned that freedom in economic affairs without which personal and political freedom has never existed in the past. Although we had been warned by some of the greatest political thinkers of the nineteenth century, by De Tocqueville and Lord Acton, that socialism means slavery, we have steadily moved in the direction of socialism . . . We are rapidly abandoning not the views merely of Cobden and Bright, of Adam Smith and Hume, or even of Locke and Milton, . . . not merely nineteenth- and eighteenth-century liberalism, but the basic individualism inherited by us from Erasmus and Montaigne, from Cicero and Tacitus, Pericles and Thucydides . . .[15]

But so widespread has become the hysterical cry for ever greater subvention, with its associated incursions by the central government into fields of local and private concern, as to suggest that the Washington planners disdainfully look upon tradi-

18

tional liberalism as a sort of oily antimacassar on the rocking chair of a hypocritical Victorianism!

I venture to say that the contributors to this symposium even have doubts about the *moral* gains that are supposed to be achieved by the legislative and administrative course on which we are headed. I believe they (or most of them) might agree that, when the sociologic debits and credits are set down in the book of history, it will be found that Hayek's analysis is not too far afield:

> People who admit that present political trends constitute a serious threat to our economic prospects, and through their economic effects endanger much higher values, are yet likely to deceive themselves that we are making material sacrifices to gain ideal ends. It is, however, more than doubtful whether a fifty years' approach toward collectivism has raised our moral standards, or whether the change has not rather been in the opposite direction. Though we are in the habit of priding ourselves on our more sensitive social conscience, it is by no means clear that this is justified by the practice of our individuals. On the negative side, in its indignation about the inequities of the existing social order, our generation probably surpasses most of its predecessors. But the effect of that movement on our positive standards in the proper fields of morals, individual conduct, and on the seriousness with which we uphold moral principles against the expediencies and exigencies of social machinery, is a very different matter.[16]

## VI

*The line of cleavage is also not between those who hold that under the Constitution Congress, through taxation, has the power to "provide for the . . . general welfare of the United States"* [17] *and those who believe the contrary.* The colorful debates among the Founding Fathers and the Presidents of the United States, as well as decisions of the Supreme Court, have long since settled the basic questions regarding the federal spending power. "Congress may spend money in aid of the 'general welfare.' . . . There have been great statesmen in our history who have stood for other views. We will not resurrect the contest. It is now settled by decision." [18] Speaking for the majority of the Supreme Court in upholding the constitutionality of the Social Security Act provision for "Federal Old-Age Benefits" for persons who have attained the age of sixty-five, Mr. Justice Cardozo said in 1937:

> Whether wisdom or unwisdom resides in the scheme of benefits set forth in Title II, it is not for us to say. The answer to such inquiries must come from Congress, not the courts. Our concern here, as often, is with power, not with wisdom. . . . The issue is a closed one. It was fought out long ago. When money is spent to promote the general welfare, the concept of welfare or the opposite is shaped by Congress, not the states. So the concept be not arbitrary, the locality must yield. Constitution, Art. VI, Par. 2.[19]

The Court admitted that "difficulties are left when the power is conceded."

> The line must still be drawn between one welfare and another, between particular and general. Where this shall be placed cannot be known through a formula in advance of the event. There is a middle ground or certainly a penumbra in which discretion is at large. The discretion, however, is not confided to the courts. The discretion belongs to Congress, unless the choice is clearly wrong, a display of arbitrary power, not an exercise of judgment.[20]

Conceding the dynamic nature of constitutional concepts, one may be permitted to wonder if, in view of the distinction between "power" and "wisdom," the Supreme Court would examine into whether or not proposed legislation for which tax resources are to be expended entails such premature and excessive expenditures as perhaps to threaten rather than promote the general welfare.[21] Professor Corwin, in considering the subject in 1934, came to the following timely, if exaggerated, conclusions:

> Two general observations are provoked. The first is that, inasmuch as the Supreme Court very inconsiderately refuses to relieve us of the responsibilities of popular government as regards national ex-

penditure, we shall probably have to assume them ourselves if we are to escape national bankruptcy; and this being so, the vital question becomes not that of the relationship of judicial review to governmental expenditure, but that of the proper relationship of the executive and the legislature in this field of power. While the theory stated by Monroe and others is that in no other field is the legislative body more representative and more immediately responsible, the truth is that in no other field is it less representative and less responsible, being constantly exposed when left to itself to be overriden by corrupt amalgamations of thievish interests. For the sorry fact is that a majority of Congressmen are entirely willing to buy votes so long as they can compound the felony by doing it with somebody else's money . . .

My second observation is that the success of the spending power in eluding all constitutional snares, goes far to envelop the entire institution of judicial review, as well as its product, constitutional law, in an atmosphere of unreality, even of futility. With the national government today in possession of the power to expend the social product for any purposes that may seem good to it; the power to make itself the universal and exclusive creditor of private business, with all that this would imply of control; the power to inflate the currency to any extent; the power to go into any business whatsoever, what becomes of judicial review conceived as a system for throwing about the property right a special protection "against the mere power of numbers" and for perpetuating a certain type of industrial organization? [22]

Whatever may be one's views regarding the desirability and scope of judicial review of legislative acts, Professor Corwin justifiably concludes that it is to the *people* and through them to their representatives in *Congress,* rather than to judicial limitation on the power of Congress to spend for what it conceives to be in the "public welfare," that we must look for curbs on what many thoughtful men regard as threatening incursions on the economic and political order.

At all events, the concern of the contributors to this symposium does not spring from any hard-hearted conviction that the central government must spend no public money for the "general welfare." It arises, rather, from the justifiable fear

21

that unless some reasonable and clear limits are placed on the conception of what *is* the general welfare and on the extent to which the financial future can safely be mortgaged to carry out immediate, special-interest, and partisan conceptions of the general welfare, it is conceivable that Corwin's prediction of national bankruptcy is in grave danger of becoming a reality in America as it has virtually become in England.

Politicians who rationalize the current trend by referring with a fine glow of pseudo-patriotism to the Constitution's specific imposition of a governmental obligation to "promote the general welfare" should read that prescient document more carefully. The *Preamble* to the Constitution, which clearly sets forth its *raison d'être,* tells us that it aims not only to "promote the general Welfare," but also to "secure the Blessings of Liberty." And those very real and very precious blessings are sought to be secured *not* selfishly and shortsightedly and exclusively for the generation of the Founding Fathers (or the political party temporarily in power) but, specifically, "to ourselves and our *Posterity."* It might be well for the sanguine spenders to take a page out of the philosophy of the wise men who established the Constitution, and give some thought to their own children and to the unborn generations. Surely, loose spending of the public resources will not only *not* assure the blessings of liberty to our posterity but, through increasingly crippling taxation, the undermining of the national financial structure, excessive inflation, and the centripetal suction of an ever more powerful "federal" government, must threaten the supreme value sought in and through the Constitution—*human freedom from governmental tyranny.*

## VII

What is to be done about all this?

Here, as in most social problems, recognition of a disease is much easier than discovery of a remedy.

By the selfish dialectic of "practical politics," the seeker of votes is often forced to take over many of the practices adopted by the party in power when those methods have been shown to entice ballots and bring election to office. Thus, in the recent elections in England, the Tory Party had to promise to retain many of the enactments of the Labor Party. But, especially in the vital matters of an unbridled program of public expenditure and centralized governmental control, the voice of the people is not the voice of God until the people have been thoroughly informed of the dangerous consequences that may flow from the present trend.

But when one calls for the "education of the people" he is merely repeating a vague and general demand that has been advanced as a universal nostrum for mankind's ills. A very popular competitor to the educator in these matters is a jolly gentleman whom, as a great American statesman once shrewdly observed, nobody wants to shoot at—Uncle Sam in the guise of Santa Claus.

How can we nevertheless bring home to the average voter that there are serious dangers in unbridled deficit spending and in an ever-growing centripetal tendency in government?

In his letter to Bruère, Brandeis offered a sound chart and compass which ought to serve well on a general journey away from the abyss of communism, the false haven of state socialism, and the hostile port of fascism:

> Seek for betterment within the broad lines of existing institutions. Do so by attacking evil *in situ;* and proceed from the individual to the general. Remember that progress is necessarily slow; that remedies are necessarily tentative; that because of varying conditions there must be much and constant enquiry into facts . . . and much experimentation; and that always and everywhere the intellectual, moral and spirtual development of those concerned will remain an essential—and the main factor—in real betterment.
>
> This development of the individual is, thus, both a necessary means and the end sought. For our objective is the making of men and women who shall be free, self-respecting members of a democracy . . .

23

> But democracy in any sphere is a serious undertaking. It substitutes self-restraint for external restraint. . . . Success . . . is possible only where the process of perfecting the individual is pursued . . .[23]

Such a philosophy of social reform, based on the dignity and the self-management of the individual, is the most consonant with ethical principles and the most likely to bring the highest standard of living, the greatest quantum of general economic security, and the least amount of social friction.

But something more specific is also needed.

How can we prevent the destructive dialectic of totalitarianism from taking control of the delicately balanced see-saw of political beliefs between Right and Left to the complete destruction of the all-important "Center"?

*"The Middle of the Road,"* for which General Eisenhower so earnestly pleads (pp. 132-155) ought to be the easiest to travel because it is the widest segment of the politico-economic highway. But the chronicles of history—especially the history of our century—have, alas!, shown it to be very hard to persuade the people that it is in the middle of the road that economic health and wealth, as well as freedom from tyranny, are most likely to be found. The center of the road is where men have to think; where they have to acknowledge that there are no magic nostrums for the solution of society's problems; that reasonable and fair compromise and accommodation usually yield greater values to all concerned than bitter-end insistence upon one extreme or the other. The middle of the road is the locale of Aristotle's "Golden Mean." It is where we must planfully travel in America in the future as we usually have in the past, for that is the only way to avoid the iron law of political or economic absolutism where—whether the motives of leaders be lofty or low—only ruin can follow rule.

How can we educate and re-educate the American people regarding the solid virtues of thrift? Of living within the

nation's means? Of the soundness of *gradual* social progress?
How can we make them modern Minutemen of freedom?

These are large questions.

It is hoped that this volume will help at least a little to
supply the ideas necessary if we would answer them.

The statements it contains were addressed, by serious-
minded leaders in many walks of life and representing no single
political party, to all sorts of special groups of thoughtful men
and women: lawyers, business leaders, social workers, college
students. It is hoped that they may be of further aid to other
voters who take their citizenship seriously by looking at the
welfare of the country as a whole and the welfare of its children
and children's children.

In truth, a modern Jeremy Bentham is needed to survey the
whole field of social control and national welfare in our time
and lay out the bounds beyond which, instead of conserving and
enhancing the goods of existence, reducing friction in their use,
and preserving a maximum of individual initiative and political
freedom, governmental action is likely to threaten the highest
value—society's interest in the healthy, happy, morally self-
respecting and free life of its members. Reflection on the
dangers inherent in our present course should cause one to con-
clude that not so much a Welfare State is called for as a Welfare
*Community;* a social milieu in which self-help and neighborly
help, and cooperation and social conscience will be the norm;
one in which the class struggle, so assiduously whipped up by
those who would destroy us, will be replaced by the recognition
of common interest in more efficient production, and in which
the value of individual freedom and initiative and opportunity
as motive-forces to the general welfare will not be forgotten.
The ideal must be to make the social fabric strong enough to be
independent of governmental tutelage and compulsion.

In the meantime, we cannot afford to take a cavalier attitude
about the ever-important and, in our day, crucial, problem of
the relationship of the State to the individual. The coming

Presidential elections should greatly help to assess the dangers that beset us and the means to be taken to minimize them. But apart from the elections, the issues which deserve exploration long after the people have spoken at the polls include the following:

(1) How can quicker and more effective action be obtained to introduce *economy in government*—not alone by carrying out the Hoover Commission's recommendations but by drastic slashing of appropriations and elimination of wasteful pork-barreling and "log-rolling" all down the line?

(2) What has been the *effect* on society in general of the existing central government's welfare services, as determined in each field by scientific, unbiased, *nonpartisan* follow-up investigations? To what extent have they contributed to better security, health, productivity? To what extent have they rather tended to bring about undesirable results?

(3) Which of the existing welfare services supported in whole or in part by the central government might safely be suspended or reduced until such time as the government (that is, the national economy, which means *all* the people instead of some specially favored pressure groups) can afford them? Which governmental subsidies and grants can be converted from mere passive "relief" and "public assistance" into devices for the active participation of prospective beneficiaries in various *social insurance* systems that will be actuarially sound and morally conducive to self-respect, through reasonable financial contributions by those insured?

(4) To what extent is it possible to plan ahead for improvements in *general societal services* from which *all* the people, instead of specially favored groups of voters, will benefit, on the basis of reliable predictions of general productivity and governmental income and the establishment of *priorities* in social needs? By what measures can there be brought about a systematic and financially sound proportioning of governmental welfare expenditures to national productivity and to noncrip-

pling taxation, so that minimal "floors" of economic and social welfare of the more underprivileged can be periodically redefined in terms of the country's solvency?

(5) Which welfare services—existing or proposed—might be more properly left to *local governmental* provision? Which *to nongovernmental, voluntary associations or to private philanthropy, community chests,* etc.? By what means can a sound division of responsibility among central government, local government, voluntary association, and private philanthropy be mapped out and then planfully assigned in fair and frank cooperation among all the interests involved?

(6) To what extent, and by what legislative, judicial, and administrative means, has an undesirable *centripetal tendency* developed in the Federal government? In what ways has it brought about or does it seriously threaten a fundamental disturbance of the balance of our federal-state system? In what ways has it tended to cripple state, municipal, and individual initiative?

(7) What means can be used to increase cooperation between representatives of capital, management, unionism in order to extend *voluntary* profit-sharing, insurance, and pension plans which will benefit society at large by providing both for increasing security and general industrial stability and for maintenance of high consumer demand, and do so with the lowest minimum of *governmental compulsion* and its accompanying bureaucratic expense and control and political over-centralization?

(8) How can the non-unionized members of the *forgotten middle class*—the teacher, clerk, small storekeeper, cobbler, haberdasher, clergyman, civil servant, small pensioner—be given a truly fair deal by curbing the twin evils of inflation and prodigious direct and indirect taxation?

(9) What devices can be developed to make the worker (whether organized or non-organized, industrial or agrarian, hand or head) and capital, management, and government, *see*

27

*the economic, social, and political problems of a free society as a whole,* instead of from the point of view of his own special interests, "and the devil take the hindmost"? How make them all more enthusiastic and wiser partners in the dynamic firm of *Free Enterprise, Free Society and Company?* [24]

(10) By what monetary, tax, and other reforms can we most quickly, but with least disturbance of the general economy, deflate inflation and enhance the purchasing power of the dollar and the stability of our medium of exchange?

Even this incomplete listing of the type of questions that require serious consideration shows that to ask them is far from answering them. They cannot all be answered on the hustings, although the basic problems involved must assuredly be the subject of discussion and debate before and after the coming Presidential nominations.

Nor can some of these fundamental questions be answered by mere exchange of views even on the part of experts in economics, political science, social work, social anthropology, and social psychology, for the simple and oft-ignored reason that sound public policy making presupposes careful, time-consuming, and *unbiased* research into relevant issues.

But in the meantime, I believe it is fair to mirror the wishes of the typical American in some such words as the following:

What the average citizen wants and has every right to expect is *ample opportunity for development.* That is the quintessence of the American way. He wants opportunity to make progress up the ladders of business, agriculture, the professions; opportunity to obtain a good education for himself, his children, and his children's children; opportunity to lay by a decent competence for his old age in dollars of sound purchasing power; opportunity, withal, to call his soul his own, the right which the framers of the Constitution "conferred, as against the Government" (in the trenchant words of that true liberal, Mr. Justice Brandeis) the right "to be let alone—the most comprehensive of rights and the right most valued by civilized men" (dissenting in *Olmstead v. United States,* 277 U. S., 238, 478, 1927). Give him that opportunity and that right and he himself will do the job of keeping all America strong and free, thus helping the rest of the world to be so.

But opportunity cannot be based on a mirage. It depends on a sound economic system and on a government that treats the people like self-respecting adults instead of holding them in leading-strings as if they were defective delinquents needing to be managed in every avenue of their lives. Government should interfere only where it is necessary for the welfare of the whole people and the people as a whole. It should encourage private enterprise in every reasonable way to keep enlarging opportunities presented by our vast natural and human resources for all who work.

An oversimplified but not invalid formula for government in this connection might be that it should emphasize the function of standing guard to see that there is no unfairness in the distribution of opportunities. The energy and imagination of the people themselves will be sufficient, as they have been in the past, to keep enlarging progress on the American scene. Schemes hatched by governmental bureaucrats are not necessarily superior, and are often definitely inferior, to those evolved through nongovernmental thinking and planning in an enterprise which holds out rewards for all.

How far the government should go beyond this is the difficult problem of our age. An ever-rising standard of living, extension of the privileges of economic security, education, good health, and opportunities for the constructive use of leisure—these are values we all desire; but for their achievement the most economical and least dangerous means must be found. Certain principles must be defined to serve as general yardsticks against which to measure the need of state intervention: (a) one limit is the line where excessive taxation does more harm in lowering incentive, and therefore total societal production, than it does good in providing a compelled purse for general programs of relief, health, education, and other governmentally directed mass provisions. (b) Another line is where the multiplication of governmental employees needed to enforce such programs threatens to saddle us with a powerful, entrenched, job-multiplying bureaucracy. (c) A third line is where the centralization of power through the colossal growth of Federal agencies in control of pursestrings threatens to transform our polity either into a single-party government or a servile rivalry in the seduction of voters through promises of governmental largesse to specially favored factions of the whole population. (d) A fourth line between governmental and voluntary social action is where mass-treatment methods threaten to substitute mechanical manipulation and red tape for the milk of human kindness and constructive individualization of treatment.

It is hard to know exactly where to draw these lines, of course; but it is not hard to see why the research necessary for the definition of governmental, local, and voluntary action should be entrusted to neutral, nonpolitical scientists rather than to governmentally paid bureaucrats who have a conscious or subconscious stake in the further extension of their power.

The above suggestions do not, of course, spell dogmatic opposition to various forms of modern, soundly administered forms of social insurance—old-age and survivor's insurance, industrial accident and disability insurance, and the like. Such devices do not pauperize. Such underwritings of common risks are based on the same sound economic principle of foresight, mutuality, and the sharing of unavoidable hazards as are ordinary fire and life insurance. They involve the ethically as well as economically sound doctrine that future benefits should be based, at least in part, on the beneficiary's own present, planful contribution in self-denial expressed in terms of payment of premiums. But even in this area, industrially sponsored protection against risk, in voluntary recognition of the economic good sense as well as the justice of such measures, is much to be preferred to colossal, unwieldy, and impersonal governmental machinery.[26]

Nor does the point of view urged here imply opposition to relief by the Federal Government on a nation-wide scale in times of such extraordinary crisis that private and local governmental resources are unable to cope with the load of need, as was the case in the depression of the nineteen-thirties. In such a rare and overwhelming emergency the central government is properly stepping in as the ultimate "insurer" of the entire socio-economic system and of our democratic institutions. It is not trying to extend the philosophy of the almshouse to all America. The leaders of industry and finance would, however, show a great deal more foresight than they have heretofore if they themselves would so plan their enterprises and reserves as to minimize the dangers of violent swings in the business cycle, thereby leaving to the central government only the ultimate and rarely used "safety-goal" function of supplying sufficient accumulated public works projects to fill in the gaps.

One thing is certain: enough historic and contemporary evidence exists throughout the world today to dissuade the true humanitarian—be he dubbed Liberal, Fair Dealer, New Dealer, or Republican—from approval of governmental action by leaders who irresponsibly insist that it is self-evident that they know all the answers; and that they are *ipso facto* entitled to push for their brand of hurried social salvation whether or not it leads more or less directly into the morass of the totalitarian Left or the ditch of the fascistic Right. This evidence suggests the high probability that the consciously sought *Center of the Road* is the way of wise men and free men; for it is the only way that compels patient and fair examination of facts and willingness to concede that the answers to socio-economic problems must often require frank compromise in order to obtain less total good at the bargain price of less danger of calamity. It is the only way that is based on the conviction that in social planning and societal reform, as in all mankind's activities, exuberant haste is very likely to make woeful waste.

At all events, the American citizen can no longer afford to remain complacent about the goings-on of the past decade. The contributors to this symposium recognize that the trend is increasingly such that unless there is, at this crucial stage in our history, a re-reading of the signposts on the confusing roads that face us, you and I and all of us may find ourselves carried along toward a fate we would want desperately to avoid.

"The storm is up and all is on the hazard."

## FOOTNOTES

[1] This is the title of the well-known book by Eric Fromm.

[2] "How the National Committee for Mental Hygiene is Saving Minds," pamphlet issued by the National Committee for Mental Hygiene, 1935; Glueck, B., "Mental Hygiene," Encyclopaedia of the Social Sciences, Vol. X, p. 320.

[3] *Recent Social Trends in the United States,* Report of the President's Research Committee on Social Trends, New York, 1933, Vol. II. The trend has greatly increased since the study was made.

[4] Cited by Pound, R., "Society and the Individual," Proceedings of the National Conference of Social Work, 1919, pp. 103-107. My colleague, Prof. Mark A. DeWolfe Howe, Jr., calls my attention to the fact that J. L. Campbell, *The Lives of the Chief Justices of England,* Vol. I, Boston, Little, Brown & Co. (1850), p. 262, quotes Coke on this passage. It is to be found in the report on "The Gun Powder Plot, A True and Perfect Relation of the Whole proceedings against the late most barbarous Traitors, Garnet a Iesuite, and his Confederates, etc.," London, 1606, 12-13.

[5] Text of Address delivered by President Dwight D. Eisenhower of Columbia University at the 195th Commencement exercises of the University, June 1, 1949, Public Information Office, Columbia University; see p. 152 of this symposium.

[6] *A Compilation of the Messages and Papers of the Presidents,* Vol. XIII, p. 5822. I have transposed the passages.

[7] Abels, J., *The Welfare State,* New York, Duell, Sloan and Pearce, 1951, p. 20.

[8] Burns, E. M., "How Much Social Welfare Can America Afford?," Bulletin of the New York School of Social Work, July, 1949, p. 13.

[9] "Why I Had to Step Aside," by Dr. Edwin G. Nourse, *Collier's,* February 18, 1950, pp. 13, 56.

[10] By L. Meriam and K. Schlotterbeck, Washington, D. C., 1950, p. 69.

[11] Cripps, S., "The Spiritual Basis of Democratic Strength," N. Y. Times Magazine, Oct. 2, 1949, pp. 9, 64.

[12] "In a period of prolonged tension, such as clearly lies ahead, there may be intervals of optimism, of better relations, of hopes for a return to normalcy. At such times, there will be strong pressure for the resumption of welfare spending experiments. But it is the peculiar attribute of social welfare spending that its costs are rigid and not easily susceptible of being diminished, should the situation again become critical. It is a commentary on this aspect of costs, and on the bias of the Administration toward welfarism, that the President in his 1951 budget message requested that the social welfare appropriation be *increased* by $105 million for fiscal 1952." Abels, *op. cit.*, pp. 55-56.

[13] *Brandeis: A Free Man's Life,* by A. T. Mason, New York, the Viking Press, 1946, p. 585. An excellent assessment of the nature of Brandeis' liberalism on the bench will be found in Freund, P., *On Understanding the Supreme Court,* Boston, Little, Brown & Co. (1949), especially pp. 49-50.

[14] de Ruggiero, G., "Liberalism," in Encyclopaedia of the Social Sciences, Vol. 9, p. 435.

[15] F. Hayek, *The Road to Serfdom,* Chicago, University of Chicago Press (1944), pp. 12-13.

[16] Hayek, *op. cit.*, pp. 210-211.

[17] Article I, Section 8, Clause 1, of the Constitution reads: "The Congress shall have power to lay and collect taxes, duties, imposts, and excises, to pay the debts and provide for the common defense and *general welfare* of the United States; but all duties, imposts, and excises shall be uniform throughout the United States."

[18] *Helvering v. Davis* (1937), 301 U. S. 619, 640, 57 S. Ct. 904, 81 L. Ed. 1307, 109 A. L. R. 1319. See also *United States v. Butler* (1936), 297 U. S. 1, 65-66, 56 S. Ct. 312, 80 L. Ed. 477, 102 A. L. R. 914.

[19] *Helvering v. Davis,* pp. 644-645.

[20] *Ibid.*, pp. 640-641.

[21] Such an inquiry may be founded on the *caveat* in the above quotation, "The discretion belongs to Congress, *unless the choice is clearly wrong.*" But such a test is still without a definition of "clearly wrong."

[22] Corwin, E. D., *The Twilight of the Supreme Court, A History of Our Constitutional Theory,* New Haven, Yale University Press (1934), Chap. 4. See also reviews of this work by Thomas Reed Powell, in 48 Harvard Law Review, 879, and Harold J. Laski, in 44 Yale Law Journal, 1126. Compare Senator Byrd's view, quoting Roswell Magill, p. 78.

[23] Mason, *op. cit.*, p. 585.

[24] See *Partners in Promotion,* New York, The Twentieth Century Fund, 1949.

[25] Such organizations as the Brookings Institution are supplying and have the opportunity to supply in the future research and recommenda-

tions which reflect the authors' honest attempts to be objective and scientific in the study of socio-economic problems. See, for example, *The Cost and Financing of Social Security, op. cit.* See, also, Glueck, E. T., *Evaluative Research in Social Work,* New York, Columbia University Press (1936). The Conference Center established at Columbia University under the leadership of President Eisenhower is the type of medium for frank and fair discussion of problems of great moment which deserves adoption at other educational centers. Great expansion of nonpartisan research, carried on with every honest effort to avoid propagandistic infection, is needed in the entire socio-economic field, where prejudices are so often substituted for facts; and popularization of such studies, as well as dissemination of solid findings and legitimate inferences drawn therefrom, are badly needed.

[26] "Two characteristics [says Hobhouse] which affect all state action occur to us at once as bearing upon the question of its legitimate sphere. These are, in the first place, that the life of the state is crystallized into the form of definite institutions, that its ordinances have to be incorporated in laws of universal application, that it must deal with men in masses and with problems in accordance with what is general and not with what is particular. Hence it is with difficulty adapted to the individuality of life; it is a clumsy instrument, as it were, for handling human variation. It is inadequate, to adapt Bacon's phrase, to the subtlety of human nature. Its sphere is the normal, the prosaic, the commonplace; its business is to solidify the substructure of society rather than to pursue its adornment. It can handle the matters upon which ordinary people usually agree better than those upon which there is variety of opinion. In the second place, the state is a compulsory form of association. Its laws have force behind them. Ordinarily the intervention of the state action does involve some sort of compulsion upon the individual . . . It is not difficult to see that functions may be useful and salutary when freely performed which would be useless and even injurious when imposed on reluctant people." Hobhouse, L. T., *Social Evolution and Political Theory,* 1911, p. 186.

# ꙮ ꙮ  FALSE GOSPEL OF SECURITY BY DEFICIT FINANCING*

## BY BERNARD M. BARUCH†

I T IS an honor to be here today.  It recalls happy memories.  Sixty-five years ago I was a student in the old City College building located here.\*\*\*

Of all my teachers, the one who influenced me most was Professor Newcomb.\*\*\*

It may strike you as quaint, even old-fashioned, that Professor Newcomb taught political economy, logic, ethics, philosophy and psychology—all in one course.  Today these subjects would be fragmented among several professors.  Such specialization is not necessarily a mark of progress.  Too many educators seem to have forgotten that you cannot teach good economics, good politics, good ethics, or good logics unless they are taught together as parts of one whole.

With over-specialization has come a tendency to mistake information for education, to turn out "quiz experts," who are crammed full of useful detail but who have not been trained how to think.

---

\* Address on the Thirtieth Anniversary of the Founding of the School of Business and Civic Administration, College of the City of New York, May 11, 1950.  The main title was "Regulating One's Behavior."  The subtitle is here used.—*Ed.*

† One of America's most respected Elder Statesmen and among the most useful and devoted citizens in the Nation's history.—*Ed.*

Nor is this defect confined to our educational institutions. Washington today is a dismaying example of Dryden's observation about those "who think too little and talk too much." For five years we have been engaged in a mighty struggle for peace and survival—the "cold war." Yet nowhere are all the tangled strands of that struggle brought together in one place to be woven into a unified global fabric. We continue to stagger from crisis to crisis, with the initiative left to the enemy. We remain too obsessed with today's details to think through the bold strategy so vital for tomorrow.

What is lacking is not so-called "information." There has never been so much "news," so many statistics, so many alleged "real inside stories." Yet the public has never been more confused.

To print all the facts collected by our great communications agencies would exhaust our paper supply. Of what avail is a forest of facts if we have lost the art of sitting on a log and thinking the facts through? We appear to have lost our ability to distinguish between the true and the false, the good and the evil.

The object of all fact-gathering is to furnish material for thought and reasoning to arrive at sound judgments which can lead to clear and constructive decision and action.

That ours is a well-intended confusion is significant. It indicates that the failure of our educational system is a double one —of bad moral habits as well as bad thinking habits. I refer to morals in the broadest, ethical sense. Too many people seem to regard good morals and good intentions as the same thing.

Morality rests upon values—what we regard as good and evil, what we live for, what we would die for. Without such values, everything would be reduced to a cynical zero. Values, in turn, rest upon discipline, on regulating one's behavior by the light of one's values and the rights of others. Morality, in other words, requires both good intentions and the strong backbone of self-discipline. Yet how many of our schools and teachers attempt to teach values without discipline!

This dual educational failure—the failure to instill in students the "know how" of thinking and a disciplined grounding in ethics—is all the more tragic because never were these two qualities in greater need.

I have already remarked on the folly of dealing with national and international problems on a piecemeal basis, without a thought-through strategy. Let me now turn to the moral dilemma which grips us all and which will grow ever sharper as the role of government grows.

Some of you who look to government action as the cure-all for our numerous ills may be startled by this statement—that our moral problems will grow more acute the more the government undertakes to do. With the revolt against the old laissez-faire do-nothing government philosophy has come a sense of community responsibility for the individual welfare, and rightly so. Civilized society cannot survive the jungle law of fang and claw, with its ruthless survival of the fittest.

But do-nothing government is dead. Virtually every phase of economic life is subject to some government intervention or regulation. The issue we now face is whether, as some say, community responsibility should be everything—and individual responsibility nothing. This doctrine ignores the human law that there are limits to the burden a community can carry. There is a point of no return beyond which government intervention and the lack of responsibility among nonproducers slow down all production and defeat their own purposes.

To lift the levels of human dignity and living is a proper function of government. I joined with both Woodrow Wilson and Franklin Roosevelt in their programs of humanitarian reform in the Adamson eight-hour day, collective bargaining, economic equality for farmers, and other "new freedoms." I opposed the conscription of labor in the recent war, even when President Roosevelt's "liberal" advisers favored it. I have favored pensions and care for the aged, infirm, and handicapped, and have urged that America take the lead in lifting wages and working standards all over the world.

Enormous advances have been made under our present system, the best in the world. These advances can be pressed further in years to come—as long as we preserve our form of government. But the way to protect human rights is not to socialize them. The chief threat to human rights is no longer one of too little government, as it may have been thirty years ago when this School of Business and Civic Administration was founded. Freedom's greatest threat today is too much government, that *all* limits to government action may be swept away.

Is there to be no line beyond which government shall not go, as it is in Soviet Russia, and becoming so in socialistic England? Is government action to be prompted by the sheer expediency of whichever greeds or pressure groups appear strongest at the moment? Or is it to be subject to higher ethical restraints and, if so, what are they to be?

That is the dilemma which will confront you through the rest of your lives. You will have to ask yourself not should the government take action, but how can the government's action be made just and fair to all?

Do-nothing government, we were told, was a cloak for powerful interests who wanted to be "let alone" to despoil the country's resources and the public. How unselfish are they who today invoke the power of government to further their own interests, or to get votes?

The plunder of our natural resources has been largely checked, though not entirely. Are we now to have a new system of plunder of the national treasury?

Is the old "let me alone" philosophy to be replaced by nothing better than a "gimme mine" philosophy?

Under the old philosophy of do-nothing government, it was not necessary to define or regulate social relations in detail. It was assumed that if each individual looked after his own interests, the end result, through a Darwinian process of natural selection, would be for the general good. That age had never met Hitler.

With government regulation, we now must consciously define man's relations to his neighbors, of the various segments of society to one another. To consciously regulate ourselves poses enormously greater problems than when taking things for granted, trusting to the automatic workings of competition.

Look at the inflation that has wracked the country in recent years, with such injury to those with fixed incomes and wages— firemen, teachers, policemen, nurses, civil servants, pensioners, the aged, and others. This inflation has not been the result of do-nothing economics. It has come from government-managed economics, from government favoritism to certain pressure groups, in disregard of the national interest.

To prevent this inflation, as you know, I urged that in war, priority controls be accompanied by an over-all ceiling over the entire economy, over *all* prices, *all* rents, *all* wages, *all* costs, with taxes high enough to eliminate profiteering. This plan would have treated everyone alike. It would have frozen all prices arbitrarily as of some fixed date. Adjustments could be made where essential to stimulate production and to relieve inequities.

Instead, under political pressure and only after much costly delay, a piecemeal price control plan was passed. This law legalized inflation. It allowed farm prices to rise to 110% of parity; it left wages free. When this broke down, the administration attempted to "hold the line" with an over-all ceiling, as had originally been recommended. By then the damage had been done.

With the war's end, we scuttled and ran. The process of inflation by pressure groups was given whirl after whirl—with the end not yet in sight.

Millions have been penalized through a cruel reduction of their purchasing power. Was that just, or fair?

What moral would *you* draw from this inflation?

Only recently, increased old age pensions were voted. This justly recognized that since 1939 living costs have risen around 60%. What good will increasing pensions do unless the spiral of inflationary policies and deficit spending are halted and pressure groups fought off?

Every form of saving has been depreciated—life insurance, government bonds, thrift accounts, annuities, and pension funds. Week after week, bit by bit, these sums were put aside by millions of persons for their old age, for buying a home, for sending a child to college. To the extent that these savings are cheapened, the ability of these millions to care for themselves and their families is weakened. They have been made more dependent upon the government. They have been made more insecure.

Yet, all this has been done in the name of "security."

This false gospel of security through deficit financing is evidence of bad thinking habits. If men and women are to provide for their futures, they must be able to put aside part of the earnings of their most productive years and be assured those earnings will not be wiped out. Saving is the first bulwark of security. Inflation is the worst enemy of saving.

In Soviet Russia, the people saved up their rubles, the accumulated sweat and hopes of a generation of work and deprivation. Then, ruthlessly, the Soviet Government slashed the value of the ruble to one-tenth. For all Russians over forty, nothing was left but to work at a bare subsistence level until they died. They could never hope to regain the savings their Government had wiped out.

In Eastern Europe, the Communists have demonstrated another form of tyranny—near-feudal slavery through inflation. Farmers, for example, are paid liberally for their crops. After the crops are collected the money is ruthlessly depreciated. To get working credit for a new crop, the farmer is compelled to join a communist-dominated organization which controls his planting and returns.

40

Wherever they have come to power, the Communists have wrecked the value of money. They have robbed savings of their value, and keep the people enslaved through a system of perpetual inflation.

Nothing quite so bad has happened here—yet. If American fiscal policy becomes a perpetual inflation machine—as "deficit financing" would make it—the result must be to enslave us to the government.

One of man's oldest delusions has been that he could avoid the necessity of working and saving by some money trick—lowering its value, printing more of it, changing lead to gold, burying gold in caves or concrete dungeons. In every instance these efforts have brought ruin.

Moreover, "deficit financing" has convicted itself as a system of practical economics. It has been tried. It has failed. England, where Keynes and his school were born, cannot finance her own recovery by deficit spending. In this country, when the recent war ended, the apostles of bigger and better deficits predicted a calamitous depression. Ten million were to be unemployed. Waging a campaign of fear against the American people, these deficit spenders pressured for and got tax reductions. Inflationary increases in prices and wages necessarily followed.

I opposed reducing excess profits taxes after the war, an action which, to date, has cost the Treasury thirty to forty billion dollars. Even before the war ended, I stated that for at least five and possibly seven years after the war, there would be more work than there were minds and hands to do—no matter what the government did or did not do. After that it depended upon the peace. If those taxes had not been reduced, there would be no budget deficit today.

Now, what I have said here is not intended to suggest that a return to do-nothing government is either desirable or possible. Nor that we should cease to strike for a more equitable sharing of the fruits of our production. I do want to impress

41

upon you that the mere shift from do-nothing government to government intervention does not, in itself, solve our problems. Unless this ever-expanding government activity is brought under the restraints of the highest moral laws, it will wreck our society.

Woodrow Wilson wrote, "It will be a bad day for society when sentimentalists are encouraged to suggest all the measures that should be taken for the betterment of the race."

Everywhere in the world today there is change. Nowhere is there peace. When I was a student here at City College, it was taken for granted that change was good, that change meant progress. None of us can believe that any longer. All of us have seen that change can be bad and oppressive.

Yours is a far more confused and difficult outlook than that which confronted my generation. You must stand amidst all the many changes pressing upon us and decide which are good and which are bad. You can take nothing for granted.

The world is always in need of leadership. Today the need is for self-disciplined leadership. With the training you have received here and the self-discipline which can only come from your own souls, you will find open to you positions of ever greater trust and responsibility—positions in which you, holding firm to the values of freedoms we cherish, can join in leading this country towards peace and a fuller life.

*EDITOR'S NOTE: In his notable appearance before the Senate Foreign Relations Committee on January 19, 1948, Mr. Baruch presented details of "A Peace Waging Program," \* with especial emphasis on the interrelationship of sound internal economic practices and economic aid to Europe, the dangers of inflation, and the prediction of future American industrial activi-*

---

\**European Recovery Program,* Hearings before the Committee on Foreign Relations, United States Senate, Eightieth Congress, Second Session, on United States Assistance to European Economic Recovery, Part 2, U. S., Govt. Printing Office, Washington (1948), pp. 555 *et seq.*

*ties. While some of the items in his program are less directly involved in the main theme of this Symposium than others, the entire list is here included to preserve the context of this significant, prophetic statement.—Ed.*

## I

\*\*\* Should we help Europe and the world recover? There is almost a unanimity of opinion, in which I join, that it is in our interest, in the interest of world peace, to do so.

Can it be done without wrecking ourselves? Yes, but only if the European peoples will help themselves and if the American people are prepared to do what needs to be done.\*\*\*

The foundations of economic stability in the world, without which peace must continue to elude us, can be brought into existence inside of two years, through an all-out production drive here and in the rest of the world. If, from today until December 31, 1949, we produced for peace as we produced for war, all-out, without interruptions, strikes, lockouts, or profit scrambling, mankind's whole lot and outlook would be magically lifted.

Work, production, thrift—they made America. They can now save the world. I would like less emphasis in this program on the mere giving of money and more on rewarding greater production.

## II

What of the future? Although sorely wanted, bread alone is not what Europe needs. Europe must also have faith, something to believe in. Only the United States can fill the vacuum of hope and courage, which sucks men down. We must, above all, make the future worth working for. This requires a bold, resolute, concerted attack against the clawing fears of inflation and of another war.

To this end, I recommend:

1. That the United States stand ready to buy all nonperishable raw materials produced anywhere and by anyone in the world for the next five years, and which cannot find normal commercial markets: Minerals, metals, and ores, both crude and refined; jute, sisal, etc.; yes, even wool and cotton. Also up to 750,000 tons of crude rubber. This should be made part of the European recovery legislation.

2. That the President's present tariff authority be extended for the next three years.

3. That the countries of Europe—as many as are willing—band themselves into a political, economic, and defense union under the United Nations. This would include the lowering of trade barriers among them.

4. That the United States and such others as will join us mutually guarantee the nations entering this union against aggression. By guarantee I mean a firm promise to go to war in joint defense if any of them are attacked.

5. That the European nations organize to liberate and use every productive resource of the Continent, with those of the Ruhr regulated under priorities and international control so as to protect the peaceful interests of Germany's neighbors.

6. Stabilization of all European currencies and establishment of realistic rates of exchange.

7. A two-year peace production drive in this country; to work for peace as we worked for war; where feasible, with longer hours and overtime; where not, to smash production bottlenecks.

8. As part of this work-for-peace drive, an across-the-Nation anti-inflation program to stabilize for peace, including:

(*a*) Reduction of major food and agricultural prices in exchange for guaranteeing farmers an assured price for their crops for the next three years, with ample soil conservation.

(*b*) Stabilization of wages, in return for this rollback.

(*c*) Restoration of the excess profits tax by 50 percent of the cut from war levels, with wartime amortization for new plants.

(*d*) Continued rent controls, with provision only for clearly justifiable increases.

(*e*) Postponement of tax reduction for two years, after which a five-year orderly reduction of personal and corporate taxes combined with the systematic, substantial lowering of the national debt which is a terrible threat to our security.

(*f*) Putting off all less essential works, including Federal, State and municipal projects, giving priority to increasing production, housing, schools, hospitals, and other more essential needs.

(*g*) Setting up of a Capital Issues Committee, with advisory powers, under the Secretary of Treasury, to review all capital issues, public and private, with a view to deferring less essential projects. The Governor of each state should appoint committees to pass on all proposed projects at the local level before going to the Federal committee.

(*h*) The setting up by Congress of a Digging Committee to scrutinize all Federal works and expenditures to determine which are postponable, also where Government spending can be cut and whether it is being done most economically. "Cut costs for greater efficiency" is a sound business maxim. It applies to governments as well.

(*i*) More production—so important that I repeat it.

9. Realistic settlement of all prewar and wartime intergovernment debts. For example, Britain and her creditors must decide what is to be done with the $14,000,000,000 of frozen pounds sterling accumulated during the war.

10. The retention by the British and others of their empire preferences for three years.

11. A General Staff for Peace to develop an over-all global strategy for America's peacemaking.

These measures, put into effect promptly, can boost production sufficiently to cover the whole Marshall plan and still break the present inflationary cycle almost immediately, cancel part of the national debt, while laying the groundwork for orderly tax reduction in the future.

## III

Almost four years ago, my associate, John M. Hancock, and I forecast[1] there would be no calamitous depression when the war ended, as so many were then predicting. We foresaw unparalleled business activity for between five to seven years. Doing what I have proposed would add another five to seven years to that "adventure in prosperity."

And if, in that time, we should succeed in making peace, a peace which enables men to face the future with hope, not fear, then I see that prosperity continuing indefinitely, with steadily improving living standards for ourselves and all other peoples, including Soviet Russia.

In taking these measures, the United States in effect would be saying this:

We stand ready to assure a market for the productive labor of all peoples for the next five years. Bring out the resources that lie in the ground. Go out into your colonies and the far reaches of the world and tap their riches. Produce. You will be able to sell it all.

This promise of an assured market will stimulate output so greatly—in Europe, America, elsewhere—that Europe's financial needs would be greatly and quickly reduced.

Men would discover new sources of supply. Assets now idle, hidden, or hoarded would pour forth. Governments, apparently hopelessly insolvent, would suddenly find their resources exceeding anything they had calculated.

The continuity of despair would be broken. A new continuity of hope would begin.***

Assurance of a stable market for five years will prove a fur-

---

[1] In Report on Postwar Adjustments to President Roosevelt and James F. Byrnes, then Director of War Mobilization.

ther stimulus to private investment, capital, and know-how for the immense job of reconstruction. There will be a new basis for credit in the world. We have been attempting to repair the devastation of the costliest war in history almost entirely through Government loans and Government institutions. The results have been pigmy proportions. Let us call into action the giant energies of aspiring and perspiring peoples everywhere.***

## IV

But dollars alone will not save Europe or win the peace. More is required of us. More is required of the European nations.

The major objective of the Marshall plan is the creation of stability in Europe, an essential condition for peace. To achieve this goal, Europeans must stabilize their currencies and establish realistic rates of exchange. I cannot stress the importance of that too strongly. They must reduce barriers to trade among themselves; they must compact together in mutual protection against aggression. Only as they become a bundle of sticks, unbreakable in unity, can security and peace be theirs. Should they remain so many individual, scattered sticks they invite being broken one by one.

Any economic aid which the United States gives will be inadequate without this common readiness of Europeans to stand up and fight for their independence and freedoms.

Given such a determination, the United States should pledge itself to come to the defense of these uniting nations in case of aggression. Let us not shy from stating now what we intend to do before any would-be warmaker has yielded to temptation of aggression. Such regional pacts of assistance are provided for in the Charter of the United Nations.

How can the peoples of Europe go to work and re-establish themselves unless freed from the fear of another scorching— economically, politically, and spiritually? How can they tackle the rebuilding of their countries with enthusiasm if they dread that their labors will be swept into a shambles before the repairs are even completed?

Other nations, I am sure, will join us in this mutual defense pact and, I hope, in time, Russia will also.

It is my own belief that the United Nations Charter, in spirit, if not letter, does commit the United States to oppose aggression with every means necessary. We should remove all doubts on that score. Our world—this country—has reached the point where there can be no assurance of peace unless the American people make clear where they stand.

I have been warned that the American people may not be prepared to make their position clear. If that is true, may I add this—if we do not take our stand today, so that the peace-loving, freedom-loving peoples of the world know where to rally, we shall be forced to do so in the future under more adverse circumstances.

V

In enacting this Marshall plan we shall be giving European nations a preference on the productive machinery which happens to be presently available only in this country. Shall this discriminate against Latin and South American nations who have always been our friends and allies? How are preferences given Europe to be balanced against the needs of China? Of the Middle East? Of the Far East, where rich stores of sorely needed materials lie untapped? How are all these preferences to be ranged alongside our own country's needs?

These are not decisions which take care of themselves. To integrate these and other problems into one all-embracing strategy, the President should create a body which will sit in continuous deliberations on these matters—a virtual general staff of peace. Only by knowing our own minds will we know what

America can do if we must stand alone, and what we can rightfully expect of other nations.

This general staff for peace might be created out of the National Security Council set up under the national security act of 1947. The important thing is to have some group constantly on the job, weighing the necessities of peace all over the globe, balancing the commitments we assume against our resources and, equally important, fully informing the American people so that we are prepared spiritually, physically, economically, and militarily to deliver on those commitments, when and where it counts.

The American people must make good all pledges. Let us not try to fool them.

## VI

The struggle we are engaged in will be many years in resolving itself. Because we face this long, grueling [struggle] for peace, America must keep sound, solid, and strong.

The great present threat to a strong America is inflation.

May I emphasize, so that it is clear beyond the slightest doubt, that even were there no Marshall plan, we still would need to take vigorous measures against this most insidious and subversive of menaces to the American way of life. We must stop inflation not to save Europe, but to save America.

Any program of inflation control, to be effective, must impose obligations on all the people, as fairly as can be devised. I offer that as a yardstick by which the public can measure the many anti-inflation plans which have been offered or which will be offered. Let the public ask, Whom does it hit? If it hits everyone, more than likely it will be a good program. If it taps here and there, touching one segment while exempting others, it will be a bad program.

Inflation can be prevented only by taking action all across

the nation. That was true in wartime when, as many of you remember, I urged an over-all ceiling over the entire economy —all prices, rents, wages—and that taxes be raised to leave the least wartime profit commensurate with getting production. Instead, efforts were made to let wages run free, farm prices to rise above the level of parity, and so on. The wartime price-control legislation actually legalized inflation.

The same principle—the national interest or the selfish interest—applies to halting inflation in peacetime.

The real and only full corrective of inflation is higher production. For supply to catch up with demand takes time. During war we do not have that time—to wait or waste. Nor do we have that time today in this struggle for peace. Therefore measures must be taken to bridge the gap between short supply and excessive demand. This requires three things:

1. Increasing supplies, particularly where most needed— more production, more work.

2. Conserving and directing what we have, to give priority to first needs first, putting off the less essential.

3. Organizing self-restraint—the enlightened self-discipline of the people—to accept the denials which winning the peace entails.

Fortunately, the scale of effort which the peacemaking requires—the magnitude of resources—is only a fraction of what war itself entails. As a consequence, nothing like the same degree of denial or regimentation is necessary. But the spirit must be the same. We must all see ourselves as contributors to, or detractors from, peace, in what we do or do not do.

Unless the rise in living costs is halted, labor will demand— and get—another round of wage increases. It won't do labor any good in the end, since prices will then be increased—a race to the abyss. Food is the critical item, for food purchases, unlike other things, cannot be put off. I suggest that farmers be asked to agree to a major cut in present agricultural prices in exchange for a guaranty of being able to sell all their crops at the price set for the next three years. That done, we can turn to labor and say, "You, too, must help hold this line on which peace and stability hang."

Labor and agriculture—through their organizations—have both assumed the position of importance in the community to which they are entitled. They are here to stay. They must accept the responsibility which goes with that position. Neither can again say wages or farm prices should be excluded from regulation, when regulation is necessary.

Through such a wage-farm price agreement, supported by the other anti-inflationary measures I have suggested, the price and cost-of-living spiral would be turned downward immediately.

Instead of having agricultural prices boom a bit longer to collapse in another bust, farmers will be better off if their prices remain steady. Every farm dollar will be worth more in the things it can buy as industrial prices drop. By working longer hours where feasible, each laborer will be able to earn more. Since he will produce more, prices will tend to drop, giving still greater real buying power to his wages.

By inclination I am opposed to governmental controls, except in wartime. However, we have no peace today. The demobilization was done too hurriedly, without adequately considering this fact: that the peace has still to be won. The country already has paid much of the price, in the throes of adjustment, for that overhasty demobilization. It is my belief that few controls would be needed today—and then for only a short time until production had caught up with demand—if inflation were tackled vigorously by putting off less essential activity both of governments and individuals, postponing tax reduction, reducing farm prices, holding wages stable, taking smaller profits, and increasing production.

If we do not show the wisdom and restraint to make these rather small present denials for greater future gains, then I can see no other alternative but to impose a ceiling over our entire economy as in wartime, to save America from being wrecked. I would not like to see that happen. But the longer the delay in acting wisely, the more severe the measures which will have to be adopted, or the country—and the world—will suffer the tragic consequences.

Instead of boom-bust fluctuation, we have within our reach the means for assured markets for an indefinite number of years ahead with relatively stable incomes of workers and farmers. The benefits for white collar workers, government employees, the armed forces are apparent.

Stability is everyone's gain. Inflation is everyone's loss.

Think of the millions living on pensions and annuities, if inflation continues. What will happen to all the hospitalization and medical care plans, to church and college endowments, to the budgets of State, county, and municipal governments which are even now being thrown out of balance because of rising costs? How long will the budget of the United States remain in balance unless the spiralling ceases?

## VII

Overhanging everything is the swollen national debt. It pressures for inflation. It imperils our national security. It is an invitation for regimentation, printing money, and repudiation. In event of a recession or some future emergency, where the expenditure of considerable resources might be necessary to prevent war, our national debt could paralyze us from action, unless accompanied by such a degree of internal controls as to create grave disorders. A nation which has destroyed its credit has no recourse other than regimentation.

The systematic, orderly, substantial retirement of the national debt is as much a measure of defense as maintaining an army, navy, or air force. Reducing that debt is as much a protection of our traditional liberties as uprooting those who spread subversive doctrines aimed at overthrowing our Government by force.

Had the excess-profits tax not been lowered—a move I opposed—the Government would have had several billions additional surplus last year. Restoring the excess-profits tax to the level suggested would permit a sizable lowering of the debt and interest cost.

While raising the excess-profits tax, wartime provisions for amortizing new investment should be restored to spur industrial expansion. At the end of this two-year peace production drive, which is so urgent, taxes would commence to be reduced steadily. This reduction should not be done all at once. Each year another 10 percent of the excess-profits tax would come off. Similarly, the 1943 increase in personal income taxes should come down 10 percent each year. After five years the whole situation should be reviewed—the debt, the threat of war, the state of our economy—to determine whether a more rapid lowering of taxes will then be wise.

Postponing tax reduction for two years is not asking too much when so much is at stake.

## VIII

Throughout this statement I have tried to stress how inextricably interwoven are the twin aspects of the problem we face —the need to help the recovery of Europe and other parts of the world and the need to keep our own economy strong for what making and keeping the peace may demand in the years ahead. Unavoidably, some conflicts between these two objectives will develop. Nor is it possible to predict in advance how the necessities of the situation may change, how much more quickly Europe can recover if her production is stimulated by measures such as I have proposed, or how much more can be safely made available from our own economy by these measures.

Confronted with such a problem I suggest the Congress lay down the broad, basic policies, giving full operating powers to a single, competent administrator heading the European Recovery Authority. On matters affecting foreign policy, the administrator would be subject to the President and Secretary of State.

It is to the interests of peace to aid Europe's recovery, and such aid should be substantial. However, the Marshall plan must be fitted into a larger structure of foreign and domestic policy, rugged enough for the uncertainties ahead. Whatever global peace strategy we arrive at will not be worth anything unless we stabilize our economy to keep America strong. Either we organize production and self-restraint to furnish the tools and materials for the peace-waging to the degree that is necessary, or the peace is lost.

During wartime the average person realized that what he or she did on the job, on the farm, in business, was a direct part of the war effort. It is tragic that so few people see the connection between the things they do in their daily lives and the peace effort. Much was made of the home front during the war. Where is our "home front" for peace?

Perhaps it is human nature—or political nature—to try to do just a little bit. A little bit may be better than nothing, but I would not be honest if I did not say here that to make and keep the peace will demand far more of all of us than merely appropriating money.

Many may cry, "What about free enterprise?" and "Aren't we being asked to do things which we condemn in others?" To them I reply, "You cannot save free enterprise if you let the system which protects it go to ruin."

What makes the police state? What makes totalitarianism? What makes dictatorship? Not the police, but the absence of law behind the police—the rule of men instead of law. I have no fears of the restraints which we adopt as free men to save our freedom as long as we uphold our laws and Constitution, as long as the people vote freely at appointed elections, as long as the press and radio are free, and as long as the American spirit of liberty remains as strong as it is today.

Gentlemen, the time has come to organize—to mobilize—for peace. It cannot be put off safely any longer. The time for courage and decision is here.

## ꙮ ꙮ ꙮ  HUMAN ENTERPRISE*

BY VANNEVAR BUSH†

THE human enterprise—the endeavor of mankind from earliest days—is to force back barriers, no matter of what sort, in order that man's life may steadily grow to be a better life, physically, intellectually, spiritually. It is an enterprise of movement, change, growth. As we look at the record of history, even the grimmest recent history, we know that over the long pull it has been a successful enterprise, and we are determined to keep it continuingly successful. To do that, we must assure its characteristics of evolution and advance. Above all, we must be ready, as in the past, to take risks for that purpose.

From this view of the human enterprise I wish to discuss a matter of which the air is full these days. It is the topic of security. The word has many meanings, of which three—distinct

---

* Address at the Proceedings of the Convocation Held in Honor of the 90th Anniversary of the Inauguration of The Cooper Union for the Advancement of Science and Art, New York, November 2, 1949. The opening pages of Dr. Bush's address are only indirectly relevant to the theme of this symposium; the directly relevant portion begins on page 60. While the 1951 election results in England affect Dr. Bush's statements on page 63, they are, considering the narrow margin of the Labor Party's defeat, still apt.—*Ed.*

† President of the Carnegie Institution of Washington since 1939, Dr. Bush is an outstanding electrical engineer, administrator, and public servant in governmental positions concerned with pioneering applications of science to the problem of peace and war.—*Ed.*

but closely interrelated—are of major interest at present. We shall need to consider all three. In all three senses, security is a good thing. And equally in all three senses it can, like most good things, defeat its own purposes if carried to excess. By carrying it to excess I mean simply putting so much emphasis on it that we lose the courage to take a risk. These two polar conceptions, security and risk, go together. They go together just as much today as they did a century ago when the wagon trains rolled west and men left their accustomed security and risked everything in the determination to have a better life out of which they expected a richer security to grow.

The first of the three senses of the word which engage us this evening is that of national security, the safety of this country in a hazardous world, where conquering armies still roll across a vast continent, where dictators curse one another, and where modern weapons have quickened the pace and filled us with dread of what may come.

We are not likely to lose sight of the importance of national security. It behooves us likewise not to lose sight of the fact that we may have in the future as we have had in the past to take calculated risks to maintain it. If we had not been bold and imaginative enough to take risks in the past decade with the development of the atomic bomb, for example, our security would not have been so well protected as it has been. We shall do well to keep this fact in mind now, with the President's recent announcement that an atomic explosion has occurred in the heart of the Eurasian continent. This came as a surprise— in its timing somewhat of a surprise even to military men with full access to information, for it was earlier than expected, not radically so, but earlier. We do not, of course, know how long it has taken Russia to produce this explosion; certainly the Russians did not start from scratch as the war closed. But this is a detail. We now do know in no uncertain terms that our monopoly of atomic bombs has ended, and insofar as this knowledge shakes us out of any Maginot Line complex, it is a good thing. To go from an initial test to a stockpile of bombs is a long hard road; this we recognize from our own experience. Even so, our approach to this aspect of national security is now on a new basis.

We have also heard much, unfortunately, of strife among our own services. However sincere its motives, it risks the security which it seeks to preserve. Thus the merits of carriers and of long-range bombers are argued in the public press and in open hearings in Congress, in neither of which places can sound judgments be rendered on intricate matters involving many phases which should not be made public. We hear of pursuit ships and anti-aircraft rockets, defensive radar networks and recoilless guns. To balance the effect of these into complete and accurate judgments is no mean task. It will require the best minds we can muster, the keenest of analysis using all modern methods. It will require unity of military approach, and teamwork, which is now being set back rather than forward. The system established by law to resolve such matters normally and deliberately has been thrown into confusion, and the public security suffers as a result.

We know that our security as a nation cannot safely rest on the defense of our own shores, that readiness to take the risks of the offense is necessary for security. Had we learned that lesson early enough, this might be a different world. But at least we have learned it. Hence we tax ourselves to rehabilitate Europe, and to furnish arms for aid to a revival of strength which can in the long run defend itself fully. This involves a new set of international relationships, not one world as yet, but a United Nations growing gradually in prestige and influence in spite of all obstacles, an Atlantic Pact, and the beginnings of a Federation of Europe. We have had to learn a whole new set of principles in regard to the motivations of men, their ambitions, and their fears. For the security of the country rests not alone upon weapons, and the hope of peace lies in understanding, boldness, risk-taking, and wise courage.

The second sense of the term "security" is closely related to the first. Through military usage the word has come to mean the inviolability of secret information, the guarding of data and documents important in the national defense. All, or nearly all, of us admit that certain secrets we must guard. We do not intend that spies and traitors among us shall operate unmolested, to pry out data on new weapons we are developing, or about our plans for using them if we must, in order to deliver that information to a potential enemy. This is proper enough, no more than sound common sense. The principle, basic in our heritage, that the defendant is innocent until proved guilty should be our safeguard against abuses of excessive zeal in carrying it out.

We may come to need a comparable safeguard in another aspect of security of secret information, which directly involves the national security, and which again points up the inescapable connection of the two antithetical ideas—security and risk. Fundamental science is essential to our industry, our economy, our whole social structure, our national strength, for it is from constant and vigorous fundamental research that there comes the knowledge which produces new applications, new implements, new industries. Shall we, in the name of security of information, severely restrict the publication of scientific results, with the idea of preventing them from aiding those with whom we are engaged in a race on new weapons? This question too takes on a new aspect now that there has been an atomic explosion elsewhere, and we can look at it in a new light. Certainly none object to our keeping secret the mass of technical and engineering information involved in manufacture of materials, and the making of an atomic bomb itself; we are not concerned this evening, for instance, with any such things as the rate of production, or the dimensions and design of the actual missiles. Does it make sense to hold back fundamental science? When the first atomic bombs exploded in Japan and brought an end to the war, the President made a very wise and far-reaching decision to take a calculated risk and release the Smyth Report. This told all that was bound to be generally known and readily found out, but went no further. It undoubtedly helped those in other countries to see important relationships. But it gave a great start to American science generally. The Atomic Energy Commission has pursued the same wise policy, releasing scientific matters broadly, and withholding only techniques. In the light of accomplishment elsewhere—for in my opinion that depended very little upon information obtained from this country, either overtly or clandestinely—the choice of working here in reasonable light appears in retrospect to have been the only sane course. Science in America cannot prosper in the dark. We can proceed only at a snail's pace on the basis of whispered confidences. But this country is rapidly progressing toward magnificent accomplishment in many fields of fundamental science, and free interchange of results is its heart's blood. There is reasonable limitation; we should not be so carried away that by stretching boundaries we publish practical matters of moment to a potential enemy. But the great danger of security of information is that it will be overdone, and militate in the long run against the security of the country in a hazardous world.

The third meaning of security is, however, the one to which I would primarily devote this talk. Here it means safety of the individual against the hazards of nature and of his fellow man, but safety only in a limited sense, and usually safety by reason of action of a paternal government. For a generation we have seen great strides in this direction, and most of it has been salutary indeed. The growth of voluntary life and accident insurance, and more recently of health insurance, and the great safety moves in industry have illustrated one phase of it. The governmental phase has involved child labor laws, safety codes, and more recently minimum wage laws, subsidies of farm products, social security, and the like. The growth of labor unions and their maturity into powerful organizations accomplished much in this direction, and a more enlightened business management deserves credit also. The most powerful influence, however, has been an awakened public consciousness, and a response of legislatures to the demands of organized groups of citizens. There is no doubt that we have come far, and no doubt also that much of the progress has been salutary. Our people are more protected against the hazards of life than ever before in history, yet we are prosperous, and our national product is twice as great as it was only a decade ago.

The blind pursuit and overemphasis of this form of security could, however, take us over a precipice. Specifically, if we outpace ourselves and overdo this phase of things, we can render this country unable to develop itself and to defend itself in a world in which we may have powerful enemies. We can seek security of the lesser sort so avidly that we lose its essence.

There is no such thing as absolute security. In this uncertain and complex world there is no workable security without the willingness and courage to take risks. We cannot protect ourselves by passing a law. We can hope to protect ourselves only if our people—our greatest resource—maintain and develop their imagination and initiative and are willing and able to take chances—often great chances.

Moreover, the search for security by action of a paternalistic government has its seamy side. Along with the advocates of good causes we at times encounter those who would get at the trough for selfish ends, and by political manipulation. The area is also one in which muddled thinking abounds.

One result of that kind of thinking appears to take the form of a belief that the Federal Government has a pipeline to some inexhaustible treasury on the moon—that it has income in addition to what it gets from the people in taxes—that the national income each year consists of something in addition to such total annual national product as we can produce. This kind of thinking looks at dollars, at money, as something significant in itself, rather than as what it is—a mechanism, a mirror

61

that reflects tons of coal, tons of steel, bushels of wheat, and so on. If we were not beguiled by this kind of false notion, we would hardly as a country regard with equanimity the things we do. Today, for example, with unprecedented expenditures for military services and for foreign aid, with a budget thrown out of balance by mounting costs, and a spiral of inflation hardly fully arrested, a session of Congress just ended with nine billion dollars of expenditure for various good causes still in the hopper. Many of these proposals came very close to being enacted into law. Would there be a rush in this direction if the citizens generally regarded each of these bills as merely a way of shifting funds from one group within the country to another, with the intervention of a growing governmental bureaucracy? Would we appropriate so freely to aid this or that if the taxpayers generally really recognized that they would pay the bill, either directly or by indirect taxes they hardly see? Not at all. There is still, in this country, some sort of belief in a magic wand.

The difficulty is that there has been a magic wand in the past, in fact two of them, and the people generally do not realize they have lost their power. One magic wand paid for new dispensations by soaking the rich. The other did so by leaning on the national credit. We are getting perilously close to the end of our tether on both of these matters, and as a country we do not yet know it.

It is strange that this should be so with the spectacle of England before us. It does not matter that England came to its present predicament by reason of war losses, and the metamorphosis of an Empire. The present situation is intense, and fully spread out for all to see. In England they soak the rich no more; there are no rich. No man can earn or keep an income which is more than sufficient for immediate needs. The national credit is exhausted, in spite of rigorous controls and valiant efforts to support it. Yet the move toward more taxes and more distribution continues. We cannot see the end,

but we clearly see the plight. But England is governed by
state socialists. They believe, very honestly and very vigorously, that all property used for production should be owned
by the state, although they proceed slowly in this direction to
avoid abrupt disruption. They believe in a superstate which
plans and regulates the lives of its citizens in detailed ways for
their own good. They believe in plenty of taxation, and plenty
of services, managed by a horde of officials. We may stand
off and wonder why anyone should wish to go down that path,
even as we realize that a majority of England's citizens have
voted to do so, with full freedom of discussion of all the merits.
But there is little difference in trend in the two countries.
We have been going down the same path for nearly a generation; we merely have not gone quite so far because of the for-
tunes of war and some difference in national temperament.
Moreover, we have been drifting unconsciously, rather than
plunging into state socialism deliberately. And the reason
that we drift is that as a people we do not understand. We
still believe in fairies. We still conceive that money in some
strange ways gives birth to more money, or that money can
merely be printed.

The fallacy that money makes money is very deep-rooted.
Like the other fallacies mentioned earlier, it persists for one
reason, because at times it has been true. In the early days
of commerce, when banking was rudimentary and the handling
of funds was done by a close-knit few, it was indeed true that
the mere control of a portion of the flow of the medium of
exchange could leave large residues in the hands of those who
controlled. Even in later times, say in this country for a long
period following the War between the States, the purchasing
value of the dollar increased over the years, and those who
held funds found them continually more valuable. This probably did not occur by chance. But today, and as far as we
can see permanently, if the conduct of financial matters is widespread, and the sharing of groups in the economy finds its

own level without artificial control, the value of the dollar decreases slowly and steadily. It has decreased rapidly in recent years, and that is inflation, but there are signs that the pattern following wars will again be repeated, and we will get back closer to the long-term trend.

This long-term trend is about such as to cancel out the interest on funds which take almost no risk. It is incorrect to believe that one can invest in a bond which has almost no risk, governmental or otherwise, and enjoy an income therefrom. One can receive dollar income, true, but in the long run the purchasing value of the whole, principal and accumulated income, will remain unchanged if the trends in purchasing value of the dollar which have persisted for fifty or seventy-five years continue, as they probably will, even if they do not become accelerated.

It is absurd to set up an organization with its endowment invested in riskless securities, and to call that organization perpetual or immortal. It is perpetual only in the sense that its dollars may be preserved, and dollars dwindle. It is doomed to extinction, very slow extinction it is true and on an exponential or asymptotic basis, so that it will go to zero only in an infinite time, by extinction of part of its size each generation. Money does not make money. But money combined with judgment, courage, and risk-taking can and does. In fact, securities which represent a share in the business of the country show, on the average and over many years, under the conditions which now exist, an income and an increment which much more than offsets the decline of the dollar. Some such securities become worthless—if the investor tries to be very smart, a very large fraction may do just that. But the grand averages, through depressions and wars, grow in value with time. They are bound to, not merely because the productivity of industry increases some two percent a year, measured in output per man hour, and may now be increasing at nearer to three percent because of increased reliance on research, but also because the effort expended in exercising wise judgment inevitably reaps a reward.

Not all of the governmental provision for personal security is by any means merely a result of a false belief that money grows on trees. Nor is all of it, by any reasoning, merely the result of clamor by pressure groups. Some of it is the result of real major problems. The question of old age pensions, now very much in the public mind, is a case in point. Here indeed, science and humanistic considerations meet. The medical profession, aided by chemistry, biology, and other neighboring sciences, has increased the life span and presented us with a severe problem. In 1925, 5 percent of the population was over 65. Now it is 8½ percent, and in another 25 years, even if the medical sciences made no progress in the meantime, it will be 11 percent.

An annuity which serves to provide $100 per month costs, at age 65, over $15,000. No wonder there is argument as to who is going to pay the bill. We can be sure of two things: first, the elderly are not to be left in distress, in the present temper of the country, and unless we lose our prosperity; second, no matter who pays in the first instance the burden will ultimately fall on those who produce. The chances are that the long-suffering taxpayer will get the bulk of the charges directly, and the question we present is how much he can stand without bringing about a collapse of the system on which all support of the unfortunate or elderly depends.

This is a good place, however, to emphasize that our present dilemma is not merely due to some long-haired group of socialists in our midst. We are all involved. In this particular instance part of the responsibility is that of the scientists, for it is their discovery of aids such as penicillin which have produced the problem by enabling us all on the average to live longer. In this instance management has also been shortsighted, taking management generally and, of course, with notable exceptions. Only half the men above 65 are at work.

It is reasonable to suppose that the same agencies which have postponed death have also improved the general level of health of the old, and postponed also the day of real incompetence to earn a living. Yet industry generally has made no move to correspond. It is still customary to retire working men at the same ages that applied a generation ago, and with surprisingly little attempt to keep old people earning, even at altered tasks and lessened income.

Undoubtedly, business men and professional men need to retire from responsible positions on time, so as not to block the path of younger men who could outperform them if given the chance. Undoubtedly, we should not artificially guarantee the old man a job at the cost of throwing the young man out of one, for the latter is primarily the one who has to produce for all. But there are plenty of skilled workmen whose loss of usefulness is postponed well beyond the time when executives begin to balk at difficult decisions, or coast in a changing environment.

There are plenty of other problems, besides that of old age pensions, where we have merely allowed a situation to creep up on us, and about every section of the population has been at fault in allowing it to occur. Now we are faced with tough decisions, and we are tempted merely to spend and spend, and hope that in some mysterious way the resiliency of the American system of production will provide. If we do so, that system may bog down, like a yoke of oxen when one too many rocks is rolled onto the sledge.

There is little doubt that this country would call a halt, if it could shake off its fallacies and face facts, if it ceased to drift because of the lure of individual benefits which are themselves desirable, without really counting the cost. Such a halt would not mean that we would turn the clock back, that we would frown on humanitarianism, that we would return to the good old days, or that we would become reactionaries. It would not mean that we would cease to strive to adjust the relations between men, so that there would be justice and reason in sharing the product which we all create. It would not mean that we would hesitate to extend the protecting hand of government to support the weak or distressed. Regaining the use of our heads would not mean that we need lose the impulses of our hearts. But it would mean that we would count costs as well as benefits. It would mean that, before we vote some special group a slice out of the federal treasury, we would balance affairs to see whether it is really just to take away earnings from some larger group, by taxing them, in order that the benefit that is clamored for may be given.

It would mean one more thing. It would mean that, in a world where harsh fighting is still possible, we will not follow a will-o'-the-wisp over a precipice into ineptitude. It would mean that we would not, in the selfish interests of potato farmers, for instance, who are doing pretty well already, hazard the over-all national strength which we may some day need sorely. For the question of whether we can avoid war depends to a great degree upon whether we can maintain our strength. The question of whether we can win a war without being set back for many generations, should we be forced into one, depends upon whether this country of ours is really strong. This is not merely a question of weapons, or armies, or appropriations. It is a question of whether the country as a whole is healthy, with a strong, vigorous, successful independent industry, with a soundly balanced budget and an unimpaired national credit, with progress on every front by pioneers and innovators. Whether we are sound depends upon how we control our selfishness, and our desire to be kind. For even good things cannot come all at once. If we build well we can have security, genuine national security. But if we are deluded into believing that security of the individual against all hazards and all ills can be obtained by fiat and by law, without limit, and without deliberate progress toward an end, we will sacrifice the foundation which makes humanitarianism possible, and start the weary climb over again, only after a long, dark interval.

The dangers of rushing headlong into a full welfare state are very practical and very immediate. Yet there is a more subtle danger than this in the present cry for personal security. A passion for personal security is an opiate which tends to destroy the virile characteristics which have made us great.

The danger of a central bureaucracy which plans all our lives, and doles out what it thinks we need, is much more than that it will plan badly, although it undoubtedly will. The greater danger is to ourselves, that we will cease to think for ourselves, that we will not exert ourselves when only a drab mediocrity lies ahead, that we will substitute the arts of petty political maneuvering for virile self-reliance.

The greatest of these dangers is the last mentioned. This country has the highest standard of living in the world by far, and it did not come about by chance. Some of it is due to our resources, some of it is due to the fact that in two world wars our land has not been devastated. A large fraction of it is due to the fact that we have a great homogeneous population which furnishes a mass market. But the greater part of it is due to the fact that we have willed it so.

We have not, as a country, been lured by the mirage of restricted output. In spite of featherbedding and other shortsighted labor moves, of which we have had too much, our men who labor have not in the past generally loafed on the job. Our business management has not in general grasped at cartels and combinations to restrict output, and thus furnish profits in a stagnant industry. The fact that we have had antitrust laws has helped in this regard. Much as they have been railed against, and much as they have at times been operated in ways that approached the ludicrous, their presence has been a large factor in preventing us from going down the path which England has pursued to its present dismay. We have, in general, had lively competition, rapid introduction of new machinery, lavish use of power, and a mounting production of goods at an ever-decreasing cost.

Now there is real danger that this trend may be reversed. If it is, it will be because the people fail to understand, and because our spirit of adventure—our readiness to run a calculated risk—fails us.

We cannot treat all phases of this problem. One that stands out is the matter of the advent of new industries. There is a distinct tendency for business to aggregate into very large units. Modern technical methods of mass production produce part of the tendency. Much of it is merely due to the very human tendency to build large structures. Many a great concern has blithely absorbed its small competitor for this reason alone, without giving thought to the fact that by so doing it was putting itself in jeopardy. We have to have large organizations for large things—our public utilities, for example, can hardly be managed soundly on a competitive basis. We also need large organizations for mass production of things that require great capital and extensive markets. But overdoing the matter leads straight to the type of monopoly which can be disastrous, not so much perhaps because it can control markets, as because in doing so it loses its vigorous nature. Much of our present safeguard against overconcentration is a legal one. As things stand we have not done badly at all—in fact the amount of present concentration is probably somewhere near the optimum for maximum progress, and we certainly have good vigorous competition in the fields where it really counts. But not all the offset to concentration in the past has by any means been due to legal restraints. A great part of it has been due to the constant advent of new vigorous small industrial units, which could often cut rings around the big fellows and keep them on their toes. This is one of the greatest contributions of the pioneering spirit—the willingness to take a risk—which was exemplified, for instance, by the "mechanic of New York" whose farseeing benefaction of ninety years ago we celebrate tonight. It is another reason why we need opportunity for that quality which will not rest content with increasing repetition of the accustomed, but strikes out on new paths, devises new undertakings, creates new things.

But that spirit is being smothered. It is far more difficult today than it was even twenty-five years ago, to set up a new successful business in this country, and the rewards for doing so are far less. There are many reasons for this, but they nearly all go back in one way or another to the search for artificial personal security, and the accompanying tendency to tax heavily those who are prosperous to make the way easier for those who are not.

One great factor is the system of taxation. This has dried up a large fraction of the venture capital which used to make small starts possible. It has also borne very heavily indeed on the successful pioneer who makes a sudden income. We fully accept today the graduated income tax, and the graduated estate tax. We have enormous military burdens, and burdens for foreign aid, enormous payments to veterans, enormous subsidies—we have to pay for them all, and it is reasonable that those who have prospered should pay a heavy share. But we have gone so far that the incentive to take a chance, to risk a novel product or boost a novel idea, is nearly gone. It takes a bold man to venture his property when a failure means a total loss, and success means a payment to government of a large fraction of what is gained.

A second factor is the tendency of courts to weaken the patent system. Patents, like other property, have been used improperly in restraint of trade, and it is correct and in the public interest when courts restrain such use. Often, however, in this country we take a broad lunge at the large misdoer and hit a lot of little fellows in the process, and this is an instance. A smoothly working effective system of patents is one of the primary reliances of the new unit in industry, making its hazardous way in a territory often previously occupied only by large industrial organizations. The tendency to restrict patent use, to interpret patents narrowly, is often no more than a matter of words. Patents set up a monopoly. Certainly they do, and their basis lies in the Constitution, where it was placed for that very purpose. A temporary monopoly, in exchange for a full disclosure, was intended to make it possible to attract capital to an infant idea, and to avoid the evils of industrial secrecy, and it has done just that very effectively throughout our industrial history. But to some any monopoly is *ipso facto* evil, and should be assaulted. There is no doubt that some of the present tendency to soften the patent system comes from this feeling. Wherever it comes from, it is one more thing that makes the way of the pioneer hazardous.

Moreover, we regulate everything under the sun, and in so doing we often waste most of the time of the pioneer filling out forms when he ought to be out in the shop studying a new device in its first steps. Most of the form-filling, and inquiries, and inspections, occurs because we are protecting somebody against something. It is usually well intentioned and often necessary. We protect the public against improper stock issues, and make it difficult for the small outfit to obtain capital. We protect labor against a thousand kinds of exploitation, and a horde of officials gather statistics and ask questions. We protect and protect—and bury the venturous pioneer in industry before he can begin to give us one of the greatest protections we sorely need—the protection of recurrent youth against industrial senility.

In the last analysis, where we go in this whole matter depends upon what we most desire in this world. It depends upon what our youth desires, for they will set the pattern. If we want a system in which, by every artifice we can command, we protect the individual citizen against all the ills of nature and of grasping man, we can have it. We can legislate and set up new bureaus, systematize life to the utmost, plan and regulate until we are insured against the hazards of existence and the injustice of our fellows in every way that we can devise. But when we have succeeded in doing so we shall have produced a dead level of existence far below our possibilities—we shall have stopped progress. We may then succumb in a world where wars are still possible.

On the other hand, if we want the kind of country that has thus far prospered well, if the youth of our land wish adventure and the conquest of new horizons, great possibilities lie before us. The application of science has much yet to offer, and a strong country can maintain our national security and give us opportunity to develop our great potentiality. If we wish to go down this path we will temper our humanitarianism with hard common sense. We will protect the unfortunate and continue to strive for justice between men. We will guard against the vicissitudes of life by new combinations to meet emergencies in our personal lives. But we will have no raids on the public purse. We will make sure that when we transfer a burden from one group to another we genuinely advance the common welfare. Above all, we will not block the path of the pioneer.

The choice is an individual one. As youth selects its path, so will the country grow. We have a magnificent asset in a whole generation of new lives, guarded against disease as never before, with educational opportunities that are unmatched. The kind of world in which we live will be built by those who take over the management of the next generation, and it will be a world either of progress or of settlement to a dead level, where the small securities have rendered impossible security in the larger sense. If that youth, in its choice of jobs, in its potential power, in its words and acts, wishes us to, we can have an increasing standard of living, a country of color and of opportunity, and we can be secure as a nation. We can continue our adventure in human enterprise.

# ॐ ॐ ॐ THE THREAT TO THE AMERICAN SYSTEM *

## BY HARRY F. BYRD†

### I

I

T IS a privilege to address the American Medical Association.***

I am told that the rules of this meeting prohibit a "partisan" approach. I submit that I can qualify as a nonpartisan, and my record proves it.***

I can say with all sincerity that when these great legislative issues come before the Senate of the United States, the only test I apply is not whether these measures are of Democratic origin, or of Republican origin, but whether they are best for the United States of America.***

What kind of a Democrat am I? I am a Jeffersonian Democrat of the old school who believes that simple honesty is still the very foundation of human character. I am an antisocialist Democrat, which means, in plain language, I am *not* a Truman Democrat.

The essence of freedom, under our American democracy, lies in our system of checks and balances. Within the federal

---

* Speech before the American Medical Association, Los Angeles, California, December 5, 1951. I have consolidated herewith certain passages from Senator Byrd's speech of January 18, 1952, before the Business Outlook Conference, Chattanooga, Tenn.—*Ed.*

† One of the ablest statesmen in the Senate, Senator Byrd is a fearless exponent of sound fiscal policy and a critic of wastefulness in public expenditures.—*Ed.*

government, checks and balances are provided through a three-branch system—the Executive, the Legislative, and the Judicial. Beyond this, still other checks and balances are provided in our system of state and local governments, which lie closest to individual citizens, from whom all governmental power and authority is derived. Our democracy has been given vitality by our system of competitive free enterprise, which, to this point, has made us, through individual initiative, the greatest nation on earth. I stand for this system, with the absolute minimum of governmental shackles. Our four foundation stones are freedom of religion, freedom of speech, freedom of the press and, last but not least, freedom of opportunity to the individual under the competitive enterprise system.

## II

Many are warning us as to what may come unless we change our governmental course, which in the late years has been proceeding steadily towards state socialism. Some call it the welfare state, but let us not be technical as to the name of this new "ism." I would call it "ruinism" because these new policies of government, unless quickly checked, will destroy the American system.

America today stands at the crossroads.

We can continue down the road to state socialism and ultimate disaster, or we can strengthen and revitalize the free enterprise system and then go forward to a nobler and greater destiny.

There are those who believe that socialism can be turned on and off as if it were water flowing through a spigot, and there are those who profess to believe we can have a little socialism and remain free.

For those who think "a little socialism" is a good thing, there is the British example. From what we see in England, we would be the most stupid nation on earth if we allowed ourselves to become further embraced by the socialism which has been creeping upon us. Socialism and free enterprise cannot live under the same roof. England thought they could but, to her sorrow, she has found it is impossible. She socialized the coal mines, and the production of coal immediately declined. For the first time in her history, England is now importing coal. She socialized the steel industry, and the production of steel immediately declined. She socialized civilian aviation, the electric supply industry, the Bank of England, the inland transportation system, the gas industry, and many other functions and enterprises essential to the welfare of her people, including socialized medicine, agriculture, and the legal profession.

A friend recently sent me a copy of the *London Times*. On the first page it had a list of 150 farmers who, the government had charged, were guilty of bad husbandry, because they had not obeyed the government bureau on what to plant, when to plant, and when to harvest. This notice said that unless these farmers mended their ways their farms would be confiscated. Not paid for, not condemned, under the law, but confiscated! And this in the land of England! For a thousand years England has boasted that the Englishman's home is his castle, and now under socialism our friends across the sea have reached such a low estate that if a farmer does not obey the order of a bureaucrat, he is subject to the penalty of having his property taken from him.

In England there are only 70 Britons who have a take-home income of $16,800 or more, after taxes. The rich have been liquidated. But to liquidate the middle classes you strike at the heart and core of any country. This, England has been gradually doing, as there are only 320,000 Englishmen now who have incomes of from $2,800 to $5,600 or more a year, after taxes.

In the face of these facts, are we going the road of England? Just recently, England, with momentous effort, decided to attempt the road back. By direct vote, she ousted the socialistic Labor Party and installed Winston Churchill, who I think is the greatest man in the world of his generation, and to whom England has so often turned in her days of peril. But I fear there is little reason to expect that even under this great leadership England can return to the free enterprise system. England has repented and all of us wish her well, as she is our friend and ally.

As I see it, the welfare state, about which we have been hearing so much in recent years, is that state of twilight in which the glow of democratic freedoms is fading beyond the horizon, leaving us to be swallowed in the blackness of socialism, or worse.

In many federal programs we are chasing a mirage of easy money in the form of deficit dollars. Some of us have been duped into believing that the easy dollars handed out by the federal government are something for nothing but, actually, these programs are adding to the public debt, are undermining the will of individuals, regimenting the production of agriculture and labor, controlling the practices of business, curtailing the solvency of states, and destroying the self-determination privileges which are traditional in our local governments and domestic customs.

Make no mistake: It is socialism which lies at the end of this rainbow and, in this rainbow, the predominating color is the red of federal deficit spending under which a whole new generation of Americans has grown and developed.

As to where we stand today, the last time the Socialist Party in the United States campaigned actively in a presidential election was in 1932. Today, virtually every plank in that 1932 socialistic platform has been enacted into federal law, and in some cases, enlarged upon. For this reason I assume the Socialist Party, as such, has not been active since they have gained their objectives. Read this platform and you will see. This is not a brash opinion of my own. Let me call to the witness stand Earl Browder, former leader of the Communist Party and an authority on communism and socialism, who recently listed 22 socializing items adopted by the federal government ranging through deficit financing, price controls, government housing, and "full employment" laws. These 22 items, he said, expressed "the growth of state capitalism . . . an essential feature of the confirmation of the Marxist theory . . . it represents the maturing of the objective prerequisites for socialism, the basic factor which makes socialism inevitable." Mr. Browder further said: "Socialism has progressed farther in America than in Great Britain under the labor government, despite its nationalization of certain industries, which is a formal state not yet reached in America."

The American system, operating in the fullest freedom of democracy, stimulates individual initiative in the development and production of more of what we need, in peace or war, at a cost we can more easily afford from the earnings of our endeavors. I am for that.

The American Medical Association needs no definition of the free enterprise system from me. It is the system which, in the relatively short span of one hundred sixty years, has brought us from the impotency of thirteen un-united colonies to our present position of world leadership. I do not concede that it should be scrapped for socialism in welfare state clothing, which never brought greatness, happiness, or security to any nation.

The American system has developed individual freedoms under Constitutional Democracy to the fullest measure ever known to man. It is the system which is always ready to supply the vital spark needed by the deserving to expand mediocrity into genius. It is the system which supplies the incentive to every American to start at the bottom and rise to the top.

It is the system which enables us with only six percent of the world's population to out-produce the rest of the world combined. It is the system which produces steel, the prime requirement for military defense, at a rate of more than two tons for every one produced by the rest of the world—at a rate of more than four tons to every one ton produced by Russia.

I challenge the socialists to offer a practical substitute for the American system's capacity to hold Russian world aggression at bay.

With our eyes wide open, will we yield to the ever-increasing socialization of those freedoms and institutions which are vital to our democratic free enterprise?

With respect to the checks and balances against Federal zealots provided in our system of state and local governments, there is pending in Congress now legislation, with Presidential approval, under which the Federal Government would usurp local police power and State control of elections.

### III

With respect to checks and balances between the Executive Branch and the Congress, the Honorable Roswell P. Magill, former Under-Secretary of the Treasury, now President of the Tax Foundation, recently testified that despite the Constitutional mandate that Federal expenditures be controlled by Congress, "Congress does not have that kind of control today." It has been chipped away insidiously over the past twenty years by give-away program after give-away program which have committed the Federal Treasury without annual review by Congress.

From George Washington's administration to April, 1945, including the Roosevelt Administration, the Federal Government took in taxes from the American people two hundred forty-eight billion dollars. In six years and two months, from May, 1945—when Mr. Truman took office—to June, 1951, the

Federal Government took from us two hundred fifty-five billion dollars.

In plain words, in less than six and one-half years, including only three months of World War II, Mr. Truman has taken from the people in the form of Federal taxes seven billion dollars more than was paid into the Federal Treasury in the previous one hundred and fifty-six years of our existence as a nation. This is the record of Mr. Truman, the tax collector.

Now let us look at the record of Mr. Truman, the spendthrift. From the Administration of George Washington to the beginning of World War II, Federal expenditures totaled $179 billion. From the end of World War II, in six years under Mr. Truman, the Federal expenditures totaled $260 billion, or $81 billion more than the entire life of our nation, excepting the three and one-half year period of World War II. When I first compiled these figures they appeared to me to be so incredible that I had them checked from official Treasury records. The figures are correct.

In fiscal 1953 the Budget Bureau estimates the Federal expenditures at 85 to 90 billions. If so, Mr. Truman will spend in one year—the year beginning July 1, 1952—more than one-half as much as all previous Presidents spent up to World War II.

It is alarming to note that in only one year in our history have we exceeded this estimated 1953 fiscal year spending. In fiscal 1945 at peak of World War II we spent 98 billion. Then we were financing the greatest war in history. Now we are engaged in a police action in Korea.

How much farther can we go in this reckless financial irresponsibility?

Now for a "Byrd's-eye" view of the Federal Budget:[1]

---

[1] The statement on budgeting requests and expected deficits which follows is from a later address by Senator Byrd, his speech before the Business Outlook Conference, Chattanooga, January 18, 1952, which I have inserted in place of the original statement.—*Ed.*

The Federal Government is spending your money at the rate of $2,000 every time the clock ticks. That is approximately the amount to be paid in federal taxes this year by a man earning $12,000, with a wife and two children.

The Federal Government is collecting taxes from you at a rate of nearly $1,600 every second of every day and every night. The per capita income in this country is now estimated at $1,625 a year.

The Federal Government is adding to our public debt, through deficit spending, at the rate of about $400 a second.

Federal expenditures this year, which ends June 30, will total nearly $70 billion. Federal revenue will not exceed $65 billion. The deficit will be approximately $5 billion.

The President of the United States on Monday, January 21, 1952, will submit to Congress his new budget for fiscal year 1953, which begins next July 1. It will call for federal expenditures totaling close to $85 billion. Even if we remain as short of all-out war as we are today, current long-range estimates by officials in Washington indicate the spending in the following year will total approximately the same amount. After taking into account the probability of further inflation, and assuming additional taxes will not be imposed, federal revenue in these next two years will be less than $150 billion. This indicates a deficit over the three-year period of approximately $25 billion. This will be added to a federal debt which is already a quarter of a trillion dollars.

In addition, our local and State taxation will be about nineteen billion dollars.

Americans are paying nearly 30 percent of the national income in taxes. Our taxes have reached the confiscatory stage, which means that new taxes will probably result in diminishing returns.

In the circumstances, it is natural to ponder the question: When does a democracy become insolvent? In a system such as ours, when and how does national insolvency manifest itself? There probably will be no milestone to mark the cross-road, but it seems to me that a democracy is approaching insolvency when:

(1) We are unable to pay current costs of Government over a prolonged period with taxes short of confiscation and diminishing returns and,

(2) When the constant cheapening of the dollar is a result of these Government operations.

If these are the symptoms, it would appear that the diagnosis of our present and prospective fiscal situation is unmistakably clear. Federal tax rates, increased three times in one year, will not meet federal expenditures this year, and the gap will get wider. The dollar is worth 53¢, and its value is going down.

A new generation has reached its majority under federal deficit financing. In 21 years the budget has been balanced three times. There is nothing but deficit in the foreseeable future.

We have not yet felt the full effect of the highest tax rates in our history. Taxes—federal, state and local—will be taking 30 percent of our income. Federal taxes alone will be taking 25 percent of it.

Federal taxes are now so oppressive they cannot be maintained for more than a temporary period, according to recent testimony by Defense Mobilizer Charles E. Wilson. Chairman Robert L. Doughton of the House Ways and Means Committee says it is doubtful whether higher taxes can be levied, and Senator Walter F. George, Chairman of the Senate Finance Committee, says we have reached our tax limit unless we embark on new and untried methods.

With a new chain of deficits reaching as far as we can see into the future, we are already carrying a federal debt greater than any other nation ever dared create. We went into World War I with a federal debt of less than $1 billion; we went into World War II with a federal debt of less than $50 billion.

We start this new deficit financing segment with a federal debt of more than a quarter of a trillion dollars.

If the integrity of the United States is to be maintained— if we are to remain solvent—we must finance this tremendous new debt at the same time we are meeting debt obligations from the past which are coming due. This must be done whether the debt was incurred for war or peace.

While we are selling government bonds to finance new deficit spending, we shall have to pay off from revenue, or more borrowing, the old debt which is coming due at the rate of $92 billion in the next five years, $16 billion in the following five years, $21 billion in the third five years, and $9 billion in the fourth five years. All this is in marketable issues, and in addition there are $82 billion in nonmarketable issues, and approximately $35 billion in special issues.

With characteristic deception, the Fair Deal economists tell us there is nothing wrong with a huge federal debt so long as "we owe it to ourselves." But when payday rolls around we find that we owe it to ourselves in the war bonds we hold, in our bank savings against a rainy day which are invested in it, the insurance we bought for the protection of our families which is invested in it, and the social security taxes withheld from us which are invested in it.

We find that more than 10 percent of the taxes the Federal Government takes from us goes to pay ourselves interest.

What would happen if we should find that we couldn't pay it off, we couldn't refinance it, or we couldn't pay the interest?

It is the federal debt that stimulates inflation. It is the federal debt that may impair our personal security. The federal debt is a vital factor in the security of our form of government. We are faced with a prospective federal debt at a height beyond management experience anywhere, anytime. There is a possibility that the statutory debt limit may have to be raised this year.

The reckless spending of the Truman Administration has

precipitated a Federal fiscal crisis which many of us may not fully realize but, unless we retrench, we can anticipate a constant deterioration of our currency and credit. There is only one road to solvency, and that is to *stop spending money we do not have* by elimination of every single nonessential disbursement. Yet, every effort by Congress to retrench is vigorously opposed by the President and his cohorts. There is, in my opinion, only one untouchable item in the Budget of the Federal Government, and that is the interest on the public debt. This we must pay as a matter of honor and to preserve the value of our bonds.

The one overshadowing characteristic of the Administration now in Washington is fiscal weakness and irresponsibility. From this springs the demand for confiscatory taxes, stifling controls, and centralization. If American democracy is destroyed, it will be the result of fiscal irresponsibility of which the present Administration is guilty, and which, even now, is being exploited by political camp followers who would centralize all power and purse control in Washington. From these come a deadly assault on the free enterprise system, the creeping socialism and the scandals which Thomas Jefferson foresaw when he said:

"I do verily believe that a consolidated Government would become the most corrupt government on earth."

As I witness the moral deterioration of our Government at Washington which has shocked and stunned the American people, once again I pay tribute to the foresight and wisdom of Thomas Jefferson, the founder of the legitimate Democratic Party.

A recent Gallup Poll headed "61% Fear National Bankruptcy," said: "A substantial majority of Americans think there is danger of Washington spending the country into bankruptcy."

Democracy cannot survive insolvency. Neither can the free enterprise system. Natural resources and human resources in terms of population, behind the Iron Curtain, far exceed those available to us. Our free enterprise system is a greater deterrent to Russian aggression than the United Nations ever will be. It is this system which is our first line of defense. Our armies, navies, and air forces are merely the tools through which the strength of this system is applied in war.

Socialism of our industry would be just as deadly to the productive capacity of our system as Russian totalitarianism. Therefore, we must protect our solvency if we are to preserve the freedoms of democracy, if we are to save ourselves and our allies from economic oblivion and military servitude under dictatorship.

All present signs indicate an engulfing global war is not in the Russian plans for the immediate future. On the other hand, their strategy seems to be a protracted period of international tension, studded with isolated disturbances, civil wars, guerrilla clashes, and subversive operations. In either event it is absolutely necessary that our military defenses should be made impregnable and, as in the past, I shall continue to support this endeavor to the hilt. Even if waste and extravagance of money and manpower by our military services were eliminated, the military costs will be staggering for years to come. General Eisenhower has estimated this period of military tension may last for 20 years.

### IV

If we are on the verge of national bankruptcy, or insolvency, as many believe we are, and if we must bear tremendous military costs as an essential to survival, what are the alternatives?

More taxes, as the President demands? Taxes are already perilously high, with diminishing returns in both revenue and production on the horizon.

Deficit financing? Besides the problems of financing and managing a debt of more than a quarter of a trillion dollars and all the other treacherous aspects of debt, more of it is bound to generate more inflation, which in itself will further undercut what little financial and economic stability there is left.

Reduction in nonessential expenditures? This, of course, is the only safe, sane, responsible and constructive alternative. But there is no reason to expect Fair Dealers to slaughter the cow they are milking, or to be safe, sane, responsible, or constructive.

If we fail to purge the federal budget of every nonessential expenditure, if we allow federal expenditures to mount to a level of $85 to $90 billion, or even somewhat less, if we are able to maintain the tax structure we have just enacted, for an indefinite period we shall be blindly following an irresponsible policy of debt and deficit spending which can lead only to insolvency.

Financial soundness is the heart of the American system, from which our social, economic, and military strength flows.

We are the last free area in the world. If free enterprise democracy in the United States goes down, there will be no place for us and our allies to turn for support and reinforcement.

## V

A trend toward socialism is inherent in continued deficit spending, increasing debt, and the resulting economic and social dislocations, including inflation, and mounting taxes.

These factors create demands for controls. Controls require more controls, and finally the pattern becomes so intricate it breaks down in confusion.

Prices rise and an inflation spiral sets in.

There is demand for additional taxes to halt inflation, and finally taxes reach a point of diminishing returns, suffocating the profit incentive of our free enterprise system in the process.

Then comes temptation to socialize the necessities of life,

such as security in old age and employment, schools, food, housing, medicine, and finally the source of livelihood—business and agriculture.

The President says it is an insult to the intelligence of the American people to say this country is on the road to socialism. I submit it is an insult to our intelligence to assume that we do not realize that adoption of the President's program will commit us irrevocably to a socialized state from which there is no retreat.

If the President is against socialism, the people of this country are entitled to receive from him satisfactory answers to these questions:

Why does he continue to pressurize Congress to adopt Socialized Medicine? He sent Oscar Ewing, at public expense, to England to get the "lowdown" on their socialistic system for propaganda use in the United States. If the President does not recognize that the British experiment in medicine is socialism, he could inform himself from the debates in England during the last election. The President calls his plan National Health Insurance, but it is socialized medicine just the same.

The cost of socialized medicine in America is difficult to estimate. We do things on a very grandiose scale when it comes to spending money, as you know. If the Federal Government undertakes to pay the expenses of our children when they are born, guard them through their lives from illness and the things that may happen to them, and then bury them, the cost will be huge. Some of the statisticians have estimated the ultimate cost at twenty billion dollars annually and, in fifty years, that amounts to one trillion dollars.

These statisticians further said that if you take one trillion dollars piled on top of another, it would extend two million ninety six thousand miles high—seven times the distance to the moon—with enough left over to pay our present national debt. I am told that is accurate, but I have not checked it.

If the President is against socialism, why is he advocating the

Brannan Plan, which inevitably means socialized agriculture? This plan not only would contribute in a huge way to the bankruptcy of America, but would create such chaos in the production, sale, and distribution of food as to make it necessary for the government to take over these functions that must remain competitive in private hands. President Truman and Secretary Brannan are now conducting a nationwide campaign to force the Brannan Plan through Congress, notwithstanding the fact that the great farm organizations such as the American Farm Bureau Federation and the National Grange, as well as most of the farmers of this country, are bitterly opposed to this plan. They realize it will be the end of free enterprise in agriculture.

The only sincere thing Mr. Brannan has said about the plan is that he could not estimate the cost of it. Testifying before a committee of Congress, he gave this glowing picture of what the Brannan Plan would do—reduce the cost of food to the consumer, pay the farmers a high profit for what they produce—but he did not fill in the gap by telling how the Federal Government could obtain the vast sums necessary to pay for the difference between food at low cost to the consumer and high prices to the farmer.

If President Truman is opposed to socialism, why is he advocating another extension of socialized housing?

These three proposals alone would mean socialization of your health, your food, and the roof over your head. If time permitted, many other trends to socialism could be cited.

If the President is opposed to socialism, why is he constantly advocating an extension of the number of those who receive payments from the Treasury of the United States? Today, there are 17 million Americans receiving regular payments directly from the Federal Government, and eight million more are on the rolls of counties, cities, and states. These twenty-five million, with their families, constitute a substantial part of our population. Socialism can be effectively promoted by constantly increasing those who are on the public payroll. A population of Government dependents is a socialized population.

Among the cardinal characteristics of socialism are Government subsidies with controls, and Government doles with regimentation. I am against that.

The Truman record for debt and deficit spending is made and it is continuing. His demand for more and more nonessential spending with more and more taxes is recurring. Complementing this record, in and out of emergencies, he has repeated demands for government allocation of commodities, government control of wages and prices, and government dictation over consumer credit and bank requirements.

To socialize the roofs over our heads, our health, and the food we eat, means we have adopted socialism. Socialism and free enterprise cannot live under the same roof.

No one can measure the extent to which we have already entered this primrose path to socialism. But this much certainly can be said. We would be much further on the road to ruin if it had not been for the frequently effective coalition between most of the Southern Democrats in Congress with some of the Republicans in voting on socialistic legislation. As one Southern Constitutional Democrat, I am proud to have been an active member of a coalition for this purpose. I believe you will endorse the stands we have taken.

## VI

As the Truman Administration has progressed, whether by plan or by caprice, more and more power, and more and more purse control, have been centralized within its easy reach at Washington. The thing most inflated in America today is the Federal Government. Big government costs big money. Big government and big spending are the source of inflation. The reckless spending of the Truman Administration has precipitated not only the trend toward socialism but also the trend toward centralization. No small part of this power and money has been centralized in give-away program after give-away program. And with each of these programs—in the form of subsidies, grants-in-aid, etc., to states, payments to individuals, and loans to just about anybody for anything—we are gradually changing from a nation built on the firm foundation of individual initiative, local self-government, and states rights, to one of peonage and servitude, to a paternalistic federal bureaucracy in Washington.

Through these programs the Federal Government takes money away from us, gives us back less than it took, and in the process it controls our lives and what we do, and makes us think we are getting something for nothing. As we stand today, states have to meet federal requirements or get federal permission to perform many of their functions. The same is true in a large measure with localities, business, agriculture, and even in the cases of individuals.

Think of these personal, economic, social, business, agricultural, and financial controls in terms of what unscrupulous bureaucrats might do with them once the Federal Government, in the name of civil rights, begins to usurp police power and exercise control over elections.

Make no mistake, the centralization of power in Washington is still increasing. Mr. Truman is constantly asking for more and more power to be taken from the states, from the localities, and from the source of all power—the citizens of the Nation.

The overshadowing characteristic of the Truman domestic policy is weakness in the fiscal situation resulting from continuing deficits and rising debt. The rest of our predicament is the result. A natural consequence of fiscal weakness in national government is autocratic control which, in our case, is manifest in the definite trend toward, and the demand for, more and more socialization of home, business, agriculture, and institutions. Fiscal weakness, paternalistic control, and socialism are the stuff of which centralization is made.

These constituents of centralization at the same time are the stuff on which those who would exploit political weakness feed their lust for power and easy money. Is any further explanation needed for the wave of scandals which, having started with Bennett Meyers, now has extended to the very vitals of the government represented by the Internal Revenue Bureau? And this moral weakness has been spreading. It spread to the Truman Democrats in Mississippi, whose appointees were selling RFD jobs to the highest bidder. It spread to high levels in the United States Army, where a Commander of a great arsenal, when caught receiving gratuities in the name of his position, assumed the attitude that he ought not to be discriminated against just because he was a "poor devil who got caught." Centralization is the breeding ground for the public scandals which beset us.

Perhaps being a conservative Virginian, I am such an old mossback that those things shock my conscience, whereas for some others, 20 years of federal paternalism have hardened them into the belief that anything you can get from the government is all to the good of the recipient, no matter who pays for it.

But we find that this moral turpitude has reached down into those operations of the government which collect the taxes— not just taxes from big corporations, but taxes from employees, taxes from everyone who buys medicine, food, gasoline, and all of the essentials of life on which we are having to levy excise taxes in order partially to pay the bill for federal programs.

## VII

Only the Federal Government can spend an unlimited amount. It alone determines the value of money and the extent of credit, because it alone is empowered to do so. As we think of the federal debt we must remember that a federal bond is not simply a loan to the Federal Government on which it pays us interest. It is a first mortgage on all we own.

Frankly, we are faced with a federal fiscal crisis and, unless we retrench, we can expect constant deterioration of our currency and credit. There is only one road to solvency, and that is to stop spending money we do not have for nonessential federal activities and programs. Neither democracy, nor the free enterprise system on which it depends for preservation against economic, social, or military attack, can survive in insolvency.***

Of course, we must arm to defend ourselves at a cost which will be unprecedented, but the military is notorious for its extravagance and its costs can be cut substantially, through economic and efficient operation, without impairment of defense. Every other item must be reduced to the absolute minimum.

We can continue down the road to state socialism and ultimate disaster, or we can strengthen and revitalize the free enterprise system with sound fiscal policies and go forward, with our head high, as the leader of those who have the will to fight for freedom and independence.

I do not concede that either democracy or free enterprise, or any other American freedom, has run the course of its usefulness in the world. They have been worth fighting for in the past against both economic and military challenge, and I do not concede that they were any dearer to those who have fought and won before than they are to us today. The battle lines are drawn. I am ready to fight. I hope you are. The forces of freedom in America need recruits.

What can we do? What can you do? I am frequently asked that question.

I would say, first, that you must stand firmly against socialistic trends, because a little socialism inevitably means more and more socialism. There are many doors to the house of socialism. It is very easy to get in but very hard to get out. Let us not be led into socialism by the back door. Let us judge for ourselves where these new "isms" will lead us and not be deluded by those who pay lip service to free enterprise and then advocate those things that would destroy it.

The American Medical Society has waged a clean, above-board, effective campaign against socialized medicine. You are fighting to preserve the great principles of our Republic. You realize, as all of us should, that socializing an important segment of our daily life means that sooner or later further socialism will encompass other activities, resulting in a complete socialistic regime.

Do not be deluded into a sense of false security. Those who insist upon committing this country to socialism are ever on the alert. Today, in the Senate of the United States, there are few votes for socialized medicine. But when the slightest opportunity opens you will find those promoting these measures ready to strike . . .

If Mr. Truman is re-elected on this platform of state socialism, he will assert that he has a mandate from the people to enact this full program into law.

Then I would say that you, the people of America, the voters at the polls, must demand that short of total war our Federal budget must be balanced. I do not ask for "pet" Federal appropriations but demand that the President and the Congress keep the Federal spending within the ability of the people to pay. Let us all recognize that we cannot pyramid deficit after deficit on an existing Federal debt of $260 billion and survive as a democracy.

Once the American dollar goes down, we will enter an age of international darkness. The American dollar is the only thing today that is holding the world together. It is the only currency that everybody, everywhere in the world, has confidence in.

Those who, wilfully or otherwise, would destroy the American system would destroy the freedoms of people everywhere. Today, we alone are bearing the standard. What nation can carry it if we fail? Without its light, freedom and progress would perish from the earth. We must not fail!

Without American solvency there would be no deterrent to

communism abroad. In the existing circumstances *it is no exaggeration to say that there is literally nothing on earth more important than the preservation of the fiscal integrity of the Federal Government of the United States and of the economic freedom of the enterprise system.*

In conclusion, let me say, we should always remember that human freedom is not a gift to man, it is an achievement by man; and, as it was gained by vigilance and struggle, so may it be lost by indifference and supineness.

## ೞ ೞ  THE DANGER OF DRIFTING *

BY DONALD K. DAVID†

**T**HERE is in this country a growing ferment of concern about the way we are drifting. It is expressed in the conversations of our most thoughtful private businessmen, in the writings of sympathetically critical observers, in the public utterances of some of our more enlightened leaders.

I am thinking, in particular, of five recent statements—warnings, indeed—which go to the heart of our present situation: (1) the remarks of Herbert Hoover on the occasion of his seventy-fifth birthday;[1] ‡ (2) the thinking of the distinguished musician, humanitarian, and philosopher, Dr. Albert Schweitzer, as reported in *Life;*[2] (3) the analysis made by the former Librarian of Congress, poet, and now Boylston Professor at Harvard University, Archibald MacLeish, in the August 1949 issue of *The Atlantic;*[3] (4) the essay in the July 1949 *Foreign Affairs* by Dr. Geroid T. Robinson, head of the Russian Institute at Columbia University;[4] and (5) Russell Davenport's article in *Fortune* for October 1949.[5]

As I examine the situation, the concern of these men, and of others of similar vision, is for the loss of human dignity, for

---

* Article in Vol. XXVIII of the Harvard Business Review, January, 1950, pp. 25-32.

† William Ziegler Professor of Business Administration and Dean of the Graduate School of Business Administration, Harvard University.

‡ See p. 112 for footnotes.

the fact that we have no positive philosophy to make explicit (to the world or to ourselves) our basic beliefs in our freedoms. Bear in mind, too, that when we talk of the loss to the individual of his dignity, of his freedoms and opportunities, we are specifying the very things which have made America great.

To what are we turning in order to make up for the loss? For what are we willing to pay such a price? Schweitzer has stated it well in one short paragraph:

> In a thousand different ways mankind has been persuaded to give up its natural relations with reality and to seek its welfare in the magic formulas of some kind of economic and social witchcraft by which the possibility of freeing itself from economic and social misery is still only further removed. And the tragic meaning of these magic formulas, to whatever kind of economic and social witchcraft they may belong, is always just this, that the individual must give up his own material and spiritual personality and must live only as one of the spiritually restless and materialistic multitude which claims control over him. [6]

Is this a picture of the so-called "welfare state"? Those who follow the mirage of the state's complete solicitude for the welfare of all its members may not recognize this unflattering description; but perhaps they have overlooked something—namely, what would be lost in the process of getting there.

As a matter of fact, all of us know that we are *against* such positive dangers as Communism. What we fail to recognize, as we drift toward the welfare state, is how perilously we are drifting away from what we are *for*.

That is why I want to focus attention here on one factor that seems to underlie and explain this situation: our apparent desire for security. As I look around, I see it everywhere—not only in the demands of labor for pension funds and so on, but also, and even more significantly, in some of the attitudes and actions of management. First, let me discuss the part taken by this desire for security in the drift toward the welfare state and let me try to explain why I think it may end by defeating the very purpose for which it is sought. Then I would like to discuss the way in which management may unwittingly be participating in the movement and to see what stand is indicated for management if the trend is to be reversed.

## SECURITY AS THE GOAL

In this country there may be comparatively few out-and-out advocates of the welfare state, but apparently there are many others who are willing to drift in that direction. The alluring promise of freedom from want and freedom from fear seems to me to be the commonly accepted goal of the welfare state. And one of the distinguishing marks of the advocates of the welfare state is that they give a categorical answer as to how security is to be achieved—that is, through the wisdom and generosity of the state.

Now there has been, we must admit, another categorical answer as to how men ought to seek security. The extreme rugged individualist asserted that it was the right and duty of each individual to look out for himself and, furthermore, that the fact that he might fail was a matter of no concern to anybody else, least of all to the government.

As one looks carefully at the security offered by these two extremes, one finds that they are not exactly the same. The one extreme offers an equal level of security for all; the other, a varying level depending upon each individual's ability and willingness to take hold of the opportunities available to him.

Now, frankly, I am convinced that both these extremes, these categorical answers to the question of how to run an economic system, are inadequate and wrong. They are wrong because they have either overlooked or misinterpreted what I conceive to be the facts. They both assume to a greater or lesser degree that man's foremost desire is for economic security—guaranteed by the state, on the one hand; self-assured, on the other.

## ECONOMIC SECURITY

I do not believe that economic security is all that man wants, or even that it is his main objective.

The development of our industrial civilization, with its factories and mass production, by its very efficiency in things economic took something away from man. To be sure, it brought him a great deal in terms of higher standards of living and cheaper and more abundant goods. But, for all that it gave, the rise of our industrial civilization also took away from man some very important noneconomic satisfactions. It removed him from his work bench and stood him in an assembly line; its technique of specialization deprived many a man of the feeling of a job well done by making it difficult for him to realize the importance of his contribution to the finished product. It became harder for many people to find in their daily work the satisfactions of participation, belonging, and achievement.

And so some men began to believe that they could expect from their jobs little more than the attainment of some degree of economic security, uncertain though it might be in the face of business cycles. They began to judge their jobs primarily in terms of the security and tenure that they offered, and looked more and more to other sources for the human satisfactions of life, especially to the government and more recently to group organizations such as labor unions.

An outstanding source of human satisfactions for many people today is the labor union, where men may feel that they are taking part in events which affect their own lives. This participation is as frequently expressed in union social and political activity as it is concerned with the economics of the individual's job. The importance of the point is that these are activities which men find satisfying—a further indication, in other words, that men seek satisfaction in a multiplicity of patterns. For in our industrial civilization—we might as well admit it—the degree of satisfaction derived from the job has diminished.

Now these, as I see it, are the facts, and I do not believe that the welfare state, with all its advertising slogans of "security" and "freedom from," even begins to face these facts. Economic security is not enough. And without additional satisfactions of the kind I have indicated, security would not mean very much.

## "FREEDOM FROM" VERSUS "FREEDOM TO"

"Freedom from" is not enough, because men want "freedom to"—freedom to engage in creative activities, to take a chance, to make their own decisions, and to take pride in their accomplishments. Fundamentally men like to feel they are able to take care of themselves, and the man who does feel that way gets a great deal of satisfaction out of it.

The welfare state stands ready to guarantee various aspects of security. It does not, and in my opinion cannot, offer opportunities for the human satisfactions that men so fundamentally desire. If our big business organizations, the producers of our economic goods and services, have failed to provide on-the-job satisfaction, I do not see how in the world we can expect an even larger and more remote government organization to be successful in providing it.

To the best of my knowledge, few advocates of the welfare state act as if they recognize this problem. Some who do recognize it claim that man will gain this satisfaction in his leisure time, which will be greatly increased by state-guaranteed security. To me this is unsound, wishful thinking, and defeatist. It is unsound because it overlooks the fact that men want to find in their jobs the opportunity for creative effort in which they can take pride. It is wishful thinking, for work completely devoid of satisfaction is drudgery, and how shall we get the world's work done unless people are tied into creative work? It is defeatist because it presumes that work can no longer furnish the satisfaction that men desire.

But if the welfare state cannot provide human satisfactions and if "freedom to" is so fundamental, why is it that many people seem to have fallen for this glib promise of "security" and "freedom from"? Obviously the complicated economic operations of recent years make it impossible for some citizens all the time and many citizens part of the time to take care of themselves. In such situations the promise of security alone is alluring. But what are the chances of the state's being able to deliver even that?

I think the chances are slim indeed, for real security depends upon work and a high level of production, which, in my opinion, America has achieved in the past through the aggressive exercise of a whole group of individual freedoms within the framework of protective government policies. The great danger is that the operation of state-guaranteed plans for security, for offering "freedom from," leads to restrictions upon and finally to removal of "freedom to," and thus to the entire collapse of production of the economic necessities which must be the basis of security.

What does that do to the promise of security? In my opinion it makes it meaningless, because the result of the welfare state is not likely to be security but rather stagnation. Perhaps some stagnation has already taken place. If so, the reasons are too many and too complex to discuss here. But of one thing I am convinced: that in a welfare state, with its appeal to the motives of security and leisure rather than to the incentives of pride in the reward for work well done, the economy would stabilize at a level where it could not provide even security, let alone the human satisfactions that men desire.

One of the difficulties of preventing society from drifting too far toward this welfare state, which must be faced by the advocates of a profit and loss or individual initiative economy, is the apparent success with which the promises of security are met in the early stages of a welfare state. As it gets under way, the welfare state has at its disposition the material legacy of the system it is succeeding; and for a while, as that inheritance is being squandered, everything looks rosy to those who do not examine the bookkeeping closely.

But sooner or later the accounts must be balanced. I believe that those who advocate and those who are willing to drift toward the welfare state are following a fruitless course, a course that can only end in moral as well as material bankruptcy. Not only have they mistaken their objective; they believe the state can guarantee something which state action alone is incapable of producing. They do not recognize the creeping paralysis temporarily obscured by the apparent success of the initial action.

## PROFIT AND LOSS SYSTEM

Now let us turn our attention to the profit and loss economy, and to what might well be the goal of a welfare *society* as distinguished from the goal of a welfare *state*. My position can be simply stated. There seems to be common acceptance of the goal of America as a society in which every human being is assured of the minimum necessities of food, clothing, and shelter; in which all the needy are cared for—the aged and the infirm, the disabled, the destitute, the delinquent, and of course the young and the deserted. There is no essential conflict between this goal and the profit and loss system. In fact, America's standard of living, the highest ever attained, is prima facie evidence that a dynamic profit and loss system is the best way we have yet discovered to attain the desired goal.

Now, is this a necessary relationship of cause and effect? Can the rise in our standard of living be directly ascribed to the system with which it is associated? Obviously there are many factors which have played their part, not the least of which is our willingness, our ingrained desire, to work, and, of course, our rich natural resources.

But even more significant is the fact that our profit and

loss system, operating within the setting of our national heritage of "freedom to," has produced what Professor Slichter speaks of as "millions of centers of initiative"—the idea that the birth rate of businesses is just as important to our society as the birth rate of babies. Whenever these centers of initiative, the red corpuscles of our society, fall below a certain minimum or become dulled in their activity for whatever reason, be it monopolistic government or monopolistic business, our society becomes anemic.

From time to time faults have developed in the system when these centers of initiative ceased to be centers of responsibility for human welfare. As these faults occurred originally, the government—more, I believe, as a practical matter to get things done than as a planned move toward the welfare state—began to assume, or to try to assume, some of the responsibility for human welfare. These attempts met a popular response, especially in votes. The faults which developed were very much like the faults which occur in the surface of the earth. An earthquake can be very damaging, but it does not mean that the whole world is falling apart. Rather, such faults are the results of stresses and strains which the system as a whole can easily withstand.

## BASIS FOR ACTION

Now, if this analysis is correct, there is real reason for optimism because there is at hand a basis for practical action. To me the solution is not for us to argue in favor of either of the extremes, but for all concerned to work toward a proper mixture of "freedom from" and "freedom to"; of individual centers of initiative and responsibility, on the one hand, and government responsibility for certain aspects of human welfare, on the other. Somewhat parenthetically, I should like to suggest that government action of this sort should be designed to support the independence and self-sufficiency of the individual citizen, rather than to discipline him and to make him dependent upon the state.

Thus we could think of government in the position of regulator of operations as opposed to dictator of them, providing restraint for the common good as opposed to domination. In this connection I should like again to recommend that excellent article by Professor Robinson in the July 1949 issue of *Foreign Affairs.*

There can be no fixed, no categorical formula for working out this proper mixture of individual and government action and responsibility because in our dynamic world no static solution can possibly be adequate. Flexibility is essential, and I believe a working solution can be found if we recognize the facts of our industrial civilization: that solution lies in the co-ordination of many goals of a welfare society *with* the operations of a profit and loss economy which has demonstrated its ability to create the multitude of vigorous centers of initiative and responsibility necessary to the foundation of real security.

It cannot be provided by any great panacea. It *can* grow out of the actions of individuals as they make day-to-day decisions about what may appear at the time to be little things. In this picture I see the businessman as having an almost unprecedented opportunity to serve his fellow man. His opportunity is twofold: (1) Within his own business he can seek new ways and means of furnishing opportunities for men to find human satisfactions on the job. (2) He can help society determine—in a continuing and purposeful program—the most effective ways of furnishing the maximum of human satisfactions and security.

The businessman's distinctive skills as an administrator fit him especially well for that job. His daily task of making it possible for the people within his business to work toward a common goal is not unlike the one society now faces on a somewhat larger scale. The businessman's skills should be useful to society. In my opinion they can be if the businessman avoids one major pitfall, and that is adopting the attitude that he alone knows all the answers.

The task is to provide the proper mixture of all the human activities which can contribute toward the goal. Business is one. It is going to be, in an industrial civilization, a very significant one. But there are obviously others. I have mentioned the government many times, but the church, the various professions, and labor, all have their parts to play in determining the proper mixture.

The mixture I advocate includes the traditional and uniquely American ideal of equality of opportunity but, because its purpose is to harness for the benefit of society the tremendous force of individual initiative, it does not include the welfare state ideal of equality of results.

On this basis there can be no real conflict between a profit and loss economy and a welfare society in contrast to a welfare state—a welfare society whose goal it is to furnish, by attaining this proper mixture of "freedom from" and "freedom to," the maximum of security *and* these very important human satisfactions.

## BUSINESSMEN AS THE LEADERS

But there is a possibility, as I suggested earlier, that businessmen may not be altogether ready to take the courageous stand and provide the kind of leadership called for. In a way many of us are participating in the drift away from what we are *for*—not intentionally, of course, and not always voluntarily. But if we practice complacency, strive to protect the status quo, and try to take profits without risks, to that extent we too are seeking security rather than exerting purposeful leadership.

## COMPLACENCY

We have no real reason to be complacent today. Our past accomplishments have been great, and we should be proud of them. At the same time, we have made mistakes—millions of them, whether measured in terms of wrong decisions, of unhappy workers, or of unrealized dollars of profits. We know such mistakes are inevitable in our kind of dynamic economy, so we should not be on the defensive about them. The fact remains that we have no way to be sure that management is now measuring up to its greatest potentialities.

The years during and since the war have been poor years indeed in which to measure the real results of management. First Hitler and now Stalin may have made a number of managements look good that perhaps are not so good. What standards of evaluation can be put to managements in times such as we have had, say, in the last ten years? How can we ever be sure, when conditions make so much difference?

There are many of us who made relatively few mistakes during the 1920's, or at least the mistakes we made were covered by good profits. Then we had the very humbling and real experience of the 1930's. Almost everything we did in the 1920's seemed to be right; almost everything we did from 1930 to 1933 seemed to be wrong. If we thought we were good in 1929, we knew very well that we were not in the middle 1930's.

I do not think that we are going to face another 1930 period; actually, the recession of 1949-1950, if that is what it is to be called, may be a most healthy thing. If we can only get off the unsoundly high plateau that we have been on without skidding too far, if we can only go down and then balance, we may all be better off. And that is exactly what I think we are going to do, unless businessmen forget some of their hardest learned lessons—and there have been some indications that businessmen here and there need to be reminded.

I am not putting responsibility for everything that is currently wrong on businessmen alone. But if my conviction about their place in society is correct, it follows that they must be in the lead in taking corrective action. By way of illustration, it is important that prices be brought down; it is important that volume in terms of tonnage and units be kept up. That *is* within the scope of businessmen's responsibility.

In any event, the time is coming when the going will not be so easy. I hope it comes fairly quickly, because it will be the shakedown period for many managements that at the moment look very good; and the sooner our weaknesses are corrected, the better off we should all be in the end. The real test is still ahead.

Let me mention, now, a few developments of the past decade which seem to me to be very unhealthy. What I have to say here may be interpreted as being critical of businessmen; in actual fact, it is. But I hope readers will recognize the sincerity of my motives in thus speaking out frankly. Believe me, I understand the difficulties of the problems involved; I have been through them myself. So this is sympathetic criticism, offered with the hope that it will be construed also as constructive criticism.

## FEATHERBEDDING OF CAPITAL

First, let us look at the lack of new capital formation in the last ten years, a phenomenon that some people think is becoming increasingly serious in its effects.

There are many aspects of this phenomenon. Take the matter of taxes. Even if we had really tried to, I do not see how we could have worked out a worse tax program than the one we now have, from the point of view of incentives and all the other requirements of a truly dynamic economy. Another crucial aspect is the imbalance which exists today in terms of values, some of which are artificial. Let us take potatoes, or onions, or the stock of a good company which is selling at two to three times earnings. There is an imbalance in our whole picture, and much of that imbalance has been created, on the one hand, by subsidy, and, on the other hand, by lack of return on investment and by fear—particularly by fear.

This lack of capital formation has, in my mind, some very bad implications in terms of management. Far too many managements today are "featherbedding," are building up reserves beyond amounts which might be considered adequate for normal purposes, as if they wanted a nice cushion in which their mistakes could be buried.

Is that good business, basically? Do not misunderstand me. Obviously, good reserves, ability to turn around, ability to make new investments and move quickly, flexibility—all are needed. But a year-after-year basis of holding back too large a percentage of earnings, purely because of fear, is hardly a constructive use of capital funds. Timidity about going ahead and investing that money, dread of taking risks and daring and venturing, are in direct contradiction to the private initiative that businessmen are supposed to stand for—and in fact must stand for if they are to be leaders.

## PROFITS AS A MEASURE OF SUCCESS

For some years at least, management is of course going to continue to be tested, as it should be tested, primarily on the making of profits. And let me repeat that profits are the lifeblood of our society; it is high time that profits be considered a downright necessity to a healthy society rather than something suspect or indecent.

But what standards can be used in evaluating these profits? When we look at corporate financial statements, should we not begin to ask, "What return is the management making on the capital that it is managing?" rather than, "What increase in profits happens to have been made this year over last year or the second half over the first half (or some similar comparison)?" The former would seem to be more consonant with leadership in a dynamic economy, and yet not less valid as a test of efficiency.

We can well afford to do some new thinking on this question

106

of efficiency or, as it is too often considered, of matching the dollar figures of previous periods. Here there is an easy error that often colors the thinking of managements and particularly boards of directors. When they immediately say, "Oh! We are off 5%, 10%, or 15% from last year," they are evidencing no concern about the tonnage, the units, the real things that the company makes and sells. The company is not making and selling dollars; it is making and selling merchandise—goods and services for people to use.

Standards of evaluation that get down to the basic function for which businesses exist would get us away from this dollar fetish, would make management feel responsible for results in terms of how well it is managing the resources entrusted to it— and I mean by resources both capital *and* labor.

## MANAGEMENT INCENTIVES

Let us take another of the unhealthy developments of the last ten years or so: the weakening of management incentives. I am thinking, of course, primarily of incentives which are economic in nature. But I want to make it clear that managements do respond to many other kinds of incentives and find satisfactions in many activities that have nothing to do with dollars and cents. We all know businessmen who have kept on devoting themselves to their companies long after they acquired all the money they wanted. The fact remains that economic incentives are important, particularly in the earlier stages of management careers, and as such they play an essential role in keeping private initiative strong and vigorous.

In regard to the weakening of such incentives, I must refer again to taxes—to be specific, high income taxes. Perhaps even more serious is something which happened to American business in 1943 and which has passed almost completely unnoticed— the so-called *Smith* decision of the Supreme Court.[7]

This decision ruled that when employees or executives

purchased stock under a stock operation at a favorable price, the difference between the price paid and the current market price was ordinary income in the year in which the purchase was made and as such was subject to income tax rates.

The *Smith* decision struck a blow at initiative in this country, the significance of which very few people appreciate. It is all the more serious because boards of directors in this country, trying to hold good men and keep management teams together, in my opinion, have gone to an extreme in offering security, usually in the form of pensions.

By making it impossible for us to say to a management, "Here is a good way for you to get an equity position; then, if you work hard, you will be increasing the value of your own property," the *Smith* decision obviated one strong incentive method. So we have turned on the line, and now we are saying, "Fine. You just stay here and work. It does not make any difference how hard you work. But if you stay with us, you can be sure to be comfortable. Our pension plan will take care of you."

I am obviously overstating this point for emphasis because I think management pension plans are basically sound. There had to be some adjustment of this kind in management's favor. Running a business takes a toll from management, and management deserves protection. But paraphrasing what President Eliot of Harvard once said about universities and mortgages, I should like to suggest that the time has come when managements no longer can afford to sit on their security. It is just as fair to say "featherbedding" in regard to management as it is in regard to capital or labor or any other segment of our economy.

For the sake of emphasis, let me put the point in very simple terms: the oat-bag out in front, the burr under the tail, *incentives* in a word, are just as necessary for businessmen as for any other kind of people, and just as American as are the basic concepts which we have always treasured and which we seek to strengthen as we drive our economy forward.

## PROTECTION

Another development of recent years which it is distressing to see is the willingness and sometimes almost the anxiety of some managements (and I am glad to be able to say that this at least is not typical) to run to the cover of government when they think they can be helped.   We blame every other segment of the community for doing it.   The businessman will get up and talk at luncheons against it.   And yet when something untoward happens outside the control of his company, one of the first things he thinks about is, "Well, let's run down to Washington and see if we can't get it fixed."   And every time he does it, he weakens the long-run basis of his own strength.

Of course we have had subsidy in this country for a long time.   Business has had it for a long time.   The railroads were originally built with land grants and subsidy.   Look at the mail, at protective tariffs.   I am not trying to point a finger, for I think tariffs are wise in some respects and in some places; and the subsidy as such is not necessarily un-American.   But we should have a minimum of subsidy.   Subsidy should not be so attractive that everybody woos it or at least is willing to accept it, for then we lose our initiative, we settle down again on our security.

Above all, we must avoid the self-protection of monopoly and restrictive trade practices.   In the type of society in which we all believe, this thing called competition is terribly important: real competition, the opportunity for competition, free competition in its best sense.   We need to make sure that in the long run large companies are not operating so that it is impossible for new businesses to start in their fields; and here I think that managements must take it upon themselves to see that this is so, rather than to force new laws by their own inaction.   The birth rate of businesses in this country, let me repeat, is just as important to us as the birth rate of babies.

This is of course not a new concept.   Every businessman is against monopoly and for competition.   If you ask him, he will tell you so; and in most cases he really does believe in the idea. The point I am trying to make is that individual managements need consciously to *act,* to carry their belief into day-to-day decisions, and not from the point of view of whether a proposal is legal or not but rather in a positive attempt to promote what they are for.   That is the kind of thing I mean by leadership.

The question is, will we get that leadership?   Our dynamic economy admits no half measures, no compromise, in that regard.   With such courageous leadership we can accomplish more for our people than we could under any other system. Without it, we will drift, and drift, and then founder.


## CONCLUSION

Now, let me start being optimistic.   I mentioned the ferment of concern that I sense in this country.   There is a growing idealism on the part of businessmen.   Unfortunately, business is not articulate; "business" is too broad, too vast; there is no single tent that will cover it.   But businessmen in this country typically want to do "the right thing."   The morals of the business community today are, I am convinced, better than they have ever been—perhaps also better than those of many other sections of the community.   And they should be.

There is no doubt that we are engaged in an ideological conflict.   I cannot believe that we are going to be defeatists. Some constructive program is going to be worked out.

I think responsibility for this program is going to be placed in the hands of the businessman, because we have, whether some people like it or not, an industrial civilization; and the businessman, whether he likes it or not, has to assume new responsibilities. The lawyer is not going to take them, the doctor cannot, the teacher cannot, and the minister (I am sorry to say) has lost some of his position. By the very fact of the businessman's past success in doing what he considered his only job, these new responsibilities will be thrust upon him. He cannot dodge them even if he wants to. His past training—the methods he has used in achieving his present position—are his best qualifications for meeting the new test successfully.

The emerging responsibility of business is, it seems to me, first, that the businessman must operate his business competently and purposefully; and, secondly, that he must make his place of business a good place to work, a good society in terms of some of the satisfactions to which I referred earlier.

What will count is the quality of the decisions that are made in the day-to-day work. Each man who has anybody else reporting to him—it does not make any difference whether only two or three people report to him, or a secretary, or an office boy—to my mind becomes an important person because he immediately has a human problem, he immediately is in charge of a society. He takes on community responsibilities for his own society; he must make it possible for those people to become part of the larger scheme of things. That, in turn, is the way we are going to begin to solve this problem.

As I have said on many occasions, the businessman can and will succeed in being a great factor in defining what America stands for if he brings to the job: (1) the abilities he has developed in business; (2) a willingness to face the new task squarely; and (3) a tough-minded humility, growing out of justifiable confidence in his own ability, on the one hand, and frank realization, on the other hand, that he does not know all the answers and that others have the interest, and skills of their own, to participate under intelligent leadership.

I sincerely believe America is making definite progress toward a positive philosophy and is successfully, if slowly, counteracting the tendency to drift.

What I have sketched is really a goal toward which to work. Since it is a goal, we may never attain it, and yet America has made real progress along the road to it. Let us not underestimate what we have accomplished and are on the way to accomplish. Certainly continuous progress by proven means is preferable to being allured by seductive mirages.

## FOOTNOTES

[1] *New York Times*, August 11, 1949; from a speech delivered at Stanford University, August 10, 1949. (See pp. 175-183 hereof.—*Ed.*)

[2] *Life*, Vol. 27, No. 4 (July 25, 1949), p. 75.

[3] "The Conquest of America," *The Atlantic Monthly*, Vol. 184, No. 2, p. 17.

[4] "The Ideological Combat," *Foreign Affairs*, Vol. 27, No. 4, p. 525.

[5] "The Greatest Opportunity on Earth," *Fortune*, Vol. XL, No. 4, p. 65.

[6] *Life*, July 25, 1949, p. 79.

[7] *Comm. v. Smith*, 324 U. S. 177, 65 S. Ct. 591 (1943).

# THE BLESSINGS OF LIBERTY*

## BY JOHN FOSTER DULLES†

### THE ISSUE

W HEN our nation was formed, the founders wrote a Preamble to the Constitution in which they expressed the hopes of the people. One hope was that the new government would help to "promote the general welfare." The ultimate hope was that it would "secure the blessings of liberty to ourselves and our posterity."

During most of our history there has seemed to be no conflict between these two goals. Liberty was looked upon as the fountainhead of welfare. But now many think of welfare as primarily material and that governmental compulsion is its best dispenser. Others think that that is bad economics and bad morals.

No doubt, this issue will be finally resolved in the heat of political campaigns. But the voters are more apt to decide rightly if, in cooler intervals, political scientists like yourselves work on the problem. So, I broach the subject with you.

### THE HISTORICAL BACKGROUND

Our nation was founded as an experiment in human liberty. Its institutions largely reflected the belief of our founders that

---

* Address at the American Political Science Association, December 28, 1949.

† Distinguished international lawyer and former senator. Architect of the treaty of peace with Japan.

men had their origin and destiny in God; that they were endowed by Him with inalienable rights and had duties prescribed by moral law, and that human institutions ought primarily to help men to develop their God-given possibilities.

Our experiment succeeded well. Out of it came great richness—spiritual, intellectual, and also material. What we did attracted world-wide attention and we were to others "liberty enlightening the world." Largely under the force of our example, the restraints of despotism were loosened and throughout the world men gained better opportunities to develop the worth and dignity of their persons. It was the great age of liberation, of true liberalism.

Then, around the beginning of the century, it seemed that a change occurred. We had to meet the hardest test of all, that of material prosperity. Our good society had borne such tempting material fruits that, to many, material things began to seem all-important. Our practices became disconnected from the religious faith that had formed them, and many ignored their duty to fellow man.

This lapse was the more serious because, at this same time, scientific knowledge was making our society more complicated and interconnected, our population was becoming more dense and more urban, and business and labor were organizing into larger units. On top of that came a world war, a world-wide depression, and a second world war. The combined result was that individuals became less self-reliant, feeling themselves tossed about by great cyclical waves. Many felt that security and social justice were dependent on the ordering of society by a strong central government. We have now gone far in that direction.

## THE INTERNATIONAL SETTING

The trend toward the all-powerful government has been even more pronounced elsewhere. In Russia the Communist

Party seized control and, as a dictatorship of the proletariat, put on their spectacular experiment in a completely socialized state. Their leaders were fanatical and purposeful in a postwar world which had largely become a moral, economic, and military vacuum.

Communist practices derive from irreligious beliefs. Orthodox Communism denies the existence of God or of a moral law. It holds that individuals are soulless members of a social group. Their individual personality is unimportant. The material welfare of the group is all-important.

Communists admit that there are nonmaterial things, ideas, and that ideas can be potent. But, as put by Stalin, "the material world is primary and mind, thought, is secondary . . . Hence the source of formation of the spiritual life of society should be sought . . . in the conditions of the material life of society." He concludes that "the strength and vitality of Marxism-Leninism lies in the fact that it does base its practical activity on the needs of the development of the material life of society" and relies upon that for "setting into motion broad masses of the people and mobilizing them and organizing them into a great army of the proletarian party, prepared to smash the reactionary forces." ("Dialectical and Historical Materialism," 1938.)


## CHALLENGE AND RESPONSE

We in the United States cannot evade that challenge, for it is now hurled primarily at us. In Soviet eyes we are the arch reactionaries to be smashed by the masses, rallying to the communist slogan: "Develop the material life of society."

What will be our response to this challenge? It catches us a little off-balance, because of the historical developments I have mentioned. Shall we promise the masses that, from now on, we too will seek primarily to develop the material life of society?

Or shall we respond with renewed efforts to show the worth of a society that puts spiritual development first?

The choice involves moral, not merely practical, factors. What is man's chief end here on earth? If, as Communists say, the goal is a mechanically perfect machine for the production and distribution of material things, then we might consider the arguments in favor of an all-powerful central government which would direct the living of the people and decide what is done with the products of their labor. That, however, would be to treat human life as little different from animal life and that, most Americans would think, is wrong and to be rejected as wrong.

Most Americans still have spiritual ideals. We want to be a society of individuals who love God and fellow man and who fear only God and not any other man; who work hard as a matter of duty and self-satisfaction, not compulsion; who gain personal and family security, not out of what government takes from us, but out of our ability and willingness voluntarily to earn and save; who are self-reliant, resourceful, and adaptable to changing conditions and for whom life is not merely physical growth and enjoyment but intellectual and spiritual development.

We know that such ideals cannot be attained by joining the life of an animal farm.

But also we know that material conditions do have a bearing on spiritual development. A measure of insecurity can be a stimulant. But dread of insecurity is a depressant. Sordid and unhealthy living conditions, and illiteracy, stunt spiritual development.

Since private efforts alone cannot deal adequately with such problems, government should not be indifferent to them. There are many governmental compulsions that, all would agree, should be accepted to help improve the material conditions of our society. We have some of them and there are other

116

public projects of national scope, like enlarged insurance against unemployment and old age ("Social Security"), that are generally acceptable. But also there is a point where increasing governmental compulsion produces diminishing spiritual returns.

Political scientists have not charted the precise location of that danger point. It is perhaps a shifting reef. But certain signs suggest that we are already near that danger.

Taxes come closest to being an objective test. Today federal income and estate taxes are highly graduated and at a near wartime peak, and we still have wartime excise taxes. Economic conditions are favorable to big tax collections. Yet the federal income fails, by about $6 billion, to pay for what the Federal Government is now doing. And the impact of federal taxes on states and cities is such that they cannot raise the money needed, at present costs, to carry on adequately their accustomed functions. Governors and Mayors come as beggars to the White House lawn.

Another danger sign is the increasing political attention paid to the assumed views of what the Communists contemptuously refer to as "masses." Some politicians seem to believe that there is here such a group, that it partakes only of materialism rather than what President Truman last week referred to as our "Christian heritage" and that, to get its votes, it is necessary to throw it raw political meat. That is an appetite that it is dangerous to cultivate.

Another danger sign is a world current so strong that none are immune from its suction. In 1917 the Communist Party ruled nobody. Now Communists rule about one-third of the human race and the end is not in sight. Never before have so few come so rapidly to rule so many. Such a world trend draws others to it unless positive precautions are taken.

It seems, then, that the time has come to "stop, look, and listen" before embarking on vast new governmental projects for compelling an increase in material welfare. We should consider not merely whether the professed end is good, but what the process of getting there will do *to* people's character, if it involves more government compulsion and less personal responsibility. Also, we should consider whether there are not alternative ways of getting to the desired ends that have more of a voluntary, less of a compulsory, character.

We have often been told, by wise men, that citizens ought periodically to check up on the tendency of government to enlarge its power at the expense of liberty. Washington, Jefferson, Lincoln, and many others whom we revere have enjoined that on us. I cannot believe that, under present conditions, it is "reactionary" to follow that advice.

Let us then briefly appraise some current proposals in relation to matters that touch the lives of us all—food, health, education, and taxes.

## FOOD

Take first our food problem—and none deny that it is a problem. Some would have the Federal Government buy from farmers at fixed high prices intended to guarantee a riskless profit. To prevent that guarantee from stimulating vast overproduction, there would be detailed regulations and restrictions.

Because consumers generally could not afford to buy in adequate quantities at the high prices paid the farmers by the government, the government would sell to consumers at lower prices.

The government would have to get from somewhere the difference between the high prices it pays the farmers and the lower prices it gets from consumers, plus its administrative costs. So, taxes generally would be increased.

I do not now question the strange economics which assume that people can pay in taxes what they cannot pay in prices.

What I now ask is: What would this program do to the character of our people?

Would it not make farmers into a subsidized class and take from them their sense of self-reliance and of dependence on their individual judgment and industry?

Would it not make consumers into a subsidized group, and take from them a sense of economic independence?

Would not both farmer and consumer live fearfully lest they incur the disfavor of those who govern them and subsidize them?

Certainly, taxpayers would increasingly be denied voice in the use of what they earn, with consequences to their character that we shall touch on later.

## EDUCATION

Take our educational problem—and none deny that it is a problem. Some would have our Federal Government levy taxes to raise funds that it would allot to all the states for use in paying for schools, teachers, and related activities.

It is claimed that this might equalize somewhat the education of our children. It might raise it in some areas that are poor or tax-lazy. It might lower it elsewhere. But what would it do *to* our children?

Would not our youth for the first time in our history be subjected to the risk of indoctrination by whoever might at a single time come into power in a single place? Would not Congress, in an effort to escape religious controversy, insist increasingly upon the elimination of religious influence from federal-aided education? Would not the result be to spread agnosticism and materialism?

Most of the advocates of "federal aid to education" deny any intent to have the Federal Government influence the kind of education that is aided. But the lesson of history teaches that those who make grants inevitably come to attach conditions.

119

## HEALTH

Take the problem of ill-health, and no one denies that it is a problem. Some would have our Federal Government collect the funds for the payment of doctors, dentists, nurses, etc., and assure their assignment to all in response to calls for medical assistance. This, it is contended, would make healing care more equally available. Whether or not this is so is debatable. But what would this do *to* people?

Healing is not just a matter of technical diagnosis and mechanical prescription. It is in large measure a spiritual task. It needs trust by the patient and kindliness, self-sacrifice, and devotion by the healers.

To socialize the healing profession might, perhaps, make doctors more generally available. But would it not take the soul out of a great profession and turn consultation into an assembly-line process?

## TAXES

Take taxes. As we have noted, the current federal budget will show a deficit of nearly $6 billion, and it would take many billions more to pay for such projects as the "Brannan Plan," "federal aid to education," and "socialized medicine." Because most of the rich cream is already taxed off the top of the bottle, the new billions will have to come from less rich levels. If Federal taxes on net incomes took everything over $10,000 a year, and if such incomes still remained as at present, that would not cover half of the present federal deficit.

What will these increased taxes do *to* people? Not merely those who pay direct taxes, but those who pay indirect taxes and costs inflated by the direct taxes others pay. What happens to human character when there is little incentive, when individuals can no longer be charitable, and when there is no need of self-control to save because taxes leave nothing saveable? What is the future of private institutions for health, education, and religion? And what happens to private enterprise, and above all to little business and new business, if there are no fresh sources of private capital and if it is impossible to save up against inevitable rainy days?

Already, in this country, steeply graduated income and estate taxes bring society close to the professed Communist goal, "from each according to his ability, to each according to his need." This is a noble ideal. It is reported that the early Christians "had all things common . . . and parted them to all men, as every man had need." (Acts 2:44,45.)

But it is one thing to do this voluntarily and another thing to do it under compulsion. Good behavior is significant when it is voluntary, but *only* when it is voluntary. When individuals voluntarily produce according to their maximum ability and voluntarily use it in an enlightened way, that exemplifies the best in human nature.

Of course voluntary action cannot be our sole dependence. But if compulsion becomes our primary dependence, the result is to dry up the finest spiritual qualities.

## THE MORAL ANGLE

This brief analysis is, I think, sufficient to show that if, on top of what is now being done and what still has to be done by government, there are added vast new governmental projects of the kind I have touched on, the result may be spiritual impoverishment. If so, such proposals should be rejected on moral grounds by those who believe that spiritual welfare is primary.

Slavery raised a moral issue and it is worth-while to recall it, even though present circumstances have none of that horrid quality.

Beveridge, in his *Life of Lincoln*, points out that slavery was powerfully supported as a welfare and social security measure. It was contended in respect of the negro slaves that:

*"They were fed and cared for from birth to the working
period, and from the beginning of old age for the remainder of
their lives, all at the owner's expense. They were far happier
than laborers in the North, better off than the peasantry of
Europe. Never for a moment were Southern slaves terrified by
the spectre of a friendless future of want and starvation. And
during their years of productive labor, they could not be discharged, as were white laborers in 'free' countries when business
was poor. No matter whether the season was good or bad, the
market brisk or slow, the slaveholder had to support his negroes
the same at all times . . . ."*

The proponents of emancipation never really met these arguments. They did not feel that they had to. They felt that
it was wrong for some to have great power over the lives of
others and over the products of their labor and that a system
that sanctioned that could not be justified by any material benefits it might confer. It was condemned by what it did *to* people.

Also they had faith that if they put spiritual ends first, then,
in some way beyond their planning, material good also would
come. They did not believe that nothing good happens unless
planners plan it.

## MATERIAL BY-PRODUCTS

You will recall that Jesus discussed men's need for food and
drink and clothing. "All these things," he said, "do the nations
of the world seek after: and your Father knoweth that ye have
need of these things." "But seek ye first the Kingdom of God
and His righteousness; and all these things shall be added unto
you."

The American people have been deeply influenced by that
Christian directive. They did not ignore worldly things, but
for the most part they did not exalt them as primary. Indeed,
at the beginning, our people accepted great material insecurity

in order to get freedom to worship God in their own way and to develop in themselves and their children what they believed to be God-given spiritual possibilities.

Of course, our society was not all good—far from it. There is, and always was, vast room for improvement and no basis for complacency. There were always those who treated material things as of first, not secondary, importance and, as we have pointed out, material selfishness at times led to much social injustice.

But our lapses have not been so grave or so prolonged as to justify sentencing the American people to shrivel, spiritually, under a paternalistic form of government.

Neither faith, reason, nor experience warrants the conclusion that, in the case of a people as religious and as educated as are the American people generally, public materialism is the way to counteract the ill of some private materialism. There is no reason to abandon faith in the great American experiment and every reason for resuming it.

That doesn't mean going back or standing still. The American people have been the most creative people in history. They are constantly pulling things down in order to put up something new and better. Their restless habits in that respect amaze people elsewhere. They have, to be sure, been kept under wraps in recent years. But their spirit is still vibrant, and to say that the American people, unless spurred by government, will keep in the same place is to be more nonsensical than Alice's Red Queen.

Of course, it is impossible to do today, on a private basis, all that should be done. More than ever before in our peacetime history government must be the means by which people cooperate. But that very fact makes it the more necessary to be selective and to stop assuming that whenever there is a social problem the way to solve it is to increase still more the power, the responsibility, and the taxes of the Federal Government.

And those who want freedom can and should put energy, resourcefulness, devotion, and enthusiasm into finding solutions that will be voluntary and not compulsory.

The great need of our time is to recapture faith in the infinite possibilities of the individual human being and to translate that faith into works. That is the way, the only way, to surmount the grave perils, domestic and foreign, that confront our nation.

If we consider such troublesome domestic situations as those we have discussed, we can see that it is possible to bring about great improvement while at the same time relying largely on private and local initiative.


## EDUCATION

Take education. There exists a vast willingness of parents, religious groups, public-spirited citizens, and local and state governments to carry the responsibility for the education of our youth. There may be a few areas where help is needed from beyond the state borders. But the Federal Government is no independent source of funds. It has to get what it gives. Whatever money it spends for education must be taken away from local communities—from individuals. Why not leave the responsibility with them, where the money is and where the responsibility is normally the deepest and most conscientious?

We can be confident that educational responsibilities will generally be discharged at the local level if federal taxes permit and if we get over the illusion that federal aid is a financially painless operation. Then our children will get education that is guided by parental and religious care rather than by remote control. And they will be kept beyond the grasp of any who, in the future, might win national power and feel that education ought to conform our youth to their particular way of thinking.

124

## AGRICULTURE

Take agriculture. Here some of the problems are so national in scope that federal action is needed. But it is not necessary to turn farmers into marionettes, with Washington pulling the strings. A system of flexible price supports would put a floor under farm prices rather than put those prices on stilts. Flexible price supports would allow natural forces to exercise a modest but not excessive influence and leave play for individual judgment and for increased rewards for those farmers who exercise good judgment and industry.

We are in an age when men increasingly live in an artificial environment made by men and saturated with men. That makes it more important to preserve the sagacity of those who live apart from crowds and close to nature.

## HEALING

Take healing. Here we already have a remarkable demonstration of what can be done through a sense of individual responsibility. Voluntary plans like the Blue Cross and Blue Shield are increasing their membership by leaps and bounds, and these plans are supplemented by all sorts of health insurance plans under industrial and other private auspices. Already over 60 million people have some form of health insurance. It still costs more than many can afford and the coverage is still too small. But only one very far gone in pessimism can fail to see the tremendous and unexhausted possibilities in voluntary plans which preserve, in healing, the spiritual qualities.

## TAXES

Take taxes. Federal taxes can be substantially reduced so as to give those who produce greater incentive and a greater material possibility of discharging social responsibilities individually and at the state and local level. The biggest single item of federal expense is due to the unstable international situation —$20 billion a year. That, and more, may be needed if, in matters of defense, we also became so materialistic that we trust only in material might. But defense would not be so costly if we had the spiritual resources to lead a moral crusade for liberty throughout the world and if we were able to achieve a greater measure of unity with like-minded people. I shall say more of that in a moment.

In other respects, federal savings in large amount can be effected by greater economy and efficiency and by the people getting rid of the notion that all of their problems can be solved by dumping them in the lap of Washington. Washington, too, can help if it rejects the view that, because the Federal Government has unlimited power to tax incomes, that implies an unlimited responsibility to try to remedy every ill.

Having been in the United States Senate, I can sympathize with the viewpoint of those who see a human need which apparently they can remedy if only they use increasingly their power to tax. In any individual situation the case for federal action is powerful. But it must be remembered that the multiplication of such acts will make taxes so heavy as virtually to deprive all of our citizenry of responsibility and, as Justice Brandeis warned:

*"Experience should teach us to be most on our guard to protect liberty when the Government's purposes are beneficent."*

## MEANS AND ENDS

In these matters, as in most others, dispute relates to methods, not ends.

Those in power usually believe that the way to get good ends is to increase their power. They lose faith in the capacity and

126

willingness of private persons and state and local authorities. They have complete faith in their own benevolence and in their own ability to withstand the corrupting influence of power.

Our founders had no such faith. They took great precautions to erect barriers against what George Washington, in his Farewell Address, referred to as "the spirit of encroachment" which

"... *tends to consolidate the power of all the departments in one, and thus to create, whatever the form of government, a real despotism.*"

They carefully restricted the powers of the Federal Government and stipulated that all others "are reserved to the States respectively, or to the people." But, in fact, the power of the states and of the people exists only on paper if those in Washington lose faith in all except themselves and, through taxes, monopolize the means of promoting the general welfare.

Professor Toynbee has recently pointed out in *Civilization on Trial* that when, as he says is now largely the case, men come to believe that "the significant and important thing in human life is not the spiritual development of souls but the social development of communities" the result has been "moral enormities."

Today, one of those moral enormities is the status of the individual in Russia, where the doctrine of social development by and through central government is most fully being put into action. Similar enormities are certain to show themselves in the West, if our peoples and governments follow down that path.

## THE RECAPTURE OF MORAL LEADERSHIP

The danger to the West is not merely the internal danger of slow but sure deterioration of the character of their people. The tendency to materialistic paternalism brings greatly increased risk from without.

We are engaged in a "cold war" with Soviet Communism. It is a war that cannot be won by material might alone. It is primarily a struggle for souls and minds of men.

Soviet Communism has won great victories by bringing discontented masses to believe that free institutions are bankrupt and that their best hope lies in the Soviet system of state socialism.

In this ideological struggle the United States has played a feeble role. Our conduct suggests that we ourselves have lost faith in the possibilities of a free society with institutions derived from a religious belief; that we, too, have come to believe, with Stalin, that material things are primary and spiritual things secondary; that we are following in the wake made by the leaders of Soviet Communism.

If the solution for agriculture is for government to buy at fixed prices from farmers and to sell to consumers at subsidized prices, then why should the farming communities of the world turn to us for leadership? We are late starters in that direction. Soviet Russia has been operating for many years on principles found in what we now call the "Brannan Plan."

If health care is best to be found by having government employ the doctors and nurses and allocate them to needy persons, then why should those in the world who want better medical care look to the United States for guidance? Socialized medicine already exists and has existed for many years in Soviet Russia and elsewhere.

If education ought to be financed and controlled by a central authority, then why should the peoples of the world look to the United States for guidance? That is the regular practice in totalitarian countries.

If people should work in accordance with their ability and deliver the fruits of their labor to the central government to be used by it to promote the social welfare, then why look to the United States for guidance? For a generation that has been the operating program of the Communist Party in Russia.

Today it seems to many peoples of the world that perhaps, after all, the most important thing is expressed in Stalin's slogan, "Develop the material life of society." If so, the Communist Party in Russia is providing the great example and offering its large experience to those who would follow.

Throughout the world, the discontented people are the more easily induced to accept this offer because even the United States, for generations the citadel of human liberty, seems to be giving endorsement to many Soviet socialist measures, endorsement which is belated and grudging, but no less impressive on that account.

Of course, practices are not to be rejected merely because they bear a Communist label. Good may be found anywhere. But a spiritual society should be able to find practices superior to those which derive from a materialistic and atheistic belief. We can never achieve moral leadership and wide following in the world if we lose our faith in the possibilities of a free society, and if we fail to find practices that distinctively reflect that faith. If we do not have that faith and those practices, then we have lost our surest defense in a dangerous world.

We are today concentrating on material defenses which are costing us nearly $20 billion a year. That is a staggering burden which itself jeopardizes our freedom and which, standing alone, is ineffective as a defense of freedom.

For a century and more the United States was a materially weak nation. We had virtually no military establishment, and we were largely dependent upon economic help from others. Never, however, were we in serious external danger because we were strong in faith and dynamically espoused the cause of human freedom. What we did caught the imagination of men everywhere, and no leaders, however personally hostile or ambitious, could have brought their people to try to crush out the great American experiment, because that experiment carried the hopes and aspirations of all the peoples of the world.

We are in the process of losing that protection and because

of that we are in great peril. A people are doomed if they think only of security and not of mission; if they seek safety in steel and not in the sword of the spirit. Our future greatness and our power lie, not in aping the methods of Soviet Communism, not in trying to contain them—and us—within walls of steel, but in demonstrating, contrastingly and startlingly, the infinitely greater worth of practices that derive from a spiritual view of the nature of man.

## THE NEED FOR ADAPTABILITY

Another aspect of the problem is the need of the West for greater adaptability. The West is today a group of many separate sovereign nations. It faces a hostile and still expanding unity that already extends from the Elbe to the China Sea and embraces some 700 million people. That unity has been achieved by methods that we would not copy, and is itself undoubtedly doomed to collapse because of the materialistic and rigid nature of its society. But it is nevertheless formidable and it could, in its own death struggle, also destroy the West, unless the West voluntarily adapts itself to the need of greater unity and the greater strength that unity can provide.

Toward the beginning of World War II, Prime Minister Attlee exclaimed, "Europe must federate or perish." He was quite right. But Europe does not federate. No one imposes it, and the independent states are socialized to such a degree that they dare not voluntarily expose their economies to new external influences that would upset present governmental planning.

Take England. There the Government is trying out many measures of socialization. That experiment requires building a wall around England which can be penetrated only as planned by the English Government. English economy cannot face the impact of external forces or natural competition. We have the strange result that the Attlee Government is a major obstacle to that federation of Europe which Mr. Attlee recognized was imperative if Europe were not to perish!

There are plans for an Atlantic Union in which the United States would participate. These plans are backed by logic that is powerful. It is said, and rightly said, that mere agreements like the North Atlantic Treaty, for action in unison, do not provide either the economies or the strength inherent in a common defense such as our federation provided for our States. But that logic will prove impotent if the members of the projected Atlantic Union, including the United States, develop domestic economies that cannot stand exposure to new conditions. Socialization demands insulation.

There is a primitive law of the survival of the fittest and fitness is found, most of all, in adaptability to ever-changing conditions. Those who live under artificial, hothouse conditions do not last for long. People become insecure when they demand and get personal security and material welfare that depend upon highly artificial conditions. No armament can protect against that type of insecurity.

People survive in freedom if their members are courageous, resourceful and self-reliant, if each carries a share of responsibility for common problems, if they are individually and collectively adaptable to changing conditions, if they have faith and vision and put spiritual values ahead of material values, and if they keep control of their own destiny.

I pray that we shall continue to be that kind of a people.

# 🙿 THE MIDDLE OF THE ROAD: A
# STATEMENT OF FAITH IN AMERICA*

### BY DWIGHT D. EISENHOWER

**E**VERY gathering of Americans—whether a few on the porch of a crossroads store or massed thousands in a great stadium—is the possessor of a potentially immeasurable influence on the future. Because America has freedom of speech, freedom of communication, the world's highest educational level, and untapped reserves of individual initiative, any group of our people, fired by a common purpose, can generate a decisive strength toward its achievement. Some of the most inspiring chapters in our history were written by a handful of our citizens who, joined together to talk out among themselves an idea or a principle, struck a note that revolutionized the world's thinking. That capacity still resides in every gathering in this country.

Those who fear that our people are bogged down in the apathy of regimented thought have never been privileged to listen to the talk of a squad of soldiers or a gandy-dancer gang on the railroad. Or—for that matter—to a conference of bankers

---

\* Address by General Dwight D. Eisenhower, then active President of Columbia University, at the second session of the Assembly of the American Bar Association, St. Louis, Mo., Labor Day, 1949. Extracts from two other addresses by General Eisenhower are appended at the end.—*Ed.*

when there was under discussion a topic of vital interest to the future of this Republic. Readiness to air a grievance, to propose a remedy, to argue the pros and cons of a plan, is an enduring—and priceless—American trait.

## LAWYERS ARE POTENT FORCE IN NATIONAL POLICIES

Few groups, however, can have so profound an impact on the course of public affairs as this Assembly. Ours is a government of law—not of despotic decree—and you who practice the law have a specialized knowledge and unique influence in human relations. Indeed, without your counsel and advice hardly a single policy decision is reached by any of the forces most potent in the American economy—by labor organizations, by management, by farm groups, by welfare and professional associations, or by governmental agencies. Your attitude today often foreshadows the facts of tomorrow.

As a consequence, a more than ordinary responsibility is on you to remain free from bias and prejudice when you consider broad social problems. If you are true to your profession and to the responsibilities of your citizenship, you view them within a framework of *three fundamental principles* of American life.

*First,* that individual freedom is our most precious possession. It is to be guarded as the chief heritage of our people, the wellspring of our spiritual and material greatness, and the central target of all enemies—internal and external—who seek to weaken or destroy the American Republic.

*Second,* that all our freedoms—personal, economic, social, political—freedom to buy, to work, to hire, to bargain, to save, to vote, to worship, to gather in a convention or join in mutual association, all these freedoms are a single bundle. Each is an indispensable part of a single whole. Destruction of any inevitably leads to the destruction of all.

*Third,* that freedom to compete vigorously among ourselves,

133

accompanied by a readiness to cooperate wholeheartedly for the performance of community and national functions, together make our system the most productive on earth.

These three principles express the common faith of loyal Americans—the shining guide that, for the vast majority, points always the straight path to America's future. In the industrialized economy of the twentieth century, that path lies down the middle of the road between the unfettered power of concentrated wealth on one flank, and the unbridled power of statism or partisan interests on the other. Our agreement in these three great fundamentals provides the setting within which can always be composed any acute difference.

Yet there are some who build out of catchwords and fallacies a testament of inescapable conflict within our economy. Should misguided or vicious persons gull us into acceptance of this false dogma, the fault—criminal and stupid as it is—will be our own. We shall have been victimized by the crude technique of the brazen lie, often repeated. You, of the legal profession, are uniquely fitted to expose this fraud, and thereby prevent senseless cleavage and hostility among us.

## AMERICAN LABOR IS PART OF TEAM THAT BUILT AMERICA

Labor Day itself poses an immediate challenge. In every state of the Union, this day is set aside to honor the men and women who in factories and shops, in transportation and communication, in all the technical areas of our economy, have wrought the material marvel of our time—industrial America. By their labor—teamed with the know-how of management and the vision of investors—they have produced a wealth of goods and aids to human existence, widely distributed and possessed, beyond precedent in history and without parallel anywhere.

Because of our productivity and insistence upon fairness in human relations, we have largely—though far from wholly—freed ourselves from the tragic contrast of abject pauperism lying in the shadow of gluttonous luxury. That appalling picture could not be, and never will be, long tolerated by a people who believe in the dignity of man and the legitimate aspirations of all men.

And, let us not forget, our freedom from degrading pauperism is due to America's deep-seated sense of fair play translated into adequate law; to American industrial initiative and courage, to the genius of the American scientist and engineer, and to the sweat, the organizing ability, and the product of American labor in a competitive economy. It is *not* the result of political legerdemain or crackpot fantasies of reward without effort, harvests without planting.

## MISTAKES OF PAST HAVE BEEN CORRECTED

Acknowledged and glaring errors of the past, committed by those who prided themselves as leaders of great industrial empires, have at times justified and compelled drastic action for the preservation of the laborer's dignity—for the welfare of himself and his family.

Selfishness and cupidity—the source of those errors—will never be wholly eradicated from our midst. But just as we do not, today, seek to solve international problems in terms of wartime passion, let us not confuse present industrial difficulties with the mistakes and failures of past decades, long since wholly or partially corrected. In the infancy of our modern industrialized society, management and labor and the neutral observer were often equally ignorant of sound practice, of economic trends, of the effect of mass production on human standards of living. However, guided by these great principles and lighted by the spirit of fair play, the builders of our industrial economy have achieved success that confounds the prophets of disaster.

A little more than a century ago the Communist Manifesto of Karl Marx was published, preaching the falsehood of an inescapable class warfare that would continue within such a society until by violence the workers erased all traces of traditional government.  If Marx were right, this day should be, in all our great country, an annually recurring provocation to riot, physical strife, and civil disorder.  The factual evidence of his blunder is so clear that it ought not to require emphasis.

## "CLASS WARFARE" DOCTRINE IS FALSE

Nevertheless, with a full century of contrary proof in our possession and despite our demonstrated capacity for cooperative teamwork, some among us seem to accept the shibboleth of an unbridgeable gap between those who hire and those who are employed.  We miserably fail to challenge the lie that what is good for management is necessarily bad for labor; that for one side to profit, the other must be depressed.  Such distorted doctrine is false and foreign to the American scene, where common ideals and purpose permit us a common approach toward the common good.  It must be combated at every turn by both clear word and effective deed.

Of course, our path in places is still obstructed by unfinished business, the debris of inequities and prejudices not yet overcome.  But strong in the fundamental principles of American life, we have, in less than two centuries, accomplished more for the community of men than was won in the previous forty.

For us today, those principles still dictate progress down the center, even though there the contest is hottest, the progress sometimes discouragingly slow.  The frightened, the defeated, the coward, and the knave run to the flanks, straggling out of the battle under the cover of slogans, false formulas, and appeals to passion—a welcome sight to an alert enemy.  When the center weakens piecemeal, disintegration and annihilation are only steps away, in a battle of arms or of political philosophies.  The clearsighted and the courageous, fortunately, keep fighting in the middle of the war.  They are determined that we shall not lose our freedoms, either to the unbearable selfishness of vested interest, or through the blindness of those who, protesting devotion to the public welfare, falsely declare that only government can bring us happiness, security and opportunity.

## MIDDLE OF THE ROAD REPRESENTS HOPES OF AMERICAN PEOPLE

The middle of the road is derided by all of the right and the left. They deliberately misrepresent the central position as a neutral, wishy-washy one. Yet here is the truly creative area in which we may obtain agreement for constructive social action compatible with basic American principles, and with the just aspirations of every sincere American. It is the area in which are rooted the hopes and allegiance of the vast majority of our people.

Thus, the American system, in line with its principles, can and does, by governmental action, prevent or correct abuses springing from the unregulated practice of a private economy. In specific cases local governments have, with almost unanimous approval, provided needed public services so that extraordinary power over all citizens of the community might not fall into the hands of the few. In all cases we expect the government to be forehanded in establishing the rules that will preserve a practical equality in opportunity among us.

We, in turn, carefully watch the Government—especially the ever-expanding Federal Government—to see that in performing the functions obviously falling within governmental responsibility, it does not interfere more than is necessary in our daily lives. We instinctively have greater faith in the counterbalancing effect of many social, philosophic, and economic forces than we do in arbitrary law. We will not accord to the central government unlimited authority, any more than we will bow our necks to the dictates of uninhibited seekers after personal power in finance, labor, or any other field.

## Extremists Would Use Subsidies to Destroy Free Economy

Extremists hope that we lack the stubborn courage, the stamina, and the intelligent faith required to sustain the progress of the attack. By appeals to immediate and specialized selfish advantage, they would blind us to the enduring truth that no part of our society may prosper permanently except as the whole of America shall prosper. They use the cloying effect of subsidy as well as the illusory promise of an unearned and indolent existence to win our acceptance of their direction over our lives. They believe that the intricate interdependencies of our highly industrialized economy will drive us to desert principles in favor of expediencies—particularly the expediency of governmental intervention.

Thus far the record belies their hopes. Consider the abundance of courage and faith, manifested thousands of times each year in union meetings when workingmen penetrate the ideological complexities, parliamentary maneuvers, entangled plottings of Communist agitators, exposing and defeating them. Consider also the many thousands of times each year in meetings of management when businessmen—though primarily charged with concern for cost, production, distribution, and profit—subordinate these material things to increasing the welfare of their employees. Were it not for those, in both management and labor, who fight and work to keep us from the ditches on the right and on the left, then indeed this day would be a symbol of class warfare, and the City of St. Louis—and every other great metropolitan center—would be a battleground for what Marx called the proletariat.

But, in public places, soon only the specious promises of the extreme right and the left may make themselves heard. The truth can be lost if the peddlers of lies go unchallenged. To defeat them in their campaign of falsehood, we must first destroy their stock in trade—the shibboleth of an irreconcilable difference between those who manage and those who operate.

## There Is No Proletariat in the United States

Marx appealed to the self-pity, the justifiable resentments, of the proletariat in the Europe of his day. He could not imagine a great nation in which *there is no proletariat,* in which labor is the middle class that he so much despised and hated. He could not foresee that millions of plain people would in two world wars stake all they possessed in defense of ideas and ideals that were hardly more than shadowy dreams to most Europeans of a century ago. He could not imagine that one day the grave of an unidentified soldier would become a symbol of our dedication to political, economic, and social freedom.

American workingmen are principals in the three-member team of capital, management, labor. Never have they regarded themselves as a servile class that could attain freedom only through destruction of the industrial economy. With only rare exceptions, they have striven within the framework of our laws and tradition to improve their lot through increased production that profited all Americans.

To the achievements of organized labor my four brothers and I can testify, remembering the eighty-four hour week and skimpy wages of our youth. But we likewise remember with gratitude the opportunities presented to us by the American environment—opportunities so rich, so profuse, that we scarcely were aware that the circumstances in which we lived could be classed only as meager. Among these opportunities was and is that of education.

## Education Has Prevented Growth of Inherited Caste

By promoting literacy and understanding, our schools have made it impossible for a specially privileged leisure class to prey on those who work. By opening the sciences and professions to all our people, our colleges and universities have destroyed the curse of inherited caste and made our society the most fluid yet attained by man. Though the time has not yet arrived when all men will, as a matter of course, begin their careers in the lowest positions, and from there go upward in accordance with their individual value to society, yet this opportunity today spreads itself before every intelligent, educated, and energetic working-man of America.

The great body of American teachers daily increases our understanding and appreciation of democracy in economic action. Even the divisions and cleavages that still exist—the unfinished business still before us—are increasingly bridged in our classrooms. Each year education does a little more to promote the efficiency of our system and therefore the opportunities, security, and prosperity of our people. My experience as President of Columbia University has fortified my conviction that in the welfare of our teachers, of our whole educational fabric, we find the welfare of future America.

### LAWYERS CAN PROMOTE PEACE BETWEEN LABOR AND MANAGEMENT

You of the legal profession can likewise be effective in eradicating false, though sometimes persuasive, propaganda from the day-to-day relations of labor and management. You constitute a unique body of agents and umpires whose counsel is needed—and sometimes heeded—by members of our industrial team.

You realize that the interests of labor and management in most situations are identical. Differences are centered almost exclusively in the annual bargaining conferences. But even here the true differences are more apparent than they are real. Intelligent management certainly recognizes the need for maximum income to workers, consistent with reasonable return on investment. With equal clarity, labor cannot fail to recognize the need for increasing amounts of risk capital to provide jobs for our constantly growing population. And—make no mistake about it—no group in our country is more firmly dedicated to the retention and development of our system of private enterprise than is American labor.

The vast majority of Americans, moreover, respects your historic role in the development of our American way of life and your unique position in relation to its continued progress. For one thing—if you set yourselves to do the job—you can clean out the ambush of catchwords, tags, and labels in which the plain citizen, including the old soldier, is trapped every time he considers today's problems. How can we appraise a proposal if the terms hurled at our ears can mean anything or nothing, and change their significance with the inflection of the voice? "Welfare state," "national socialism," "radical," "liberal," "conservative," "reactionary" and a regiment of others—these terms, in today's usage, are generally compounds of confusion and prejudice. If our attitudes are muddled, our language is often to blame. A good tonic for clear thinking is a dose of precise, legal definition.

## KEY TO WELL-BEING OF ALL IS INCREASED PRODUCTIVITY

Above all, we need more economic understanding and working arrangements that will bind labor and management, in every productive enterprise, into a far tighter voluntary cooperative unit than we now have. The purpose of this unity will be—without subordination of one group to the other—the increased productivity that alone can better the position of labor, of management, of all America. No arbitrary or imposed device will work. Bureaucratic plans, enforced on both parties by government, pave the road to despotism. Laws that needlessly impose stifling controls and inflexible rules beyond the codes necessary to fair play may be necessary in a dictatorship, but in a democracy they are futile at the best and the cause of rebellion at the worst.

You, however, using your recognized position as guardians of the law and counsel to both parties in dispute, can work out voluntary solutions in our industrial problems—that now sometimes appear to be no better than in a state of armed truce, punctuated by outbreaks of industrial warfare. Such a condition is a criminal absurdity, since the participants possess a common stake in the prosperity of industry. Moreover, they possess common political concepts, common social purposes, common economic attitudes, and, above all, identical aspirations for themselves, their families, their country.

They are Americans—all.

*EDITOR'S NOTE: At his installation as President of Columbia University on October 12, 1948, General Eisenhower made clear the core of his political and social philosophy in an important address in which man's ancient concern with human freedom is ringingly renewed. The following major extracts from this notable address are here included:*

\*\*\* I feel a sense of high personal distinction that I am privileged to participate in this ceremony. If this were a land where the military profession is a weapon of tyranny or aggression—its members an elite caste dedicated to its own perpetuation—a lifelong soldier could hardly assume my present role. But in our nation the Army is the servant of the people, designed and trained exclusively to protect our way of life. Duty in its ranks is an exercise of citizenship. Hence, among us, the soldier who becomes an educator or the teacher who becomes a soldier enters no foreign field but finds himself instead engaged in a new phase of his fundamental life purpose—the protection and perpetuation of basic human freedoms.

## CHALLENGE TO FREEDOM

Today's challenge to freedom and to every free institution is such that none of us dares stand alone. For human freedom is today threatened by regimented statism. The threat is infinitely more than that involved in opposing ideologies. Men of widely divergent views in our own country live in peace together because they share certain common aspirations which are more important to them than their differences. But democracy and the police state have no common purposes, methods, or aspirations. In today's struggle, no free man, no free institution can be neutral. All must be joined in a common profession—that of democratic citizenship; every institution within our national structure must contribute to the advancement of this profession.

The common responsibility of all Americans is to become effective, helpful participants in a way of life that blends and harmonizes the fiercely competitive demands of the individual and of society. The individual must be free, able to develop to the utmost of his ability, employing all opportunities that confront him for his own and his family's welfare; otherwise he is merely a cog in a machine. The society must be stable, assured against violent upheaval and revolution; otherwise it is nothing but a temporary truce with chaos. But freedom for the individual must never degenerate into the brutish struggle for survival that we call barbarism. Neither must the stability of society ever degenerate into the unchained servitude of the masses that we call statism.

Only when each individual, while seeking to develop his own talents and further his own good, at the same time protects his fellows against injury and cooperates with them for the common betterment—only then is the fullness of orderly, civilized life possible to the millions of men who live within a free nation.

The citizenship which enables us to enjoy this fullness is our most priceless heritage. By our possession and wise use of it, we enjoy freedom of body, intellect, and spirit, and in addition material richness beyond the boast of Babylon. To insure its perpetuation and proper use is the first function of our educational system.

143

## ESSENCE OF CITIZENSHIP

To blend, without coercion, the individual good and the common good is the essence of citizenship in a free country. This is truly an art whose principles must be learned. Like the other arts, perfection in its manifold details can never be attained. This makes it all the more necessary that its basic principles be understood in order that their application may keep pace with every change—natural, technological, social.

Democratic citizenship is concerned with the sum total of human relations. Here at home this includes the recognition of mutual dependence for liberty, livelihood, and existence of more than 140,000,000 human beings. Moreover, since we cannot isolate ourselves as a nation from the world, citizenship must be concerned too with the ceaseless impact of the globe's 2,000,-000,000 humans upon one another, manifested in all the multitudinous acts and hopes and fears of humanity.

The educational system, therefore, can scarcely impose any logical limit upon its functions and responsibilities in preparing students for a life of social usefulness and individual satisfaction. The academic range must involve the entire material, intellectual, and spiritual aspects of life.

Underlying this structure of knowledge and understanding is one immutable, incontestable fact: Time and again, over the span of the last 700 years, it has been proved that those who know our way of life place upon one thing greater value than upon any other—and that priceless thing is individual liberty. This requires a system of self-government which recognizes that every person possesses certain inalienable rights and that rules and regulations for the common good may be imposed only by the ultimate authority of the citizens themselves.

This individual freedom is not the product of accident. To gain and retain it our forefathers have sacrificed material wealth, have undergone suffering, indeed have given life itself. So it is with us today.

## ALERTNESS ESSENTIAL

But it is not enough merely to realize how freedom has been won. Essential also is it that we be ever alert to all threats to that freedom. Easy to recognize is the threat from without. Easy too is it to see the threat of those who advocate its destruction from within. Less easy is it to see the dangers that arise from our own failure to analyze and understand the implications of various economic, social, and political movements among ourselves.

Thus, one danger arises from too great a concentration of finance, the power of selfish pressure groups, the power of any class organized in opposition to the whole—any one of these, when allowed to dominate, is as fully capable of destroying individual freedom as is power concentrated in the political head of the state.

The concentration of too much power in centralized government need not be the result of violent revolution or great upheaval. A paternalistic government can gradually destroy, by suffocation in the immediate advantage of subsidy, the will of a people to maintain a high degree of individual responsibility. And the abdication of individual responsibility is inevitably followed by further concentration of power in the state. Government ownership or control of property is not to be decried principally because of the historic inefficiency of governmental management of productive enterprise; its real threat rests in the fact that, if carried to the logical extreme, the final concentration of ownership in the hands of government gives to it, in all practical effects, absolute power over our lives.

There are internal dangers that require eternal vigilance if they are to be avoided. If we permit extremes of wealth for a few and enduring poverty for many, we shall create social explosiveness and a demand for revolutionary change. If we do not eliminate selfish abuse of power by any one group, we can be certain that equally selfish retaliation by other groups will ensue. Never must we forget that ready cooperation in the solution of human problems is the only sure way to avoid forced governmental intervention.

## DANGER IN DEMAGOGUERY

All our cherished rights—the right of free speech, free worship, ownership of property, equality before the law—all these are mutually dependent for their existence. Thus, when shallow critics denounce the profit motive inherent in our system of private enterprise, they ignore the fact that it is an economic support of every human right we possess and that without it, all rights would soon disappear. Demagoguery, unless combated by truth, can become as great a danger to freedom as exists in any other threat.

It was loss of unity through demogogic appeals to class selfishness, greed and hate that Macaulay, the English historian, feared would lead to the extinction of our democratic form of government. More than ninety years ago he wrote of these fears to the American historian, H. S. Randall. In a letter of May 23, 1857, he said, ". . . when a society has entered on this downward progress, either civilization or liberty must perish. Either some Caesar or Napoleon will seize the reins of government with a strong hand; or your republic will be as fearfully plundered and laid waste by barbarians in the twentieth century as the Roman Empire was in the fifth;—with this difference, that the Huns and Vandals who ravaged the Roman Empire came from without, and that your Huns and Vandals will have been engendered within your own country by your own institutions."

That day shall never come if in our educational system we help our students gain a true understanding of our society, of the need for balance between individual desires and the general welfare, and of the imperative requirement that every citizen participate intelligently and effectively in democratic affairs. The broadest possible citizen understanding and responsibility is as necessary in our complex society as was mere literacy before the industrial revolution.

It follows, then, that every institution built by free men, including great universities, must be first of all concerned with the preservation and further development of human freedom— despite any contrary philosophy, or force that may be pitted against it.

At all levels of education, we must be constantly watchful that our schools do not become so engrossed in techniques, great varieties of fractionalized courses, highly specialized knowledge,[1] and the size of their physical plant as to forget the principal purpose of education itself—to prepare the student for an effective personal and social life in a free society. From the school at the crossroads to a university as great as Columbia, general education for citizenship must be the common and first purpose of them all.

I do not suggest less emphasis on pure research or on vocational or professional training; nor am I by any means suggesting that curricula should be reduced to the classical education of the nineteenth century. But I deeply believe that all of us must demand of our schools more emphasis on those fundamentals that make our free society what it is and that assure it boundless increase in the future if we comprehend and apply them.

Love of freedom, confidence in the efficacy of cooperative effort, optimism for the future, invincible conviction that the American way of life yields the greatest human values—to help the student build these attitudes not out of indoctrination but out of genuine understanding, may seem to some to be education in the obvious.

Of course, the reverse is true. There is a growing doubt among our people that democracy is able to cope with the social and economic trials that lie ahead. Among some is a stark fear that our way of life may succumb to the combined effects of

---

[1] Compare the views of Mr. Baruch, pp. 35-37.—*Ed.*

creeping paralysis from within and aggressive assault from without.

Fear of the future with a concomitant sense of insecurity and doubt of the validity of fundamental principles is a terrible development in American life—almost incredible in the immediate aftermath of America's most magnificent physical and spiritual triumphs. Only by education in the apparently obvious can doubt and fear be resolved.

Here lies a heavy obligation on Columbia University and all her sister schools; unless such fear is banished from our thinking, the sequel will be either the heavy curse of tyrannical regimentation or the collapse of our democratic civilization in social anarchy.

Love of freedom, confidence in cooperative effort, optimism, faith in the American way will live so long as our schools loyally devote themselves to truly liberal education. To assign the university the mission of ever strengthening the foundations of our culture is to ennoble the institution and confirm the vital importance of its service.

Historical failures in the application of democratic principles must be as earnestly studied as the most brilliant of democracy's triumphs. But underlying all must be the clear conviction that the principles themselves have timeless validity. Dependence by the country upon the schools for this vital service implies no infringement of academic freedom.

Indeed, academic freedom is nothing more than specific application of the freedoms inherent in the American way of life. It follows that to protect academic freedom, the teacher must support the sum total of the principles which, among other things, guarantee freedom for all. The teacher's obligation to seek and speak the truth is further safeguarded by university custom and commitment.

There will be no administrative suppression or distortion of any subject that merits a place in this university's curricula. The facts of communism, for instance, shall be taught here—

its ideological developments, its political methods, its economic effects, its probable course in the future. The truth about communism is, today, an indispensable requirement if the true values of our democratic system are to be properly assessed. Ignorance of communism, fascism, or any other police-state philosophy is far more dangerous than ignorance of the most virulent disease.

Who among us can doubt the choice of future Americans, as between statism and freedom, if the truth concerning each be constantly held before their eyes? But if we, as adults, attempt to hide from the young the facts in this world struggle, not only will we be making a futile attempt to establish an intellectual "iron curtain," but we will arouse the lively suspicion that statism possesses virtues whose persuasive effect we fear.

The truth is what we need—the full truth. Except for those few who may be using the doctrine of communism as a vehicle to personal power, the people who, in our country, accept communism's propaganda for truth are those most ignorant of its aims and practices. Enlightenment is not only a defender of our institutions, it is an aggressive force for the defeat of false ideologies.

America was born in rebellion, and rebellion against wrong and injustice is imbedded in the American temper. But whatever change our rebels of the American past may have sought, they were quick to proclaim it openly and fearlessly, preaching it from the housetops. We need their sort, and here at Columbia we shall strive to develop them—informed, intelligent rebels against ignorance and imperfection and prejudice. But because they have sought the truth and know it, they will be loyal to the American way, to the democracy within which we live. They will never tire of seeking its advancement, however viciously they may be attacked by those content with the status quo. Their loyalty will be enhanced by each day they spend at Columbia.

## WORKING PARTNERSHIP

The American university does not operate in an unreal world of its own, concerned solely with the abstract, secluded from the worrisome problems of workaday living, insulated against contact with those other institutions which constitute our national structure. Just as the preservation of the American way demands a working partnership among all 146,000,000 Americans, its continued development demands a working partnership between universities and all other free institutions.

The school, for example, that enjoys a partnership with the manufacturing industries and labor unions and mercantile establishments of its community is a better and more productive school in consequence of its non-academic associations. Its influence permeates the entire community and is multiplied many times over, while the school itself, energized by the challenge and dynamism of community life, grows and broadens with each problem it helps surmount.

Together, the university and the community—the entire record of human experience at their call, able to apply academic, technical, and practical knowledge to the problem, joined in voluntary cooperative effort—together they can analyze and evaluate and plan. By such partnership, it is not too much to hope that the university—losing none of its own freedom, but rather extending its academic horizons—will in time help develop a new freedom for America—freedom from industrial strife.

Partnership is the proof and product of unity. In a free democracy, unity is obtained by our common approach to fundamental principles regardless of even sharp differences with regard to details. A unified America is the greatest temporal power yet seen upon earth, a power dedicated to the betterment and happiness of all mankind. Columbia shares in that dedication.

Columbia University, like so many others, has been established and is voluntarily maintained and supported by free people. In no other environment could it in the space of two centuries have attained an international stature as a home of learning and research.

## BOUND BY LOYALTY TO TRUTH

Columbia University, consequently, an independent gift-supported institution, free from political and sectarian obligation, will forever be bound by its loyalty to truth and the basic concepts of democratic freedom. It shall follow, then, that Columbia will always be characterized by: First, an undergraduate body of men and women schooled in the broad expanse of human knowledge and humble in their heritage —resolute that they shall pass both on with some increase. From among them will come scholars, executives, statesmen. But Columbia shall count it failure, whatever their success, if they are not all their lives a leaven of better citizenship.

Second, Columbia will be characterized by a graduate body of men and women who, each in his own field, shall advance frontiers of knowledge and use the techniques of science in the service of humanity. From among them will come skilled surgeons, engineers, lawyers, and administrators, great leaders in every profession and science. But again, we shall count it failure, if they, by specialization, become blinded to human values and so ignore their fundamental duty as citizens.

Third, Columbia University will be a dynamic institution as a whole, dedicated to learning and research and to effective cooperation with all other free institutions which will aid in the preservation and strengthening of human dignity and happiness. Our way of life and our university are the flowering of centuries of effort and thought. Men of the ancient world —in Jerusalem and Athens and Rome—men of all epochs, all regions, and all faiths have contributed to the ideals and ideas that animate our thinking. Columbia University is, and shall continue, both heir of that past and a pioneer in its future increase.***

*EDITOR'S NOTE: On June 1, 1949, at the 195th Commencement exercises of Columbia University, in New York, President Eisenhower addressed the graduating class. Extracts from that address are here included:*

*** The impact on us of every international fact and crisis is immediate. We are seldom free from anxiety as each day's events crowd instantly upon our attention. Pressure groups often pretend to a moral purpose that examination proves to be false. The vote-seeker rarely hesitates to appeal to all that is selfish in humankind. Ruthless individuals, whether they classify themselves as capitalists, spokesmen of labor, social reformers, or politicians, glibly promise us prosperity for our support of their personal but carefully concealed ambitions. False teachers, who magnify acknowledged errors in the practice of democracy, attempt to destroy our faith in man's right to self-government. As we seek to conserve what is good and sound even while we boldly explore and test new ways, we are belabored by the demagogues of right and left, both of whom would turn back the clock of history to the days of regimented humanity. In such a maelstrom of facts and crises and false counsel, the guideposts to individual duty and action become obscured.

Infallible counsel for each of us is to be found within our valid hopes and aspirations and ideals as human beings, so clearly understood by our colonial forebears. The simple faith, the unshakable conviction they held in man's individual rights and his equality before the law and God, is the most priceless jewel in all the vast spiritual and material heritage those men and women bequeathed to us. We cannot afford to lose their sharp sense of basic values—expressed by Patrick Henry in one imperishable sentence.

152

Millions of us, today, seem to fear that individual freedom is leading us toward social chaos; that individual opportunity has forever disappeared; that no person can have rightful title to property; that we have reached the point where the individual is far too small to cope with his circumstances; that his lifelong physical security against every risk is all that matters. More than this, we hear that such security must be attained by surrendering to centralized control the management of our society. In short, to these fearful men, the free human individual is a social anachronism.

On every count the fearful men are wrong. More than ever before, in our country, this is the age of the individual. Endowed with the accumulated knowledge of centuries, armed with all the instruments of modern science, he is still assured personal freedom and wide avenues of expression so that he may win for himself, his family, and his country greater material comfort, ease, and happiness; greater spiritual satisfaction and contentment.

When even the rudiments of knowledge were possessed by only a privileged few, when man's appalling ignorance handicapped his participation in government, there was ground to believe that an all-powerful state had to rule each subject's life from the cradle to the grave. That ground has diminished with each year of our Republic's existence. None remains today. The free individual has been justified as his own master, the state as his servant.

In World War II, we Americans welded into a cooperative unit the enterprise, initiative, spirit, and will of many million free men and women; we crossed the oceans and, joined with our Allies, crushed two regimented tyrannies whose power was frightening; at the same time, we rescued from industrial disaster an ally whose communist economy, we are *now* told, is the only means to a world of plenty.

If, in the tragic waste of war, we could so magnificently prove the strength of our system, founded on human freedom, what challenge is there in the future that we cannot meet? The worker of miracles is teamwork.

Every American is a free member of a mighty partnership that has at its command all the pooled strength of Western Civilization—spiritual ideals, political experience, social purpose, scientific wealth, industrial prowess. There is no limit, other than our own resolve, to the temporal goals we set before ourselves—as free individuals joined in a team with our fellows; as a free nation in the community of nations.

The modern preachers of the paternalistic state permit themselves to be intimidated by circumstances. Blinding themselves to the inevitable growth of despotism, they—cravenlike —seek, through government, assurance that they can forever count upon a full stomach and warm cloak or—perhaps—the sinister-minded among them think, by playing upon our fears, to become the masters of our lives.

In the years ahead of you graduates, the fundamental struggle of our time may be decided—between those who would further apply to our daily lives the concept of individual freedom and equality and those who would subordinate the individual to the dictates of the state. You will participate in the fight.

We believe that Columbia has effectively trained you for the practice of your chosen profession—your diplomas are evidence of our confidence in that training and your successful completion of it. But beyond the purely academic or professional—and more important to humanity—is your readiness for responsible citizenship.

We trust that Columbia has strengthened within you the conviction that human freedom must be treasured beyond all else—even life itself—for any diminishment of it is a tragic backward step. We hope that this school has inspired within you a resolution to live the full lives of American citizens, good neighbors in every community task and in your aid to those less fortunate than yourselves; forever building a stouter teamwork within our people. We hope, too, you will always be sharply conscious that the great rights you possess are accompanied by inescapable obligations; that you can most surely preserve your own rights by defending the rights of others.

And we hope that your faith has been strenghtened in the wealth of opportunity our country and civilization spread before the individual; that you have grown in courage to defend the old when it is good, to move forward fearlessly on the path of proved principle, undaunted by the pitfalls to left and right. Today our stark need is courageous and wise men and women, who conserve their goodly heritage while they add new richness to it.

If it has done these things, if it has helped you to both wisdom and understanding as well as to knowledge and techniques, then Columbia University has accomplished its mission toward this class and toward the free democracy of which you are a part.

*EDITOR'S NOTE: On October 24, 1949, at the opening session of the 18th Annual* New York Herald Tribune *Forum in New York City, General Eisenhower delivered an address suggesting a promising vehicle for exploring the perplexing dividing line between governmental and voluntary social planning. Extracts from that address follow:*

\*\*\* Under the atomic shadow, the world dwells in two hostile camps. The one is dedicated to human freedom and human rights, founded in the dignity of man. The other is committed to a dictatorship of the proletariat where the state decides *what* rights, *what* freedom the individual may enjoy. This basic cleavage, of itself, would apparently involve no irreconcilable antagonisms. But communistic leaders openly declare that individual freedoms and free enterprise, as we practice them, cannot long exist in the same world with communism. They leave us no doubt on this point. In their declaration is a tragic and continuing threat to our kind of government—"The Kind of Government Ahead." In view of the dynamic force with which those leaders are prosecuting their aims, we scarcely need further incentive to concentrate our thinking, our planning, and our actions toward preservation of freedom against threats from without.

At home, we face the complex social, economic, and political problems that have been highly complicated for democracy by the industrial revolution. We have had to adjust precepts, doctrines, and methods developed in an agrarian frontier age to the industrialized economy and civilization of the 20th century. This has not been easy. Perfection has not been attained, but we will continue to seek it, using every means available to us.

A century ago, the year of the discovery of gold in California, the average American citizen typified a sturdy independence. He had faith and confidence in himself and in the limitless potential of his country's resources, readily available to his use. While he was vaguely aware of his government's existence, it had little to do, either good or bad, with his day-by-day living. With a mite of help, the citizen built his own house from materials at hand. He raised his family's food —and good land was to be had cheaply. His clothing was made by his wife; his transport was his horse. Given health, initiative, and stamina, he could always find for himself and his dependents subsistence—even abundance. Taxes were low, opportunity was everywhere, life was good—even if frequently filled with risk and danger to life and limb. In a sense, the aims of the framers of our Constitution seemed to be almost perfectly achieved.

Nevertheless, the essential dignity of man and the mastery of man over his institutions were less expressed in the facts of American life in 1849 than they are in 1949. Then, luxuries were for the very few, and grinding hardship was, in some season of every year, the lot of most. Recurrent epi-

demics scourged alike our cities and our frontiers. A few
men of industrial power could throw a region into a panic;
a single person could, on a whim, shut down the mills of a
community and self-righteously judge himself guiltless of the
suffering imposed on workmen and their families. The moral
crime of human slavery was legalized. Millions of human
beings were subject to barter and sale. In 1849 we practiced
democracy somewhat in the fashion of the ancient Athenian
experiment, and woe to him who was born of black or red
skin. For him there was only the master's whip or the sword
of the exterminator.

Americans in the century just past have used the power of
self-government to the progressive advantage of our people.
Our fathers, and we, have fought disease, suffering, injustice,
and license in all its forms so that all of us might win larger
freedoms, including freedom from economic calamity with its
consequences of widespread want and human misery. In doing all this we have used, whenever necessary, the government
as our servant and laws as our instrument. But so far as possible, we have depended upon the force of public opinion,
without direct government intervention, to bring about reform and progress—responding to our instinct that "The best
government is the least government."

Certainly, the American Dream demands that we continue
the search for betterment in the cultural and material standards of our people, using, where absolutely necessary, specific
powers of law and government. Because of the complexity
of the problems involved, it may be impossible for any individual to define accurately the line dividing governmental and
individual responsibility in this quest. This is typical of collective activity. Two great American industries are today
shut down because a few men cannot see eye to eye on specific items of employee and employer responsibility. If they
—of undoubted loyalty to America—can dare calamity by their
failure to agree in a far more simple decision, how can the

plain citizen determine the dividing line between his own and the government's responsibilities?

To help us, I believe that nothing could be more effective than a convocation of leaders in every field with the faculties of some of our great universities. I should be proud to see Columbia cooperating in such an effort, its purpose to develop a clear and authentic chart of this dividing line. The result might not satisfy the mind and conscience of each of us, yet the question would be rescued from the domain of prejudice, emotion, partisan politics, and selfish interest and be subjected to logical analysis and enlightened judgment.

The task is to promote social and economic welfare without jeopardy to individual freedom and right. The conclusions of any such convocation would be transitory in their application, but based upon principles with which we are all familiar. The first of these is the American conviction that men are created equal; that governments are instituted to secure to man their rights to life, liberty, and the pursuit of happiness. Another is the danger inherent in concentration of too much of any kind of power in too few hands.

The leaders in our convocation would be guided also by the truth that the American Dream implies the fullest possible exploitation of American resources for the good of all. They would so locate the dividing line between government and citizen as to provide full play to the American qualities of initiative, courage, inventiveness, which, in their sum, have won us a productivity without a parallel in the world. The need for economy in government would require guards against excess of bureaus at the seat of government. Their conclusions would certainly emphasize the truth, "More and more bureaus, more and more taxes, fewer and fewer producers; the final result is financial collapse and the end of freedom."

The basic difference between the obviously important external and internal factors affecting "What Kind of Government Ahead?" is that the former is a threat, the second a trend. But when freedom is threatened from without, it is more than ever necessary that we, here at home, watch with a critical eye every slightest reason or excuse for moving the line that separates governmental from individual responsibility. Moreover, highly intensifying the need for alertness is the communistic practice of boring from within. Communistic agents, within our own borders, seize upon any difficulty in our constant process of adjustment and particularly upon every sign of failure and of weakness to lead us further astray in our own thinking—exploiting every excuse to claim that "the government ahead" must conform to their creed. How they must be congratulating themselves when they read that one of our cabinet officers foresees, because of current industrial deadlocks, 5,000,000 will be out of work by December 1—for them, confirmation of their predictions that free enterprise will disintegrate!

Our foremost need is strength, and *proof* of strength: moral, intellectual, and material strength. We must cling ever more closely to the fundamentals of the American belief in human dignity and rights. So, as we consider measures designed to affect the status or the security of the workingman, we must ask these specific questions: "Does the proposal push the worker one step closer to regimented labor? Does it ease the way to governmental control over his life and his livelihood?" As we strive to devise measures intended to lessen the shocks and privations incident to old age, to sickness, to unemployment, to natural disaster, let us choose among the several proposals that which best protects our heritage of freedom.

In revising the governmental structure, in approving new appropriations and new governmental ventures, in reforming tax laws, in considering a multitude of glittering proposals—each of which is held by its author to promise eternal happiness and prosperity—let us hold ever before our eyes the simple truth that to men who have lived in freedom there is nothing in life so valuable as freedom—not even life itself.

If, today, we never give up the effort to determine—so far as each of us can—the probable effect of every new governmental proposal upon our personal freedom, we will be discharging one of our most acute responsibilities as American citizens. But thereafter it is still necessary to act, to use all the detailed political machinery, including the two-party system, intended to give each of us a voice in his own government. In precinct or district caucuses, in party councils, in all the ways that are open to us, we must act decisively and within the limits established by our own understanding of freedom's requirements. Only thus will be answered wisely —each day—"What Kind of Government Ahead?"

Put all of this into the language of practical action and we would say to ourselves:

> Our American heritage is threatened as much by our own indifference as it is by the most unscrupulous office-seeker or by the most powerful foreign threat. The future of this Republic is in the hands of the American voter.

And we would further advise ourselves:

> Stop shrugging off politics as only the politicians' business; stop banking on American luck to get us good government and good policy —some time it will run out.
>
> Stop using the alibi, "one vote doesn't count." It won't, only if not used! And our neighbor's won't, unless we make him use it.
>
> Dishonest political promises to selfish groups—not rebuffed at the ballot box—can make a nightmare of the American Dream.
>
> But wise and determined performance of our civic duties can make that dream come true.

# ꙮ ꙮ ꙮ ꙮ THE LAST MILES TO COLLECTIVISM *

## BY HERBERT HOOVER†

I AM glad to come to Ohio Wesleyan University today to take part in the formal installation of my friend Arthur Flemming as your President. I know more about him than I do about John Wesley. But every American knows Wesley as the founder of a great movement which has inspired millions to righteous living.

I am, however, concerned with Mr. Flemming. I need not tell you that he is a son of this University, or of his years of public service in war and peace.

I have worked with him intimately for the past two years. He was better fitted for the work of the Commission on Organization of the Executive Branch of the Government than any of the rest of us. He brought high statesmanship and great understanding of its human problems. I can condense the many things I could say of Dr. Flemming into two short sentences:

* "Give Us Self-Reliance or Give Us Security," address at Ohio Wesleyan University, Delaware, Ohio, June 11, 1949, from *Addresses upon the American Road,* 1948-1950, Stanford, California: Stanford University Press (1951), pp. 8-31, 174-176.

† A distinguished engineer, public administrator, and humanitarian, ex-President Hoover continues to devote his time and thought to problems of prime concern to the welfare of the United States and the world.—*Ed.*

President Flemming will be one of the great American university presidents. That is one of the highest positions of leadership in our American life.

This season you and a mighty host of 500,000 other American graduates are lining up to receive your college diplomas.

Once upon a time, I lined up just as you are. For me, it was a day of lowered spirit. The night before we had omitted the cheerful song about "The Owl and the Pussy Cat," and chanted of "Working on the Railroad" and that immortal college dirge about going "Into the Cold, Cold World." The dynamic energy and the impelling desire to crack something up had sunk to low action levels.

I had to listen to an address made up of the standardized parts which were at that time generally sold at Commencements. It took over an hour for the speaker to put the parts together. We were warned that our diploma was an entrance ticket to jungles of temptation and hard knocks. Our speaker dwelled upon the Founding Fathers, the division of powers, upon Herbert Spencer and John Stuart Mill. He said we were living in a New Era in the world. He described it as Liberalism. The idea had to do with free minds and free spirits. It included the notion that America was a land of opportunity—with the great ideal of being a land of *equal* opportunity. We were told that life was a race where society laid down rules of sportsmanship but "let the best man win." The encouraging note in his address was emphasis upon Christian in *The Pilgrim's Progress* and Horatio Alger.

I confess my attention on that occasion was distracted by a sinking realization that I had to find a job—and quick. Also, I knew a girl. Put in economic terms, I was wishing somebody with a profit motive would allow me to help him earn a profit, and thus support the girl. At the risk of seeming revolutionary and a defender of evil, I suggest that this basis of test for a job has considerable merit. It does not require qualifications either of good looks, ancestry, religion, or ability to get votes.

It is true that I had some difficulty in impressing any of the profit and loss takers with the high potentialities of my diploma. But I was without the information at that time that I was a wage slave. I was buoyed up with the notion that if I did not like any particular profit taker, I could find another one somewhere else.

And let me add, that under that particular New Era I did not find a cold, cold world. I found the profit takers a cheery and helpful lot of folks, who took an enormous interest in helping youngsters get a start and get ahead in life. And you will find that is also true today. Indeed, their helpfulness has improved, for as technology becomes more intricate, they are searching for skills, and your diploma commands more respect.

And now voices tell us that we are in another New Era. In fact, we seem to have a newer era every little while.

Incidentally, I entered the cold, cold world in the midst of what the latest New Era calls a "disinflation." We mistakenly thought its name was "depression." But as I did not then know that governments could cure it, I did not have the additional worry of what the Government was going to do about it.

The new era of today seems united in the notion that they have just discovered real Liberalism and that all previous eras are reactionary. Some tell us that, in their New Era, life is still a race, but that everybody must come out *even* at the end. Another modernistic school adds to this that life still may be a race, but that each step must be dictated by some official or unofficial bureaucrat with Stop-and-Go signals. They hold out the attraction that with this security you will finish with an old-age pension and your funeral expenses from the Government.

Whether these newest eras are right or wrong, "security," which eliminates the risks in life, also kills the joy that lies in competition, in individual adventure, new undertakings, and new achievements. These contain moral and intellectual impulses more vital than even profits. For from them alone comes national progress. At all times in history there have been many who sought escape into "security" from self-reliance.

And if you will look over the workings of these newest New Eras throughout the world, you may notice that the judgment of the Lord on Adam has not been entirely reversed, even by the Supreme Court of the United States. Moreover, governments have not been able to fix the wages of sin. Nor have they found a substitute for profit and other personal stimulants.

America has not yet embraced all these new ideas. The reactionary notion of equal opportunity with the right of everyone to go as far as his ambitions and abilities will take him, provided he does not trespass on others, still holds in the American dream.

How far he can get has been damaged by two great wars and inefficiently organized government, which we have to pay for. To pay it, you will need to work two days out of the week for the Government for a long time. The Commission upon which President Flemming and I have taken part is trying to take a few hours off that penalty.

And there is something more to be said for the old reactionary notions which held to basic freedoms of mind and spirit, holding aloft the lamp of equal opportunity. In the years since the Founding Fathers, a God-fearing people, under these reactionary blessings, built up quite a plant and equipment on this continent. It teems with millions of comfortable farms and homes, cattle and hogs. It is well equipped with railroads, power plants, factories, highways, automobiles, and death warnings. It is studded with magnificent cities and traffic jams. The terrible reactionaries have filled the land with legislatures, town councils, free presses, orchestras, bands, radios, juke-boxes, and other noises. It has a full complement of stadiums, ball players, and college yells. Furthermore, they sprinkled the country with churches and laboratories, built ten thousand schools and a thousand institutions of higher learning. And somehow, these reactionary-minded taxpayers are squeezing out the resources to maintain a million devoted teachers, a hundred thousand able professors, and to keep over two million of you in colleges and universities. Possibly another ideology could do better in the next one hundred and seventy-three years. But I suggest we had better continue to suffer certain evils of free men and the ideal of equal opportunity than to die of nostalgia.

It is very sad, but did it ever occur to you that all the people who live in these houses and all those who run this complicated machine are going to die? Just as sure as death, the jobs are yours. The plant and equipment comes to you by inheritance ready to run. And there are opportunities in every inch of it. But the best of these jobs are never filled by security seekers.

Moreover, there are other vast opportunities for those who are willing to take a chance. If we just hold to our reactionary ideas of free minds, free spirits, and equal opportunity, we have another glorious opening for every young man and woman. Science and invention, even during these troubled years, have given us further mighty powers of progress. New discoveries in science and their flow of new inventions will continue to create a thousand new frontiers for those who still would adventure.

You have the blood and the urge of your American forebears. You are made of as good stuff as they. I have no doubt of your character and your self-reliance. You are better trained and equipped than we were. I know you are champing at the bit to take your chance in an opening world.

Do not fear it will be cold to you.

*EDITOR'S NOTE: The following pertinent extracts are from Mr. Hoover's much-discussed Address before the United States Junior Chamber of Commerce, Chicago, Illinois, June 16, 1950:*

\*\*\* Some of your officers asked me to speak on the relation of Government expenditures, deficits, and taxes, to jobs and to national life.

## THE FIVE QUESTIONS

They propounded to me five questions:
1. Who pays these taxes?
2. Can taxes be sufficiently increased to meet these deficits?
3. Will deficits not lead to more inflation?
4. Can expenses be reduced?
5. What stands in the way of reductions?

It is these five questions, plus the activities of the different breeds of collectivists, which plague the American people today.

Before I attempt to answer these questions, I will make a few preparatory observations.

Today we are blessed with some kind of prosperity. Whatever kind it is, we all want stability without inflation. We want a system that finds jobs for 1,000,000 new workers each year.

## DEFICITS IN GENERAL

In 1932 I did the suffering from an unbalanced budget. The reverberations of a European panic had pulled the tax revenues out from under us, and we were compelled to make large recoverable loans to support our credit structure. Outside these subsequently recovered loans our modest deficit was about $1 billion. In the midst of this grief, Mr. Roosevelt, in denouncing our deficit, made an uncomfortable remark to the effect that, too often, liberal governments have been wrecked on the rock of deficits. However, we only heard this remark once.

About this time, Lord John Maynard Keynes came up with his new intoxicant of deficit spending in years of unemployment. It had a good political flavor. Having got the habit, we keep drinking in times of presumed prosperity. With the exception of two years in the 80th Congress, we have had deficits and increasing debt for all 17 years since Keynes helped us out.

The consoling answer of the inebriated is that there is really no such thing as Government debt. They say, "We owe it to ourselves." Any government which follows this will-o'-the-wisp will sometime break its neck over the precipice of inflation. Some have already done so.

## DEFICITS IN PROSPECT

We cannot appraise these questions without using facts, figures, and the word billions. But to be sure the billions I mention are free of political bias, I use only those from Democratic Senators.

Senator Harry Byrd says that if we include all Federal expenditures, both in and outside of the President's formal budget, they will amount to about $44 billions for the present fiscal year, with a deficit of about $5 billions. Our State and local expenditures amount to about $15 billions. That would be around $60 billions of various current Government expenditures.

Beyond this Senator McClellan calculates that if all the recommended Federal legislation is passed, it will increase the annual Federal expenditures by $20 to $25 billions more. Senator McClellan is against this phantasmagoria of the Promised Land which he so well appraised. Even without this phantasmagoria, the Federal deficit will probably be greater next year, and there are also powerful urgings to state and municipal governments for increased expenditures.

## WHO PAYS THE TAXES?

The first of your questions was, "Who pays the taxes?" Here we enter a land of twilights and illusions. We can illuminate it somewhat if we divide the taxpayers into the sheep and the goats. The sheep are the families who have a gross income of less than $7,000 a year before taxes. The goats are those who have a gross income of more than $7,000 a year. Various studies show that almost 80 percent of Governmental revenues come from the sheep. It also shows that each sheep family on the average pays about $1,400 a year in taxes and deductions. Therefore even the $7,000 top figure for the sheep is not $7,000.

Your second question was:

## CAN TAXES BE INCREASED TO MEET
## THESE DEFICITS?

I suppose taxes could be increased until the whole population can no longer buy enough food or clothes. The real question is how far our people can be taxed and still have jobs and a decent standard of living. We can apply four tests as to whether the patient can stand any more tax mixtures.

*First.* Because of the average $1,400 annual taxes on the sheep families, a large number of them are already prevented from reaching the standard which the Labor Department insists is "desirable."

*Second.* But how about the goats who have gross incomes of more than $7,000 a year? The answer is easy. If the Government confiscated their *entire* personal incomes, it would

168

not pay the present Federal deficit—and that does not include Senator McClellan's phantasmagoria of a Promised Land.

*Third.* One of the illusions of our times is that corporation taxes come from the stockholders. Sometime the American people will realize that corporation taxes are passed on to the customers, which are the sheep. Otherwise, the corporations would in the end go bankrupt.

Therefore, any substantial increase in taxes must come by shearing more from the sheep.

*Fourth.* It is my belief that even present taxes are so draining the savings of the people into the Government as to undermine new jobs for the future. It is possible to calculate the present Government take as theoretically over 60 percent of the people's savings after deducting the cost of a possible decent standard of living. If the phantasmagoria described by Senator McClellan came into action, the Government take would be over 80 percent.

The fact that taxes have already definitely shrunken venture and equity capital for small business would seem to be proved when the Government proposes to furnish such capital. Never before, in 165 years, did small business depend on Government. Small business is the plant from which big business grows.

That is also proof that the Government is becoming more and more the source of capital and credit. To which the socialists applaud.

Big business can finance itself by borrowing money, especially while the Government is inflating credit. But big business only employs about 25 percent of the working population.

The answer to the question, "Can our economy stand substantially more taxes and still make substantial progress?" is just simply No, unless you believe a collectivist state is progress.

Your third question was:

## WILL DEFICITS LEAD TO MORE INFLATION?

Financing Government deficits by borrowing, if continued long enough, has only one end—inflation. That has been proved by a dozen nations.

We ourselves have already decreased the purchasing value of the dollar by over 40 percent and we are still creeping along that road. The five-cent telephone call went a few weeks ago and the five-cent fare had already gone, and the five-cent candy bar has shrunk even more lately. A new round of inflation is now appearing in direct or indirect wage and salary increases and rising commodity prices.

If we keep on this road, we are certain to reach the President's ideal of $4,000 a year to every family. But it will not have $4,000 purchasing power.

To this question of further Government borrowing to meet deficits, my answer is that it is the road to disaster for every cottage in the land.

Your fourth question was:

## CAN WE REDUCE EXPENSES?

To that, the answer is YES.

The first move in that direction is to stop the phantasmagoria described by Senator McClellan in its tracks. That is easy if we take a holiday in new Government services until the deficit is overcome. No doubt many things the Government can provide are desirable. Most every family would like to add desirable things to its living. But getting them by borrowing money is the way the old homestead was lost. Most families shy off that method. And the Government should be even more shy, or it will come to a bad end.

The second and most simple device to reduce expenses is

for Congress to cut proposed expenditures to the very bones of necessity; also to suspend the sports of log-rolling and pork barrels.

We are generally told that these enormous Government expenditures and deficits are mainly the inheritances of the war and cannot be helped. It is true that of the present budget of $44 billions, about $32 billions go to pay interest on the debt, veterans, national defense, and subsidies to other countries to keep them comfortable in the cold war. Those items have been increased by only 15 percent in the last three years.

To get some look at expenditures not created by the wars, and to avoid any partisan flavor, we may start from a Democratic fiscal year of 17 years ago. This non-war part of the Government has increased expenditures 400 percent in 17 years and 50 percent in the last three years. No amount of claims that the purchasing value of the dollar has decreased or that the population has increased can explain these increases.


## REORGANIZATION OF THE EXECUTIVE BRANCH

The third way to reduce expenses is the more efficient organization and the cutting out of waste in government on the lines proposed by the Reorganization Commission.

Through the cooperation of the Administration, the Congress, the Citizens' Committee, and such organizations as yours, we have already made substantial progress in these reforms of the Executive Branch of the Government.

The major accomplishments are:

Unification of the Armed Forces,
Reorganization of the State Department,
Unification of the General Services,
Reorganization of the Government Merchant Marine.

They represent big money. In additon, a number of minor reforms have been accepted.

171

## MAJOR REFORMS STILL TO DO

We still have many major reforms to accomplish. They include our proposals:

To reorganize the whole Civil Service into an honest-to-goodness career service based on merit, with justice and encouragement in promotion. The experienced chairman of our task force unhesitatingly stated we could save 10 percent of the Federal payroll. That would be a little item of $600 millions.

To put the Budgeting and Accounting of the Government on a business basis. There would be many savings possible if the Government could see itself in the mirror of an adequate accounting system.

To organize the Post Office into a modern business concern, with management free from politics. With this reform and some increase in rates to special commercial users, I believe its deficit of half a billion could be overcome.

To reorganize the structure of the departments of Treasury, Agriculture, Commerce, Labor, Interior, and Housing so that each of them has, cheek by jowl, the agencies devoted to a related major purpose. That would fix responsibility for policies, create checks and balances, eliminate overlaps, competition, and waste inevitable in activities now scattered all over the Government. The chairman of only one of those task forces said that $300 millions could be saved by that one unification.

To unify the Government Hospital Services so as to save $400 or $500 millions of unnecessary construction now authorized; at the same time to provide better medical service and better preparedness for war.

And there are scores of other reforms which are pointed at greater efficiency for less money.

These recommendations were founded upon two years of study by 18 task forces comprised of independent leading men and women of experience whose reports, recommendations, and reasons are open to everybody.

172

These reforms are in the lap of the gods in Washington and the pressure groups at home.

## WHAT STANDS IN THE WAY OF REDUCTION OF EXPENDITURES?

The next question is, "What stands in the way of these reforms and reductions?"

Over 25 years ago, I served on a Commission of Reorganization of the Executive Branch. I saw those reforms go to their burial with the following remarks:

". . . Practically every single item has met with opposition from some vested official, or it has disturbed some vested habit, and offended some organized minority. It has aroused the paid propagandists. All of them are in favor of every item of reorganization except that which affects the activity in which they are specially interested. In the aggregate, these directors of vested habits and propaganda surround Congress with a confusing fog of opposition. Meantime, the inchoate voice of the public gets nowhere but to swear."

Here ended that funeral sermon of 25 years ago.

But we are doing better this time than 25 years ago, as we had little public or Congressional support at that time.

Among our public supporters, the Junior Chamber of Commerce has given its fine energies to educating the misguided lay members of obstructing pressure groups, and yours is a splendid, intelligent appreciation of what economy in government means.

## PROBLEMS DEEPER THAN REORGANIZATION

But the problems which face us in fiscal questions are deeper in American life than reorganization of the executive departments.

We need to make an appraisal of some of the forces which

173

produce these dangers from expenditures, deficits, inflation, and drainage of savings into the Government.

It is possible to denounce public officials for all these dangers and ills. But do not overlook the fact that public officials get elected because they satisfy their constituents. Among their constituencies are the special groups who want something from the Treasury. Many of them are on guard to protect their members from losing established privilege. They all wear the clothing of public interest. They are active in electing their man while the other citizen sleeps.

We bitterly fought special privilege in business. This idea of special privilege in groups is a more modern development.

There are probably 200,000 voluntary associations in the United States of some kind or another, most of which give voice for or against something of public importance. Except for the collectivists, they are one of the essential foundation piers under the American system of life. They perform millions of services in developing public understanding and public action. They also serve the country by neutralizing each other before the Congressional committees.

The number of associations interested in increasing or preventing the decrease in Government expenditures is very small, probably not 50 of much consequence, but they are a powerful minority.

Nor do all these pressures come from the voluntary associations. The municipalities press the State governments and the State governments press the Federal government.

If such an unexpected thing were to happen as all these groups keeping their hands off expenditure questions and these reforms in government for twelve months, both in Washington and in the election districts, the Congress would do a great job not only in decreasing expenses but in the common interest of the nation.

## MORALS AS WELL AS ECONOMICS

There is something else involved in all this problem.

Out of the war, as from all wars, the nation has had a spell of moral and spiritual sickness. It has been a period of great cynicism. With the lowered moral resistance of this period, unfair burdens have been placed on the people by particular groups. Too frequently do we hear a repetition of the excuse, "They got theirs; we will get ours," or Ben Franklin's remark about "God helps those who help themselves."

But if Ben were alive today he would say, "Free men were not created by drives of pressure groups on the public treasury."

## CONCLUSION

Nations must inevitably suffer from their mistakes. But their survival depends upon their will, their courage, and their moral and spiritual fibre. If these qualities live, then unbalanced budgets and ideological disputes can be but a passing froth on the surface. The rise of American civilization was out of a people of such qualities. It has been sick but it is not in its decline and fall. All around us we see signs of moral and spiritual strength in the oncoming youth.

There is a difficult word I could use here—atavism—that is, the latent qualities which we inherit from our ancestors. They are coming back. Your organization is one of their expressions. In your leadership of American youth lies the hope and confidence of our country and of my generation.

*EDITOR'S NOTE: The following extracts are from Mr. Hoover's Birthday Address ("Think of the Next Generation") at the Reception Tendered by Stanford University, August 10, 1949:*

\*\*\* Some of you will know that during the past two years I have added somewhat to my previous knowledge of the currents of government in this Republic. Beyond the immediate problems of efficient organization of the Federal Departments, there arise from these investigations some grave questions relating to the next generation and indeed to our whole future as a nation.***

## THE GROWTH OF GOVERNMENTAL SPENDING

We must wish to maintain a dynamic progressive people. No nation can remain static and survive. But dynamic progress is not made with dynamite. And that dynamite today is the geometrical increase of spending by our governments—Federal, state, municipal and local.

Perhaps I can visualize what this growth has been. Twenty years ago, all varieties of government, omitting Federal debt service, cost the average family less than $200 annually. Today, also omitting debt service, it costs an average family about $1,300 annually.

This is bad enough. But beyond this is the alarming fact that at this moment executives and legislatures are seriously proposing projects which if enacted would add one-third more annually to our spending. Add to these the debt service and the average family may be paying $1,900 yearly taxes. They may get a little back if they live to over 65 years of age.

It does not seem very generous to set up an "acceptable" standard of living and then make it impossible by taxes.

## THE GROWTH OF BUREAUCRACY

No doubt life was simpler about 147 years ago, when our government got well under way. At that time there was less than one government employee, Federal, state, and local, including the paid military, to each 120 of the population. Twenty years ago, there was one government employee to about 40 of the population. Today, there is one government employee to

176

about every 22 of the population. Worse than this, there is today one government employee to about 8 of the working population in the United States.

## THE GROWTH OF DEPENDENCY

Twenty years ago, persons directly or indirectly receiving regular monies from the government—that is, officials, soldiers, sailors, pensioners, subsidized persons, and contractors' employees working exclusively for the government—represented about one person in every 40 of the population.

Today a little more than one person out of every 7 in the population is a regular recipient of government monies. If those of age are all married, they comprise about one-half the voters of the last Presidential election.

Think it over.

## WORKING FOR THE GOVERNMENT

In the long run it is the Average Working Citizen who pays by hidden and other taxes. I have made up a little table showing the number of days which this kind of citizen must work, on an average, to pay the taxes.

|  | Days' Work |
|---|---|
| Obligations from former wars | 11 |
| Defense and cold war | 24 |
| Other federal expenditures | 12 |
| State and local expenditures | 14 |
| Total thus far | 61 |

But beyond this the seriously proposed further spending now in process will take another 20 days' work from Mr. and Mrs. Average W. Citizen.

Taking out holidays, Sundays, and average vacations, there are about 235 working days in the year. Therefore, this total

177

of 81 days' work a year for taxes will be about one week out of every month.

You might want to work for your family instead of paying for a gigantic bureaucracy.

Think it over.

## CONFISCATION OF SAVINGS

To examine what we are doing, we must get away from such sunshine figures as the gross national income. We must reduce our problem to the possible savings of the people after a desirable standard of living. If we adopt the Federal Government's estimate of such a desirable standard, then the actual, and the seriously proposed, national and local government spending will absorb between 75 and 85 percent of all the savings of the people. In practice, it does not work evenly. The few will have some savings, but the many must reduce their standard of living below the "acceptable" level to pay the tax collector.

And it is out of savings that the people must provide their individual and family security. From savings they must buy their homes, their farms, and their insurance. It is from their savings finding their way into investment that we sustain and stimulate progress in a dynamic productive system.

One end result of the actual and proposed spendings and taxes to meet them is that the Government becomes the major source of credit and capital to the economic system. At best the small business man is starved in the capital he can find. Venture capital to develop new ideas tends to become confined to the large corporations and they grow bigger. There are ample signs of these results already.***

Another end result is to expose all our independent colleges and other privately supported institutions to the risk of becoming dependent upon the state. Already it is more and more difficult for these institutions to find resources. Then through politics we will undermine their independence, which gives lifting standards and stimulus to government supported institutions.

No nation grows stronger by such subtraction.

Think it over.

## GOVERNMENT BORROWING

It is proposed that we can avoid these disasters by more government borrowing. That is a device to load our extravagance and waste onto the next generation. But increasing government debts can carry immediate punishment, for that is the road to inflation. There is far more courage in reducing our gigantic national debt than in increasing it. And that is a duty to our children.

## INCREASING TAXES

And there is no room for this spending and taxes except to cut the standard of living of most of our people below the "acceptable" level. It is easy to say, "Increase corporation taxes." That is an illusion. The bulk of corporation taxes is passed on to the consumer—that is, to every family. It is easy to say, "Increase taxes on the higher personal income brackets." But if all incomes over $8,000 a year were confiscated, it would cover less than 10 percent of these actual and proposed spendings.

The real road before us is to reduce spending and waste and defer some desirable things for a while.

## WE CANNOT HAVE EVERYTHING AT ONCE

There are many absolute necessities and there are many less urgent meritorious and desirable things that every individual family in the nation would like to have but cannot afford. To spend for them, or borrow money for them, would endanger the family home and the family life. So it is with the national family.

So long as we must support the necessary national defense and cold war at a cost of 24 days' work per year to Mr. Average W. Citizen there are many comforting things that should be deferred if we do not wish to continue on this road to ruin of our national family life.

Think it over.

## THE BACK ROAD TO COLLECTIVISM

The American mind is troubled by the growth of collectivism throughout the world.

We have a few hundred thousand Communists and their fellow travelers in this country. They cannot destroy the Republic. They are a nuisance and require attention. We also have the doctrinaire socialists who peacefully dream of their Utopia.

But there is a considerable group of fuzzy-minded people who are engineering a compromise between free men and these European infections. They fail to realize that our American system has grown away from the systems of Europe for 250 years. They have the foolish notion that a collectivist economy can at the same time preserve personal liberty and constitutional government. That cannot be done.

The steady lowering of the standard of living by this compromised collectivist system under the title "austerity" in England should be a sufficient spectacle for the American people. It aims at an abundant life but it ends in a ration.

Most Americans do not believe in these compromises with collectivism. But they do not realize that through governmental spending and taxes, our nation is blissfully driving down the back road to it at top speed.

In the end these solutions of national problems by spending

are always the same—power, more power, more centralization in the hands of the state.

Along this road of spending, the Government either takes over economic life, which is socialism, or dictates institutional and economic life, which is fascism.

We have not had a great socialization of property, but we are on the last miles to collectivism through governmental spending of the savings of the people.

Think it over.


## FOOLING THE PEOPLE'S THINKING

A device of these advocates of gigantic spending is the manipulation of words, phrases, and slogans to convey new meanings different from those we have long understood. These malign distortions drug thinking. They drown it in emotion.

For instance, we see government borrowing and spending transformed into the soft phrase "deficit spending." The slogan of a "welfare state" has emerged as a disguise for a collectivist state by the route of spending. The Founding Fathers would not recognize this distortion of the simple word "welfare" in the Constitution. Certainly Jefferson's idea of the meaning of welfare lies in his statement "To preserve our independence . . . we must make a choice between economy and liberty or profusion and servitude. . . . If we can prevent government from wresting the labors of the people under the pretence of caring for them we shall be happy."

Another of these distortions is by those who support such a state and call themselves "liberals." John Morley would not recognize one of them.

Out of these slogans and phrases and new meanings of words come vague promises and misty mirages, such as "security from the cradle to the grave." In action, that will frustrate those

181

basic human impulses to production which alone make a dynamic nation.

Think it over.

## WHERE BLAME MUST BE PLACED

It is customary to blame our Administrations or our legislatures for this gigantic increase in spending, these levies on the nation's workdays, and this ride to a dead-end of our unique and successful American system.   A large cause of this growing confiscation of the work of the people by our various governments is the multitude of great pressure groups among our own citizens. Also the state and municipal governments pressurize the Federal Government.   And within the Federal Government are pressure groups building their own empires.

Aggression of groups and agencies against the savings of the people as a whole is not a process of free men.   Special privilege either to business or groups is not liberty.

Many of these groups maintain paid lobbies in Washington or in the State Capitols to press their claims upon the Administrations or the legislatures.

Our representatives must run for election.   They can be defeated by these pressure groups.   In any event our officials are forced to think in terms of pressure groups, not in terms of need of the whole people.

Perhaps some of my listeners object to somebody else's pressure group.   Perhaps you support one of your own.   Perhaps some of you do not protest that your leaders are not acting with your authority.

Think it over.

## IN CONCLUSION

And finally, may I say that thinking and debate on these questions must not be limited to legislative halls.   We should debate them in every school. We should resort to the old cracker barrel debate in every corner grocery. In those places these phrases and slogans can be liquidated by common sense and intellectual integrity.

A splendid storehouse of integrity and freedom has been bequeathed to us by our forefathers. In this day of confusion, of world peril to free men, our high duty is to see that this storehouse is not robbed of its contents.

We dare not see the birthright of posterity to individual independence, initiative, and freedom of choice bartered for a mess of collectivism.

My word to you, my fellow citizens, on this seventy-fifth birthday is this: The Founding Fathers dedicated the structure of our government "to secure the blessings of liberty to ourselves and our posterity." A century and a half later, we of this generation still inherited this precious blessing. Yet as spend-thrifts we are on our way to rob posterity of its inheritance.

The American people have solved many great difficulties in the development of national life. The qualities of self-re-straint, of integrity, of conscience and courage still live in our people. It is not too late to summon these qualities into action.

*EDITOR'S NOTE: The following relevant extracts are from Mr. Hoover's speech, "The Government Cannot Do It All," delivered at the Greater New York Fund's Twelfth Annual Campaign Dinner, the Waldorf Astoria, New York City, April 25, 1949:*

\*\*\* We have a steady expansion of government into welfare activities. I am not here criticizing the expansion of govern-mental welfare agencies. They have a place in American life —provided the cloak of welfare is not used as a disguise for Karl Marx. But parallel with this expansion, we have stupendous taxation to support the hot and cold war. That makes it difficult for the citizens to support the voluntary welfare agencies. It requires more personal sacrifice than ever before.

From all this, many citizens ask themselves: For what reasons must we continue to support the voluntary agencies? Why not let the Government do it all?

The first short answer to this question is that you cannot retire from the voluntary field if you wish our American civilization to survive. The essence of our self-government lies in self-government outside of political government. Ours is a voluntary society. The fabric of American life is woven around our tens of thousands of voluntary associations. That is, around our churches, our professional societies, our women's organizations, our businesses, our labor and farmers' associations —and not least, our charitable institutions. That is the very nature of American life. The inspirations of progress spring from these voluntary agencies, not from bureaucracy. If these voluntary activities were to be absorbed by government bureaus, this civilization would be over. Something neither free nor noble would take its place. The very purpose of this Fund is to keep voluntary action alive.

The second answer to this question is that it is our privately supported and managed hospitals and educational institutions that establish the standards for similar governmental agencies. It is the voluntary institutions which are the spur to official progress. Without them, our governmental healing and educational agencies will lag and will degenerate. Your sole purpose is support of the private institutions.

The third answer to this question is that morals do not come from government. No government agency can create and sustain a system of morals. You perhaps are not working specifically in the religious field, but your works confirm religious faith and morals. You do support the development of sports in our youth. The ethics of good sportsmanship are second only to religious ethics.

There is a fourth answer. Governments and bureaucracies

184

cannot build character in our youth. With the brutalization which is inevitable from war, revitalized character building has never been as necessary as it is today. Over half the organizations for which you are appealing are, directly or indirectly, for character building.

There is a fifth answer. The greatest and, in fact, the only impulse to social progress is the spark of altruism in the individual human being. "And the greatest of these is charity" has been a religious precept from which no civilized people can depart without losing its soul. If governments practice charity, then it is solely because it rises from that spark in the hearts of the people. The day when altruism in the individual dies from lack of opportunity for personal expression, it will die in the government. At best, charity by government must be formal, statistical, and mechanistic. Yours is charity in its real sense—not obligatory but from the heart.

There is a sixth reason. The world is in the grip of a death struggle between the philosophy of Christ and that of Hegel and Marx. The philosophy of Christ is a philosophy of compassion. The outstanding spiritual distinction of our civilization from all others is compassion. With us, it is the noblest expression of man. And those who serve receive in return untold spiritual benefits. The day when we decide that the Government is our brother's keeper, that is the day the personal responsibility for our brother has been lost. If you fail, New York will have lost something that is vital to its material, its moral, and its spiritual welfare.

But a simpler answer than all this lies in the Parable of the Good Samaritan. He did not enter into governmental or philosophic discussion. It is said when he saw the helpless man "he had compassion on him . . . he bound his wounds . . . and took care of him."

That is your mission.

185

ॐ  ॐ  WHAT LIBERTIES ARE WE
LOSING?

BY RAYMOND MOLEY*

C LEARLY disturbed by a rapidly growing apprehension among the people that the current Truman program points toward socialism and away from personal freedom, Administration orators, including the President, are resorting to an old trick known as a "poser." A poser in political usage is a question framed in such a manner as to allow either no answer at all or an answer favorable to the person who asks the question.

The current poser is: "What liberties are you losing?" The manifesto issued in Chicago by the Democratic National Resolutions Committee puts the issue in affirmative form: "The achievements . . . in the past seventeen years" have been accomplished "without depriving one single American of one single liberty."

In reply, let us begin with a primary material liberty—the right to use personal income for purposes determined by the earner of that income. This liberty has been steadily, rapidly, alarmingly narrowed.

* Raymond Moley was one of the influential leaders in the early New Deal days. A noted student of crime, he has long been professor of public law at Columbia University and is Contributing Editor of *Newsweek*. The following extracts are taken from his well-known column, "Perspective," in the May 29, June 5, 12, 19, and 26, 1950 issues of that periodical.—*Ed.*

Twenty years ago, according to Herbert Hoover, all units of our government were taking less than $200 annually from the average family. Today, government costs that family $1,300. The various programs now proposed would greatly raise the cost, perhaps by a third. Meanwhile, the number of people receiving government money has risen to something like 15 percent of the population. If we add dependents, the figure will be two or three times as high. All these people are becoming increasingly dependent upon government. Their liberty is thus ebbing away.

The ratio of government expenditures to the total national income is moving upward. The percentage has not yet reached the 40 percent figure of Britain, but it is in the mid-20s.

All this means that government has taken from the people more and more of their personal property and has determined how it should be distributed. Those in power, cynically hiding their purposes behind the good word "welfare," take the substance of all the people and return it to some of the people. Their assumption is that they know best. The liberty to have and to hold and to dispose of what is earned is vanishing.

And the program for the future set forth by the President and his stooges on the national committee is an ominous threat to contract still further the boundaries of personal economic liberty.

Ah, but a rich promise goes with this proposal to spend more. The gross national product will be increased to $350,000,000,-000. That may be true, but it is speculative. The proposals to spend more are not speculative.

The reality of taxation is never explained by these self-professed defenders of liberty. A farmer in Georgia, for instance, who believes he is getting something for nothing from the government, is not told what he pays for his benefits. The fact is that on one item, gasoline for his car, he pays 192 taxes. A similar mass of taxes is hidden in other things that he buys. Since the clear intention is to increase these taxes, the tide is

running toward complete expropriation. That means socialism—nothing less. The disciples of Marx have always held that
the most direct nonviolent means to a socialist state is through
taxation. And there are no personal liberties under socialism.

Inflation is another means of curbing personal liberty. Savings have already suffered a tremendous shrinkage in real value.
The prospect is terrifying. For if the program outlined by the
President and the national committee should be adopted, at least
three-quarters of the people's savings will be taken. That
means that thrifty people who provided for their own future
will have to fall back on the protective bounty of government.
The man who wants to enjoy freedom to start a business will
find little venture capital and must mortgage himself to government. Colleges and other free social and educational institutions will find fewer donors and will have to turn to government.

All these are among the material liberties we are losing.\*\*\*

But the more the whole question of personal liberty is considered, the more it becomes apparent that property or material
rights cannot be set off from nonmaterial rights, such as worship,
speech, petition, and assembly. The individual's inalienable
rights are also inseparable. They depend upon each other and
they are, moreover, equal in importance.

This principle of inalienable, inseparable, and equal rights
was once firmly established after a long struggle to secure man's
basic freedoms. It was established in the custom and fundamental law of free nations such as England, France, and the
United States. The Constitution of the United States associates
the three fundamental liberties: life, liberty, and property.

From John Locke onward, the essential nature of property
was described as something of value which the individual had
created by mingling his mental or physical effort with some material gift of nature in such a manner as to make it a personal
attribute. It is the individual's because into its creation has

passed some of his own personality.  It stands on all fours with his rights to worship, speak, and otherwise express his thought and feeling.  And it is limited only by the similar rights of other individuals.

Those who would quarrel with this definition on the ground that some property is inherited or received as a gift overlook two elements in such property.  One is the fact that the right of the creator of such property involved his choice of its disposition.  It is still private property.  Another factor is the element of trusteeship, in which possessors of such property are bound by an obligation to those who have transmitted it.  All this is embodied in our law and all of it is rooted in the basic tradition of our Constitution.

All this, however, is denied in the philosophy of the superstate and socialism.  The Communist, of course, is perfectly frank in denying not only the individual's right of property, but all other rights.  The Socialist has either less realism or less honesty.  He argues, and I have heard Prime Minister Attlee expound on this at length, that while government may proscribe private property, it leaves all other rights in the individual. The citizen may lose his shirt, but he can still go to church, make speeches, and publish his opinions.  His liberty is even enhanced, argues the Socialist, because, presumably, he has less responsibility to look after his property and can spend more time worshiping, speaking, writing, and petitioning.

The fallacy of this is shown in the financial predicament in which British Socialism now finds itself.  The cost of government has moved to prodigious heights, partly because government has been an inefficient operator of industry and partly because government beneficiaries have taken more than the goverment anticipated.  The result is that the Socialist government is now moved to curtail rights.  Labor unions are forbidden to quit work in strikes.  In one instance, the government threatened action if a strike vote were held.  Free medicine has become so expensive that government must, as its next step, tell the doctor whom he will serve and the citizen what doctor he may have.* The essential indivisibility of rights has been demonstrated in every Socialist experiment.

American sponsors of the superstate are in accord with the philosophy of the British Socialists in assuring us that property can be set apart from other rights. Their approaches, however, are even less candid than those of their British brethren. One of their insidious tricks is to arrange rights in an order of descending importance. Another is to substitute the vague word "security" for "property" in the enumeration of human rights.***

The American sponsors of superstatism have had a great deal of trouble getting around the constitutional guarantees of the rights of life, liberty, and property. For when these are joined in an indivisible triangle of liberty, they constitute our most powerful defense against the invasion of socialism. The one which they need to eliminate or breach, of course, is the right of property.

Three methods of attack have been used for this purpose in legislative and judicial action. The first is to break down the defenses of property through a wide, almost unlimited use of the general-welfare clause in the Constitution. The second is to rate the three rights of life, liberty, and property in a descending order of importance. The third is to attempt to disassociate the right of property from the rights of life and liberty and to substitute for it a "right" of security.

The first two of these methods have found help and sympathy not only in the legislative declarations of Congress but in the Supreme Court as reconstructed over the past thirteen years. The third method, which is especially emphasized in the effort

---

* The new Churchill regime has had to demand a fundamental change in this aspect of British polity—the requiring of the payment of at least partial fees by patients.—*Ed.*

of the United Nations Commission on Human Rights, has reached the point of inclusion in the FEPC bill endorsed by President Truman and urged by his representatives in Congress.

The term "general welfare" appears twice in the Constitution. It is in the Preamble: "promote the general welfare," and in Article 1, Section 8: that Congress may tax to provide, among other things, for the "general welfare of the United States." Under an interpretation of the reconstituted Supreme Court, a great number of Federal grants, benefits, and regulations for all sorts of groups and purposes have been allowed. *The point seems to have been forgotten by all but a minority of the Court that the words "general welfare" mean something more than the sum of all little welfares. For if enough little welfares are provided, the general welfare of the nation will be hopelessly impaired.* But an opening has been made in the Constitution for almost anything a political Congress and President may find it expedient to provide.

Another trend has been a disposition of a group of Supreme Court Justices, notably Murphy, Rutledge, Black, and Douglas, to regard the three rights of life, liberty, and property in an order of descending importance. This tendency was vigorously resisted by the late Chief Justice Stone without avail. Justice Frankfurter has more recently protested about this "preferred position" of life and personal liberty, over property. This double standard has also been pointed out—not to say deplored —by the notable and respected Judge Learned Hand. He has very forcefully pointed out the truth that has been assumed for nearly a century and a half: that there is a strict equality of all three rights.\*\*\*

While President Truman and his Fair Deal supporters have studiously avoided saying that they are seeking to put into effect a planned economy for the nation, if they succeed in electing a Congress that will enact their program, the fact is that we shall have an economy as planned as the British Socialists were able to achieve in five years of power. This can easily be shown by adding together the major items of the Fair Deal.\*\*\*

Let us begin with compulsory health insurance. Here the government collects a tax, sets up the machinery for providing services, pays the doctors, directs patient participation, and foots the bills for all services, including drugs, hospitalization, eyeglasses, and so forth. The spurious claim is made that the patient may, among other things, select his doctor, and the doctor his patient. In practice, this choice would be very limited, and in the end, as Britain is learning, there could be no freedom of choice at all.

Innumerable proposals have been made to provide easy credit for small businesses through government loans. Careful analysis makes it plain that this plan to set up government-financed businesses in competition with privately financed businesses will strike at the very heart of a free economy. For it will support inefficient businesses and burden the efficient. And as one of its sponsors has admitted, much of the productive plant of the country will under foreclosure ultimately be owned by the government.\*\*\*

The operation of a great Federal political machine, with hundreds of thousands of jobholders and vast patronage, impairs free elections in every state.

The trend of pension and welfare legislation takes from the individual the responsibility and power of providing for himself.

The Brannan plan for agriculture pushes still further a limitation upon the farmer in a free market. It penalizes larger farms. And in its provisions for perishables, it subsidizes every grocery basket at the taxpayer's expense and in effect tells the farmer what he shall receive for his product.

The most gigantic example of planning, however, is the proposal for a series of river-valley authorities which would ultimately cover the nation. These are to follow the pattern of the TVA. The Columbia Valley Administration is first on the list, and President Truman vigorously argued for it on his recent Western trip. Under the Columbia plan, there would be three board members, virtually irremovable during a six-year term, with vast powers over electric-power production, navigation, irrigation, and many related activities. States would be denied their traditional control over their rivers, their land, and their resources generally. Local communities would be compelled to accept grants from the CVA in lieu of taxes. Almost every business and individual enterprise, from the small farm to the vast lumber industry, would be subjected through the control of electric energy. As a major spokesman for the plan has said: "He who controls electric power controls people."

These are a few of the aspects of the American grand plan.***

The immense paw of the tax collector is already upon us. He takes at least $60,000,000,000 annually now. As Herbert Hoover pointed out last week, this means at least 60 percent of our possible savings, after we have paid for a reasonable standard of living. But the President and his party ask for more. Senator McClellan, a Democrat, tells us that the President's program calls for an additional $20,000,000,000 to $25,000,000,000. That would increase the bite from our savings to a possible 80 percent. That means that the individual's freedom to invest or otherwise dispose of his surplus earnings is approaching the vanishing point.

Meanwhile, our past savings, laid aside in years when taxes were not so oppressive—contemptuously referred to by the President as years of darkness, denial, and despair—are shrinking in real value under inflation. For government's needs are not met by taking from what we earn this year. A larger and larger amount is taken from what we have earned and saved in past years. A deficit reaches a long arm back and grabs what government failed years ago to take in taxes. Thus, government forecloses the future, robs the present, and sacks the past.

Government must, in putting over its program, knock down

or chisel away the constitutional right of an individual to the property he has created or earned. This, as we have seen, is done by making property a third-class right or by substituting for it the idea of security through government. Thus, our serene highness, government, takes what you have and hands you a vague promise that has no binding force on future holders of power.

The alleged benefits bought by our money consist of a long list of government activities, each of which shears away some of our liberties.***

The prospect is enchanting. A tight little life with everybody equal. Hordes of officials peering into every corner of our lives. A barren plain of uniformity, over which ride the inspectors and police of a superstate. A fine end for a nation of once self-respecting pioneers! As Churchill once exclaimed in another connection: "What kind of people do they think we are?"

In 1947 Prime Minister Attlee admitted that seventeen ministries had the power to enter private houses without search warrants. That is the ultimate picture of a planned state.

But, says the planner, you still have freedom of thought and expression. Let us see. As freedom of choice ceases in the use of earnings, in occupation, in the things bought and sold, in caring for ourselves and our dependents, our minds lose the habits of freedom. The superstate hires a greater and greater number of us, and we learn that it is best to keep our mouths shut and our opinions to ourselves. The businessman whose customer is the government must realize that the customer is always right. Our private cultural, educational, and religious institutions, denied contributions from vanishing private savings, become government dependents.

In the end, there must be very little left for free expression and thought. Somebody else does all the thinking about everything important in life. Moral and intellectual atrophy sets in, and self-reliance evaporates in the thin air of absolutism.

*The planning of things ends in the planning of men.*

# THE MARCH OF PROGRESS— ECONOMICALLY

## Monetary and Fiscal Tricks
## Have No Power of Magic*

### BY EDWIN G. NOURSE†

WHEN I saw the first outline of your program, I was impressed with the strong note of courage and optimism which it expressed. Fifty years of progress by the association; "the march of progress" in manufacturing; "the march of progress" in agriculture, in farm mechanization, and even in Government—with Senator Byrd as its prophet. Compared with his assignment, mine should be easy—"The March of Progress—Economically."

The economic progress of this country has been almost fabulous since its founding, or during the last century, or in the fifty years spanned by the life of your organization. All these records of progress are matters of common knowledge. As we come closer to the present day, the tempo of progress seems to be accelerating, not being arrested. Against the somber backdrop

---

* Speech delivered before the National Retail Farm Equipment Association, Washington, D. C., October 18, 1949.

† Eminent economist, former Chairman, Council of Economic Advisers.—*Ed.*

of the depression 30's, the stimulus of war touched off a blaze of new achievement. It revealed latent powers for production not demonstrated before, powers which were inherent in our natural resources, our high-grade labor force, our accumulated capital, and our capacious credit reserves. That enlarged economic power made us the decisive contributor to victory and at the same time permitted the masses of our people to enjoy a higher average of consumption than they had ever known before. As I remarked in another connection about a year ago, even a war of such gigantic proportions did not reduce us to the blood, sweat, and tears that were the lot of England and our other allies. "While individual deprivations and family losses were grievous, it could be said of the Nation as a whole that we lost some blood, shed a few tears, and got up a healthy sweat."

After the war, many people, reasoning by analogy, prophesied that we would have a postwar slump, that demobilization would throw 8 or perhaps 10 million workers into the ranks of the unemployed. But we passed from victorious war to vigorous peacetime reconversion with amazingly little lost motion. Assembly lines were switched back to peacetime goods, pipelines were filled, and trade relations were re-established. Consumers, with plump pay envelopes and an unprecedented reserve stock of liquid savings, resumed their normal but now enlarged role in the market as stimulators and guides of the productive process.

The Employment Act under which I have the honor to serve is a march-of-progress act. It calls for maximum production, employment, and purchasing power, engendered by free competitive enterprise complemented by prudent but vigorous public enterprise and sustained over the years with only moderate ups and downs. I am not prepared to say that 1948 and 1949 precisely measure the maximum of production, employment, and purchasing power for the United States, but I venture the thought that they may be accepted as at least "a reasonable facsimile thereof."

196

As we now approach the year end, I am not prepared to offer you any assurance, private or official, that we shall do precisely that well next year, throughout the decade of the 50's, or for the rest of this century. It is notable, however, that the events of the last ten years or so, taken in the perspective of preceding decades, have given many thoughtful persons confidence to make projections that are about hat optimistic. I need cite only two, which come from particularly significant sources and, by coincidence, both from persons whom I may call "colleague."

My former and long-time colleague, President Moulton of the Brookings Institution, in his recent book, *Controlling Factors in Economic Development*, envisages a doubling of population during the next century and an eightfold rise in general standards of living. My more recent colleague, Vice-Chairman Leon Keyserling, in his address "Prospects for Economic Growth" at the Democratic Party Conference on Land, Water, and Jobs in San Francisco, a month ago envisaged a march of progress for the next ten years "founded conservatively upon rates of growth that we have achieved during good years in the past." On this basis, he said, "we can lift our total annual output of goods and services from 262 billion dollars in 1948 to ... about 350 billion dollars by 1958."

This, he estimates, would permit almost all families to "reach a minimum income level of around $4000," with more than $40 billion left to "improve income in the higher brackets." Farm incomes would gain "almost 35 percent ... a somewhat more rapid relative gain than the population as a whole, because our rural areas have not yet attained the parity of income and opportunity which is both just and essential for an economy healthful in all its parts."

Furthermore, social security would be improved, health and education better provided for, the long-range resource development program enlarged, and "home building for all income groups stepped up to a pace which would provide a decent home for every American family." Finally, Mr. Keyserling argued

that that projected national production would also "be enough
to achieve balanced budgets, make large retirements on the national debts, . . . and leave substantial room for tax reduction."

I am not too clear as to how Mr. Moulton derived his factor
of 8. Nor am I altogether sure that Mr. Keyserling could simul-
taneously raise wages, farm incomes, and business profits so fast
and at the same time reduce the public debt and cut taxes. But
"hitching our wagons to the stars" has been good American
practice, and it is not my purpose to quibble with the precise
terms of either of these courageous projections. I want to call
your attention rather to the fact that in both cases, the prospect
of great progress is made conditional.

Mr. Moulton says plainly that his projection is only "concerned with economic *potentials,* as governed by resources and
productive power." He thereupon turns to consider the kind
of economic organization and practices, public and private, that
would be needed to bring these potentials to actual fruition.
"What principles, methods, or policies," he asks, "must be pursued in order to realize in fullest measure our national economic
goals?"

Mr. Keyserling, too after outlining his ten-year targets, undertakes to put them in the perspective of reality by adding that,
to achieve them, "we need ever-improved cooperation between
labor and management," price and wage policies "which will
allow enough capital accumulation to expand productive facilities and provide enough purchasing power to buy the full product, . . . a satisfactory program for completing the postwar
adjustments of agriculture," and government programs "to conserve and build up our security against the hazards and risks of
modern industrial life, and to maintain that regulatory vigilance
which prevents any one group from seeking to benefit unfairly
at the expense of another."

Now, what does all this review of predictions of progress lead
up to? To me, it proclaims an almost self-evident truth that,

with our traditions, our training, and our resources, the march of economic progress from here on *should* be even greater—much greater—than the quite creditable record of the past. But that does not mean an easy life for a generation born with a silver spoon in its mouth. No, it underlines a tremendous responsibility. Those dreams of progress will go a'glimmering unless they are intelligently and diligently brought to pass. The free world looks to us to be the pacemakers of that progress, to be the rock on which the non-Soviet future can be built. To falter or to lag in our task would be to dishonor our fathers and to defraud our sons. But in all seriousness, I must say that as I look about me I am filled with real concern. I cannot indulge in easy optimism.

As an economist, I do not see standards of life being raised adequately out of enlarged production when a great labor organization sees the current situation as "the occasion for a reduction in the hours of work" (to 35 or 30), lest the productivity of the labor force "exceed the power of the market to absorb the total production under prevailing and impending conditions," or when the czar of coal orders a 3-day week (21 hours) with full pay for a redundant labor force, and when pensions at 60 are demanded for a population steadily becoming longer-lived.

I am filled with apprehension too when I look to management and see it choosing the costs of banked fires and the demoralization of the delicate adjustments of supply lines and distribution patterns rather than capitalistically venturing some re-examination of its practices of accounting and its theories of price-making.

I am uneasy when I see farmers demanding stimulative prices whilst Government accumulates gigantic surplus holdings, pays subsidies out of federal deficits, and imposes production allotments and marketing quotas.

I am not happy either when I see Government slipping back into deficits as a way of life in a period when production and employment are high, instead of putting its fiscal house in order and husbanding reserves to support the economy if less prosperous times overtake us.

In sum, if we are to maintain the march of economic progress, we must, individually and as groups, in private business and in politics, display industry, prudence, and self-discipline, recognize that we can't get more out of the economic system than we put in, that collective bargaining in good faith and on solid facts is the road to a workable distribution of total product, and that monetary and fiscal tricks have no power of magic but are a slippery road to misery.

*EDITOR'S NOTE: On May 2, 1950, Dr. Nourse delivered a notable address, "The Battle of the Budget Bulge," at the 38th Annual Meeting of the United States Chamber of Commerce, Washington, D. C., from which the following extracts are here included:*

When I learned of the proposed title for this session—The Battle of the Budget Bulge—I was struck by its suggestiveness and pleased to echo it in the title of my remarks. I recall very vividly that, when our papers and radio carried the news of the break-through at Bastogne, many fireside generals and military amateurs began clamoring for an immediate containment. Then, as day followed day without news that the enemy had been routed, they registered fear verging on panic. It was much like the vicarious athletes in the bleachers at a football game who yell "Hold that line!" "Don't give an inch!" "Throw 'em back!" But more is needed than mere protest to overcome a dangerous military thrust or a threatened gain by the opposing team. It takes coolness, method, and competent strategy.***

## NATURE OF THE BREAK-THROUGH

What does the word "bulge" mean in connection with our session this afternoon? To my mind, it means that our complacent expectation of returning to something approaching post-war fiscal normalcy was upset by a new military threat in the spring and summer of 1948. We were at that time running a Treasury surplus and enjoying a justifiable measure of confidence that we would be able to manage a debt of the enormous size necessitated by the war and that we would continue such level of Treasury surpluses as would operate effectively to damp off the fires of inflation. But on March 17, 1948, the President went before the Congress with news that a Russian breakthrough on the diplomatic front would necessitate a check of the rapid disarmament which we had planned and had had under way. The Congress shortly responded with an increase of 3.5 billion dollars of added military authorizations.

Even before this we had heeded the cry for help from Western Europe and launched the Marshall Plan to strengthen its industrial and commercial structure so as to make a solid civilian base for military security against possible Russian aggression. Together the cost of the cold war and our economic cooperation with the non-Soviet world account for sums as great as or greater than the budget bulge, measured by current and prospective deficits. Stated from the other side, the current level of deficits is about the same as the amount of tax reduction voted in the summer of 1948. Such was the financial breakthrough with which we are still contending.

Now, there are government officials, members of the Congress, economists (including some of considerable prominence), and possibly even some businessmen who are not concerned about the present state of government finances. They might say that the Chamber's program-makers have relied on a false analogy and employed "scare words" in phrasing the title of this session. In essence, they argue that if we do not become unduly alarmed, the threatening tide of increasing debt will shortly abate. The pending budget, with its estimated deficit of another 5.1 billion dollars on top of this year's deficit of 5.5 billion (more likely 7) is described by the Administration as "a sound basis for moving toward budgetary balance in the next few years." In other words, those menacing Germans will shortly turn around and march back home. They were just out for a little healthful exercise.

I happen to belong to a different, a more old-fashioned, school of thought. I admit "I do not understand deficit financing" in this bland and complacent sense. I think that slipping into deficits as a way of life is threatening the industrial security of our country, on which we have to rely if the cold war goes on, and still more if a hot war develops. Continued deficits will threaten the value of, or public confidence in, the Nation's basic monetary unit. And it is only upon confidence in that unit that the sustained activity and stable prosperity of all kinds of business can be built.

## FOUR PHASES OF STRATEGY

Half my cards are already on the table in thus showing you exactly the premises from which I proceed in suggesting a national economic strategy for meeting a danger which I believe to be greater in its scope and menace than was the local bulge across the Roer. Now, I'll put my remaining cards down in a series of brief propositions about a strategy for victory in correcting the budget bulge.

First, we can't correct the budget bulge if we yield in the matter of military expenditures every time Joe Stalin throws a scare into us. We must have the imperturbability of a General McAuliffe to say "Nuts" when an industrially primitive and illiterate country tries to bluff us as to our respective abilities to wage industrialized warfare. I do not venture an opinion as to just what figure should be set for the military budget. I have not even seen the voluminous diplomatic and military data whose study is indispensable to judge that issue. But I do feel qualified as an economist to raise a note of warning when the issue is decided unilaterally without weighing all the economic data and analysis of economic capacities and impacts over and against the military and diplomatic yen for impregnable strength.

As I emphasized in a series of speeches at successive citizen orientation conferences at the Pentagon, security is a global concept. It is not attained by building up a military machine at the expense of a sound economy—which is no stronger than the financial foundation on which it rests. We all see the folly of the Mississippi steamboat owner who put on such a big whistle that the engines stopped when he blew it.

This is no issue between Democrats and Republicans, but between economic statesmanship on the one side and fear complexes and power drives on the other.***

Second, whatever the final decision on military expenditures (and the higher they are, the more this will apply), we can't win the battle of the budget bulge without tightening our belts in matters domestic and civilian. Cutting out deadwood and raising efficiency in government agencies will be important, but by no means enough. We have to forego many things we would like and could have in the absence of foreign drains. These civilian purposes come under three general heads: resource development, social welfare, and personal security.

I am not going to get impaled on the thorny question of just how far or how fast we should go in any of these directions as a long-run matter. The point I want to make is simply that we can't eat our cake and have it too. If we believe there is danger in persistent budget deficits in times of prosperity (and I do), then we have to hold these development, welfare, and security expenditures down in proportion as military and foreign aid expenditures rise. To do this, we need to start with frank recognition that some of the development projects and some of the welfare outlays are just good old-fashioned "pork" and some of the welfare is of the enervating "dole" kind, and some of it is of the ill-chosen Lady Bountiful kind. From the economic or business standpoint, these expenditures are of course the ones to prune. That is, from the broad and basic business viewpoint, they should be drastically pruned. But unfortunately, there is also a narrow business viewpoint. From that approach, any market dollar is to be sought or promoted just because it gives a chance of private profit. That is why you businessmen, who demand that the Government balance the budget by cutting expenditures, swarm down here to see to it that you don't lose any gravy in the process. I'll return to this phase of budget balancing in the latter part of my remarks.

Third, to win victory in the battle of the budget bulge, we must have industrial peace. Only if payrolls are full and steady, only if plants run continuously above that "high break-even point," only if goods move in full volume and promptly away from the factory platform and off the dealers' shelves will we have the high national income out of which to meet heavy government expenditures. An industrial impasse, with numerous, frequent, or long strikes, will lower government revenues and increase government costs, particularly those for social security benefits. Then the tide of the budget battle will turn against us.

Don't tell me that putting industrial peace as one of the four major strategic requirements for budget balancing is idealistic to the point of being impossible. So labor's demands *"are* unreasonable and labor leaders tough people to deal with." So "employers *do* demand inordinate profits and accept lower volume of operations rather than making wage or price adjustments which maintain volume operation." The pot can go on endlessly calling the kettle black. But if we don't find ways of employing collective bargaining in good faith so that we keep public and private revenues at full tide, we won't win the budget battle, and if we lose that, we will lose the cold war.

To say this is not to pass judgment on anybody or to criticize anybody. It is simply stating a simple mechanical fact which the Kremlin understands whether we do or not. If our First Army is fighting our Second Army, we won't have so much strength to resist the common enemy.

Fourth, the strategy of victory requires that we do not take the easy road of tax reduction while there is still a serious deficit problem. I know how unpleasant it is to pay taxes, and I know that there are glaring inconsistencies and inequities in our present tax structure. They may be so serious as to cripple some firms and actually cause others to pass out completely. But they are not preventing prosperous operation for the economy as a whole. We can better postpone reform of the tax system than insist on getting relief at the expense of adding another billion or so to the deficit, which is a more basic threat to our prosperity. The men who won the Battle of the Bulge were tired and hungry, many of them sick, and some of them lost their lives. But they did not put their own safety and comfort above the great objective of winning the battle.\*\*\*

## MORALE FOR VICTORY

While my title employed the word "strategy," treatment of the theme has called for passing over at points into discussion also of some tactical issues. The winning of battles in fact rests upon three factors: sound basic strategy, skillful tactics, and high morale. The operations of a democratically organized economy are something very different from the processes of a military organization. There is no supreme command to devise a unified strategy, no corps of staff officers to execute local tactics or of lesser officers to enforce discipline. The possibility of winning the battle of the budget bulge comes down therefore in the last analysis to an issue of self-discipline. This self-discipline must be based on understanding of economic means and ends on the part of millions of businessmen and workers at points of individual responsibility, large and small.

As I view the current scene, I cannot regard the state of economic morale of our people as being high. We were not severely disciplined by the war, and we have tended to fall into even more self-indulgent ways of thinking and acting since. I am by no means sure that the battle of the budget bulge can be won at all without radical change in our behavior and in what we demand from the economic system under present conditions in return for what we put into it. Speaking at Philadelphia a few weeks ago, I summed this situation up in the following sentence: "It strikes me that the United States today is indulging in the lazy relaxation of an Indian summer daydream instead of facing the stern realities of clearly foreseeable storms and dangerous weather for business."

## TIMING IS OF THE UTMOST IMPORTANCE

The general argument that I have been presenting to you is that the strategy of the budget battle calls for (a) holding both external and internal expenditures down and (b) holding our productive contributions and our tax participation up by respective amounts which will bring the two into balance at the earliest practicable time. Timing in economic strategy and tactics is no less important than in the military area. It was not possible to throw the Germans back to the Roer in a day or in a week. First there had to be a succession of steps planned out and then a timetable drawn up so that moves would be synchronized and a series of limited objectives achieved that in an orderly and cumulative process reached the major and final objective. Similarly, we cannot pull expenditures down or push taxes up or combine the two movements in such a way as actually to balance the budget in 1950 or probably in 1951. If we tried to do so in any such drastic fashion, we would bring on a depression, perhaps a rather severe one. Our last state would be worse than our first.\*\*\*

Of course we believe that if we could stop the government from spending so much, private spenders could employ all our resources to supply goods and services the people prefer. But, granting all that, the switch cannot be made overnight. So we have to show a good sense of timing in our strategy and work out a practical timetable. Then we shall have to put our backs into meeting that timetable. If we fail we will simply trade a deficit for a depression. And if depression gets started, it could spread fast. Or those who want to see government take over could move in fast on the wave of fear engendered by rising unemployment. In fact, you wouldn't even trade a deficit for a depression. The depression thus brought on would bring its own new deficit with it.

It might be a rough guess that stopping 3 or 4 billion dollars of government disbursement and its resultant business and promptly substituting 3 or 4 billion dollars of private business at the necessary points to prevent disruption of markets and production would be a pretty good performance for a single year. This would give us at the minimum a two-year timetable for balancing the Federal budget—that is, fiscal '52. But we would have to start now, have a timetable we take seriously, and do a lot of vigorous and skillful private enterprising clear down to the little company and the local community. Here is a task in which local Chambers of Commerce under wise leadership from the national Chamber may well take a major part.

In fact, a pretty good estimate of whether we are or are not going to win the Battle of the Budget Bulge can be made by ascertaining how sincerely the central and local chambers here represented really want to win it and can be counted on to do their part in winning it. Success will call for intelligent and courageous leadership and for voluntary cooperation all down the line. Your GHQ made a truly admirable start. When the first honest-to-goodness economy drive was put on by Secretary Johnson in the Defense Department under the specific direction of the President, the United States Chamber of Commerce gave full acceptance and support. President Herman Steinkraus wrote to Secretary Johnson:

On behalf of this organization and its underlying membership of 2500 chambers of commerce and 500 trade associations, I wish to extend to you our sincerest congratulations and appreciation of the courageous and patriotic action you are taking in making substantial savings for the taxpayers of this country.

We, therefore, support your action and are advising the many thousands of our members in our underlying membership of 1,300,000 who are engaged in every phase of business and industry, to support your stand in their respective communities.

Mr. Steinkraus then sent a letter to the 2500 chambers all over the country, saying in essence: "You have been asking for economy. Well, here it is. Don't foul it up. Don't come to Washington or wire or telephone trying to get your community exempted from cuts which have been carefully considered in relation to the whole picture." But even better than this negative counsel to local chambers, he gave a positive admonition. He said: "Do get busy studying in advance just what cuts will be made in your community and how many people of what kinds will be disemployed in the process. Then immediately bestir yourselves to see that these people are moved into productive jobs elsewhere."

I know of at least one State Chamber of Commerce that vigorously reinforced the stand of the national chamber. President Weaver of Ohio wrote Secretary Johnson:

Objections to your reduction order . . . from some organizations in local areas where the temporary decline in private business and employment would have its first impact . . . should not be interpreted as representing the views of business generally. It is our best judgment that the great benefits to our economy which would flow from the establishment of a well-ordered fiscal program to which your order points the way, far outweigh any temporary local dislocations which may arise . . . Our Board of Directors, representing the entire membership of this organization, warmly welcomes this evidence of governmental economy and ventures the hope that it will be equaled or surpassed in scope by subsequent reductions in other Federal departments."

Furthermore, the Ohio Chamber wrote its members urging them to see that private jobs were planned in advance to take up any unemployment. If that sort of constructive private business leadership is followed generally, I believe we can get from the situation of deficit in a time of prosperity to a sound fiscal situation within a reasonable time, and with production and employment maintained at a high level.

Recent developments, however, do not look too good. I have been traveling up and down the country making speeches and hearing a lot of business talk. In southern California, they tell me local business interests are plugging hard to keep hospital building at the highest point even if there are no patients for the beds or doctors for the patients. In northern California, they tell me there is determined resistance to any cut at Mare Island, however redundant or obsolete the shore installations. In Texas, they say: Our people are invoking all their political strength to prevent any drying up of the Federal largesse we became accustomed to during World War II.

I was encouraged, even thrilled, when I read Senator Douglas' historic statement that "To be a liberal, you do not have to be a wastrel!" I was greatly impressed as he went on to elaborate the practical details of his economy program. But I am not so happy when I read in the current number of a leading news weekly [*Newsweek*, May 1, 1950] of how this Colonel of Marines has fared in his sortie in the Battle of the Bulge.

Last week a former college professor who thinks it might be a good idea to balance the Federal budget had the Senate rocking with laughter. Democratic Senator Paul H. Douglas of Illinois was deadly serious about it, too, which made him all the more comical. Up for consideration was a $1,565,000,000 rivers and harbors authorization bill. Rivers and harbors bills traditionally are pork-barrel bills; senators and representatives toss in projects without even bothering to explain why they conceivably might be necessary. The whole principle is: "Don't ask questions. You vote for my project, and I'll vote for yours."

Douglas . . . introduced twenty amendments that would have chopped the bill down to about $700,000,000, carefully explaining why each project he wanted to kill, including two in his own state, would be a waste of money. Each amendment was greeted with raucous laughter. Each was howled down, and some of the loudest shouts were from those Republicans and Southern Democrats who moan most about economy between appropriations bills . . .

While the Senate was laughing at Douglas, the House also demonstrated that in Congress *economy* is a word that rhymes with *hypocrisy*. The Republicans had promised to pare appropriations by $1,000,000,-000, but after a few test amendments party leaders became aware they couldn't even keep their own members in line for the cuts, much less pick up any appreciable number of Democratic votes, so they dropped the whole idea.

The Federal deficit this year and next will be much bigger than anyone expected. Originally the 1950 deficit was estimated at $5,500,000,000, but Treasury receipts have fallen off and even if appropriations don't exceed the President's requests, the government actually will find itself $6,700,000,000 in the red. The decrease in receipts similarly makes the 1951 deficit likely to reach at least $7,300,000,000 instead of the anticipated $5,100,000,000. Actually the situation may be much worse, for Congress not only has shown no disposition to cut appropriations, it actually is talking of raising them.*

As I said before, no strategy will win the campaign for national solvency if there is a lack of economic morale among the troops. If I were sitting in the Kremlin, I think that I would be quite complacent as I viewed the progress of the Battle of the Budget Bulge. Sitting in Washington, I am deeply concerned.

---

* That the situation has become much worse is shown by President Truman's colossal budget for 1953. It remains to be seen, at the present writing, whether Congress will interpret its *general* economy-mindedness into a willingness to remove specific items from the pork barrel, or whether it will continue to believe in economy "in principle" only.—*Ed.*

# THE RISE OF THE SERVICE STATE AND ITS CONSEQUENCES*

BY ROSCOE POUND†

A NEGRO who used to do some work for my father
had come from the West Indies and was never
weary of talking about them. "They has there," he said once,
"a drink they calls planter's punch. And, you know, Judge,
those planter's punches they creeps up on you surruptitious and
clandestyne."

The service state, the state which, instead of preserving
peace and order and employing itself with maintaining the
general security, takes the whole domain of human welfare for
its province and would solve all economic and social ills through
its administrative activities, has been creeping up on us in the
present century after the manner of "those planter's punches."
It was known earlier in Continental Europe. But although
some writers in England were calling attention to its possibilities
at the end of the last century, it was so at outs with ingrained
modes of Anglo-American thought that few tried to put the
pieces of evidence together to see what it indicated as to the

.* Address at the Forum sponsored by The Economic and Business
Foundation and The Service and Professional Clubs, at New Castle, Pa.,
June 13, 1949.

† Roscoe Pound, distinguished jurist, is Dean Emeritus of the Harvard
Law School.—Ed.

direction in which we have been moving. In the meantime, since the first world war, it has made exceedingly rapid progress and has covered already a very wide field of individual activity and of official promotion of wide welfare programs on every side.

I say service state rather than welfare state. The term welfare state seems to me a boast. Governments have always held that they were set up to promote and conserve public welfare. This is implicit in the synonym *commonwealth*—the common weal or general welfare personified in the state. So far men have agreed. But when it comes to the question how the common weal or general welfare is to be achieved, they have differed and do differ profoundly. Some think the general welfare is best promoted by a government which maintains order and administers justice, for the rest, leaving men free to do things for themselves in their own way so far as they do not commit aggressions upon others or subject others to unreasonable risk of injury, and act in good faith in their intercourse with others. On the other hand, there have always been those who have believed in a benevolent government which helps men instead of leaving them free to help themselves; who have believed in a paternal ruler or paternal state doing things for his subjects or its citizens to the fullest extent.

Understand, I am not preaching against a service state in itself. The society of today demands services beyond those that the state which only maintained order and repaired injuries could perform. In a complex industrial society it becomes more difficult to do by private initiative many things which the public wishes done and wishes done quickly. Administrative agencies of promoting the general welfare have come to be a necessity and have come to stay. It would be futile to quarrel with the idea of a service state kept in balance with the idea of individual spontaneous initiative characteristic of the American. What one must resist is not state performance of many public services which it can perform without upsetting our legal, political, economic, and social order, but the idea that all public services must and can only be performed by the government—that politically organized society and that alone is to be looked to for everything, and that there is no limit to the services to humanity which it can perform. What I deprecate is carrying to the extreme the idea of regimented cooperation for the general welfare, the exaltation of politically organized society to the position of an absolute ruler. This presupposes supermen administrators or an all-wise majority or plurality, omnicompetent and equal to taking over the whole domain of the general welfare and to determine in detail what it calls for in every situation. The service state in the English-speaking world began by performing a few major additional services beyond maintaining order and administering justice. As it has added more and more it has come to be jealous of public service performed by anyone else.

What is to be the effect of the service state upon American constitutional democracy? The service state as it develops as a superservice state must be *par excellence* a bureau state. From the very nature of administration the bureau state calls for a highly organized official hierarchy. A hierarchy calls for a superman (very likely an *ex officio* superman) at its head. Thus, unless we are vigilant, the service state may lead to a totalitarian state. It has Marxian socialism and absolute government in its pedigree and has grown up along with the totalitarian state in other parts of the world. Liberty—free individual self-assertion, individual initiative and self-help—is looked on with suspicion if not aversion by the service state, and its advocates seek a "new concept of liberty" as freedom from want and freedom from fear, not freedom of self-assertion, or self-determination. Self-help by the individual, competing with the service rendered by the state, seems an interference with the regime maintained by the government. Spontaneous individual initiative is frowned on as infringing on the domain of state action. The service state easily becomes an omnicompetent state with bureaus of *ex officio* experts and propaganda activities carried on at public expense. If the step to it is gradual, the step from it to an absolute state is easy and may be made quickly.

Bills of rights are a characteristic feature of American constitutions. Beginning with the Virginia Bill of Rights of 1776, enacted immediately after the Declaration of Independence, they have been made a part of all our constitutions, state and federal. Our American bills of rights are prohibitions of governmental action infringing guaranteed rights, that is, guaranteed reasonable expectations involved in life in civilized society. They are laws, part of the constitution as the supreme law of the land, enforceable in legal proceedings in the courts at suit of those whose rights are infringed. They are generically distinct from the declarations of rights on the model of the French Declaration of the Rights of Man which are to be found in constitutions generally outside the English-speaking world. Those are mere preachments, declarations of good intentions or exhortations to governmental authority, legally binding on nobody and unenforceable by anyone whose declared rights are infringed. But the service state is beginning to affect our conception of a bill of rights in America. In a recent proposal for a declaration of rights for a world government we get the Continental note in the very title, but also the note of the service state which is disinclined toward law. There is a declaration of a right of everyone everywhere to claim for himself "release from the bondage of poverty." It is not that he is to be free to free himself from this bondage, but that the state is to free him without his active help in the process. Also he is declared to have a right to claim reward and security according to his needs. But his claim to needs is likely to have few limits and is sure to conflict with claims of others to like needs. Such declarations are not merely preachments, not enforceable or intended to be enforced as law, they are invitations to plundering by rapacious majorities or pluralities.

In a recent book, Professor Corwin has discussed the deca-

214

dence of fear of oppression by government which has become very marked. Experience of government in seventeenth-century England and experience of government of the colonies from Westminster in the seventeenth and eighteenth centuries had made this fear a dominant consideration in our policy from the beginning till well into the present century. Growth of a feeling of divine right of majorities, akin to that of divine right of kings, has led to an assumption that concern about oppression by government is something we have outgrown. Yet distrust of absolute majority or absolute plurality is as justified in reason and in experience as distrust of the absolute personal ruler. Indeed, the latter may be given pause by fear of an uprising which an intrenched majority need not fear.

It is characteristic of the service state to make lavish promises of satisfying desires which it calls rights. If a constitution promises to every individual "just terms of leisure," those who draft it do not ask themselves whether such provision is a law, a part of the supreme law of the land, or a preachment of policy which no court can enforce and no legislative body can be made to regard. Such preachings enfeeble a whole constitutional structure. As they cannot be enforced, they lend themselves to a doctrine that constitutional provisions are not legally enforceable and may be disregarded at any time in the interest of political policy of the moment. They weaken the constitutional polity we have built up. Is there wealth enough in the world reachable by taxation imposed by a world government, or even reachable by wholesale confiscation by a world state, to guarantee "just terms of leisure" during life to the whole population of the world or even to four hundred and fifty million Chinese?

Setting forth such things in a constitutional declaration of guaranteed rights makes a farce of constitutions. How can a government release the whole world "from the bondage of poverty?" What organ of government can be made to bring about that enough is produced and is continuously produced to insure plenty for everyone everywhere? How can a court compel legislative or executive or individuals or organizations of individuals to bring this about, or how can executive or legislative compel either or anyone else to do it? Such pronouncements proceed upon a theory which used to be preached by social workers that law is a protest against wrong. Protests against wrong may be very effective in spurring lawmakers to find remedies and enact laws making them effective. But protests themselves lack the quality of enforceability and machinery of enforcement which are demanded for a law in any advanced society. On one occasion Hunt, the agitator, appeared before Lord Ellenborough while sitting at circuit and insistently demanded to be heard. When recognized by the court, Hunt explained that he appeared on behalf of the boy Dogood. On Lord Ellenborough telling him that there was no case of the boy Dogood upon his docket, Hunt exclaimed theatrically: "But, my Lord, am I not in a court of justice?" "No, Mr. Hunt," replied the Chief Justice, "you are in His Majesty's Court of Oyer and Terminer and Jail Delivery to deliver the jail of this county." "Then," said Hunt, "I desire to protest." "Certainly, Mr. Hunt, by all means," said Lord Ellenborough, "Usher, take Mr. Hunt to the corridor and allow him to protest as long and as much as he likes." A law which is simply a protest against wrong is as futile as were the declamations of Hunt in the corridor of Lord Ellenborough's court.

A power to act toward a general equality of satisfaction of wants and a policy of developing such an equality are something very different from a provision in a declaration of rights that a world government guarantees to bring such a policy to fruition. No one can seriously believe that in such time as we can foresee the western world can provide complete social security for the rest of the world, a great part of which is always close to the brink of starvation.

I have spoken at some length of proposals for declarations of rights for a world political organization because the propositions drafted by enthusiastic promoters of a world constitution are followed sometimes in recent proposals for constitution writing in the development of the service state in America. A state which endeavors to relieve its people of want and fear without being able to relieve its individual citizens of the many features of human make-up which lead to poverty and fear is attempting what the colored preacher aptly called unscrewing the inscrutable. How can we expect a state to bring about a complete satisfaction of all the wants of everybody in a world in which we all want the earth, but there are thousands of millions of us and only one earth. Guarantees which are no more than promissory declarations of policy can do no more than deceive. Some years ago, when in one of our states a "modern code" was being urged and propositions for promissory declarations for wide amelioration of human ills were presented, a wise and experienced lawyer suggested that one additional article would make the whole perfect: Be good and you will be happy. Hell is paved with good intentions. An extensive pavement of that material is far from a solid foundation for a politically organized society. The service state is a politically organized society and cannot, as could Baron Munchausen, pull itself up by its own long whiskers.

This does not mean, however, that our nineteenth-century bills of rights cannot be supplemented to meet conditions of the urban industrial society of today. The two new articles in the bill of rights of the New Jersey Constitution of 1947, articles 5 and 19, directed to questions of segregation and discrimination on grounds of race, color, or creed and to rights of organization and collective bargaining, are models of what may be done by constitutional provisions, part of the effective law of the land, enforceable and meant to be enforced, as compared with preachments and promises and wishful declarations of ideal policy.

Promissory bills of rights that create expectations of the politically and economically unachievable and weaken faith in constitutions are a step toward the totalitarian state. The strong selling point of that state is its argument that a strong man, a superman leader, can do what a government hindered by constitutional checks and balances cannot do. When a constitution declares rights as claims to be secured by government which it can't secure, it invites centralization of power in an absolute government which claims ability to secure them. The service state, taking over all functions of public service, operating through bureaus with wide powers and little practical restriction on their powers, through government positions for a large and increasing proportion of the population, and through systematic official propaganda and a system of subsidies to education, science, and research, can easily be taking strides toward an absolute government, although under forms of democracy. Indeed, the extreme advocates of the service state insist that constitutional democracy is a contradition in terms. A democracy must be an unrestricted rule of the majority. The majority must be as absolute a ruler in all things as was the French king of the old regime in France or the Czar in the old regime in Russia. As the seventeenth century argued that a monarchy must in the nature of things be an absolute not a constitutional monarchy, on the same logical grounds it is argued that a democracy must be an absolute not a constitutional democracy.

General welfare service by the state, becoming service for strong aggressive groups or for politically powerful localities at the expense of the public at large, has been the ladder by which absolute rulers have climbed to power and the platform on which they have been able to stay in power. Louis XIV held down France by holding down Paris by distribution of bread at the expense of the provinces. The Spanish absolute monarchy long held itself in power by using the wealth of the New World for service to its subjects at home. Napoleon III used state workshops. Totalitarian Italy used the theory of the service of the corporative state. Totalitarian Russia promises proletariat rule at the expense of the rest of the community. Indeed, in antiquity the Roman emperor held down Italy by extortion of wheat from Egypt.

Since the first world war we have preached a great deal and promised much as to the rights of minorities and of oppressed racial groups. But the lavish promises and administrative absolutism of the super-service state (or shall we say service super-state?), with the absolute ultimate rule of majorities or even of pluralities which they involve, are a menace to the guarantees that a constitution which is a legal document, not merely a frame of government promising welfare services which it cannot be made to perform, is able to give those groups. The attempt to make all men equal in all respects instead of in their political and legal rights and capacities is likely to make them more unequal than nature has done already. Unless we give equality the practical meaning of our American bills of rights, we are likely to be thrown back to a proposition that all men are not born equal but are born equally.

There has been a tendency of men in all history to worship their rulers. In the society of today this takes the form of faith in absolute rule of the majority or, indeed, of the plurality for the time being. We forget that majority or plurality are only a way out when we cannot get entire agreement. The founders of our polity, with long and bitter experience of absolute rule behind them, sought a government of checks and balances by which absolute rule by anyone was precluded. As Mr. Justice Miller put it, in the centennial year of the American Revolution, the theory of our governments, state and national, is opposed to the deposit of unlimited power anywhere. Today we are told that this doctrine is outmoded. What called for the pronouncement was legislation imposing a tax for subsidy to private manufacturing enterprise. That was regarded as unconstitutional in 1875. But in the service state of today expensive service to some at the cost of others is regarded as a service to the public, as indeed it may be in some cases, and this tempts aggressive groups to obtain legislation providing service to them for which others must pay.   A group of this sort easily, in its own mind, identifies itself with the public.   Obviously the conception of public service needs to be carefully defined and limited if we are to avoid being led into absolute rule by majority or plurality.

A government which regards itself, under pretext of extending a general welfare service to the public, as entitled to rob Peter to pay Paul, and is free from constitutional restraints upon legislation putting an element or group of the people for the whole, has a bad effect on the morale of the people.   If government is a device for benevolent robbery, a would-be Robin Hood of today is not likely to see why his benevolently conceived activities are reprehensible.   Based on colonial experience of legislation imposing burdens on some for the benefit of others rather than of the public as a whole, our older constitutions and substantially all constitutions in the nineteenth century forbade special or class legislation.   The omission of this provision from recent constitutions is significant.   No doubt the restriction in the nineteenth-century constitutions was applied too rigidly and was made to stand in the way of proper welfare legislation.   But entire omission points to a feeling that government is intended to be unfair to minorities and that there should be no limit on the ability of organized groups to make their fellow men pay for special service to them.

A service state must be bureaucratic.   Bureaus are characteristically zealous to get everything in reach under their control.   Would it be a great public service to have a bureau of psychologists to examine us for our aptitudes and assign us, whether we like it or not, to the calling for which they find us fitted?   Before the advent of psychologists such a state was argued for by Greek philosophers.   The later Eastern Roman Empire stabilized society by putting and keeping men in callings somewhat in this way.   An omnicompetent state postulates omnicompetent bureaus.   Why in the perfect all-regulating state allow human energy to be wasted by permitting individuals

220

to engage in futile efforts to employ themselves in callings in which they cannot succeed? Is not that the next move after subsidizing them to persist in these callings in which they are failing and bound to fail?

So much for the service state in its relation to our American constitutional polity. Now let us turn to the effect of the service state on the professions. By a profession we have meant, until the rise to prominence of the professional athlete obscured our ideas, a group of men pursuing a common calling as a learned art and as a public service—nonetheless a public service because it may incidentally be a means of livelihood. From the standpoint of a profession there are three ideas: A common calling, a learned art, and a spirit of public service. Gaining a livelihood is not a professional consideration. Indeed, the spirit of a profession, the spirit of a public service, constantly curbs the urges of that incident. An organized profession does not seek legislation relieving it of duties or liabilities incumbent upon it. It does not seek to advance the money-making feature of professional activity. It seeks rather to make as effective as possible its primary character of a public service. An engineer may patent his inventions. A manufacturer may get legal protection for his trade secret or patent his discovered process. What a member of a profession invents or discovers is not his property. It is at the service of the public.

A tradition of duty of the physician to the patient, to the medical profession, and to the public, a tradition of the duty of the lawyer to the client, to the profession, to the court, and to the public, authoritatively declared in codes of professional ethics, taught by precept and example, and made effective by the discipline of an organized profession, makes for effective service to the public such as could not be had from individual practitioners not bred to the tradition and motivated as in a trade primarily if not solely by quest of pecuniary gain. Nor can this professional tradition be replaced with benefit to the public by a political tradition of officeholders owing primary

221

allegiance to political parties and depending for advancement on the favor of political leaders. Moreover, the professional organization and tradition are even more to the public interest in their effect on the learned arts which the professions follow as callings.

All advances in science, in arts, in learning, in short, all progress in civilization—in the raising of human powers to their highest possibilities—is the result of trial and error, that is, of experimentation. Thus, every physician, every hospital, can and is impelled to experiment and invent, and as the professional spirit of public service leads to promulgation of the results of experiment and investigation and putting the results at the service of others, they are not individual trade secrets and are not patented, and they do not need to be argued to bureaus nor do those who would use them have to await official adoption of them. They are open to free use and make their way on their intrinsic merit.

Huge bureaus of graduates of medical schools, brought up to seek public office, and organized in the civil service as employes of the service state, can be no effective substitute for a profession. With the multiplication of services rendered by the state comes a multiplication of officials; and ideas of official omnicompetence and majority infallibility come also. When every form of public service becomes at least potentially a state function, the difference between a public service performed by a profession and a public function performed by a bureau becomes crucial.

If callings have making of a livelihood for their primary concern, in an economic order in which the great majority of the community are on the payroll of either the government or of some corporation, public, public service, charitable, or private, it follows that most individuals will be in a sense employees and so liable to be caught up in a regime of employees' organizations, collective bargainings over wages, and strikes. Organization of physicians for advancement of medicine, organization of lawyers for advancement of justice, and organization of teachers for the advancement of teaching must give way to organization of employees of every grade and kind of employer for the advancement of wages and dictation of the conditions of employment. Already the two major labor organizations are carrying on a campaign to unionize the "white collar workers" in industry and business. This may well presently take in the younger members of the bar in the legal departments of big companies. Already the American Federation of Labor has organized municipal employees, and in Los Angeles the probation officers, whom we had been thinking of as members of a rising profession of social workers, are members of a Probation Officers' Union, a branch of a Municipal Employees' Union, affiliated with the national organization. Are the young lawyers in the office of the city attorney, along with the clerks and stenographers, the municipal probation officers, the clerks, secretaries, and typists in the various city departments, the firemen and the policemen, to be in a Union of Municipal Employees and from time to time to strike for increased pay as collective bargain contracts expire or when one of their number is removed or discharged? Apparently we must say this is entirely possible. The National Labor Relations Board has held and was upheld by the Supreme Court of the United States in holding that plant guards during the war, enlisted at first in the Army and later made part of a city police force, could be organized in unions by the Congress of Industrial Organizations. Next county employees may be organized as such so that the clerical force in the courthouse may go on a strike and tie up the administration of justice. Why should not the assistant district attorneys be organized also? May we not see unions of state employees and find the secretaries of the judges of the Supreme Court striking? Already there are unions of federal employees, and these may come to include the young men, members of the bar, who are secretaries to the judges of the highest court in the land. Every department and major administrative agency of the federal government has many lawyers on its roster. Unions of federal employees may very likely seek to include them. The service state in its zeal to serve the employed by promoting organization and collective bargaining is threatening the general security by allowing them an extreme development.

Teachers in the public schools have been unionized in more places than one and members of university faculties are now active in a teachers' union in some of our old historic institutions. Are we to see closed shops of higher learning, with union faculties collectively bargained with, check-off for union dues, and all the concomitants of organized pursuit of higher wages in what had been thought a learned profession? Here, again, zeal for a service to the employed by promoting organization and collective bargaining threatens the effective performance by the state of the function of public education which it had been carrying on well from almost the beginning of our polity.

Thus, as things are coming to be in an era of bigness, large-scale organization of all activities, and strenuous acquisitive competitive self-assertion, the professional idea must contend with the rise to power of organizers of an expanding class of employees. Thus, more and more, as things are, as individuals in the professions have come to be regularly retained or, nowadays, regularly employed by great corporations, or appointed to substantially permanent positions under the federal government or state and municipal governments and administrative agencies, a constantly larger number of practitioners in their capacity of employees are enlisted in organizations with the trade spirit of emphasis on wages rather than the professional idea of pursuit of a calling in the *spirit of public service*. Unless we are vigilant it may well be that this prevailing of the trade idea will make straight the path toward absorption of the professions in the service state.

The course of that path is not hard to chart. We can see three possible stages: (1) Unionizing of all callings which may be taken to involve employment, at least so far as some in the

224

calling are not capable of classification as employers; (2) by government subsidies getting control of professional education and thus subordinating the professions to bureaucratic management; (3) seeking to bring cheap professional assistance to everyone's back door by government taking over of the callings pursuing learned arts.

Such a consummation may be pictured as a carrying of the idea of the service state to its furthest logical development. The service state began by performing a few major services. In time it has undertaken more and more. Now it has become jealous of public service being performed by anyone else. The advocates of the omnicompetent state will say that in primitive or pioneer societies certain public services are rendered by anyone who seeks to try his hand on the basis of such qualifications as he deems sufficient. Later, as society advances, such services are rendered by well-qualified practitioners organized in professions, the qualifications, as these professions develop, being prescribed and ascertained by governmental authority. Ultimately, it will be said, as political organization of society reaches maturity, all public services of every sort are to be exclusive governmental functions to be exercised by governmental bureaus.

Very likely not all of those who are teaching or preaching the doctrine of the super-service state will, at the moment, admit this conclusion. But I submit that before we go far with them on the path in which they are marching we should pause to see whither it leads. As I said above, it should be remembered that the rise of the totalitarian state was coincident with the general reception of the idea of the service state and that both have Marxian socialism in their pedigrees. Each in its way postulates an omnicompetent administration by supermen. If experience may be vouched, that means in the end supermen under the direction of an *ex officio* superman.

Even more the professional ideal is menaced by the development of great government bureaus and a movement to take over the arts as practiced by the professions and make them functions of the government to be exercised by its bureaus in a service state which may become a service super-state. For the idea of a profession is incompatible with its performance of its function, exercise of its art, by or under the supervision of a government bureau. A profession presupposes individuals free to pursue a learned art so as to make for the highest development of human powers. The individual servant of a government exercising under its supervision a calling managed by a government bureau can be no substitute for the scientist, the philosopher, the teacher, each freely applying his chosen field of learning and exercising his inventive faculties and trained imagination in his own way, not as a subordinate in an administrative hierarchy, not as a hired seeker for what he is told to find by his superiors, but as a free seeker for the truth for its own sake, impelled by the spirit of public service inculcated in his profession.

Let us consider next the effect of the service state upon business and industry. A writer on administrative law tells us that administrative agencies set up by legislation were intended, and as he seems to think, justly intended, to be unfair. They were intended to render service to a group or element of the voting public assumed to be identifiable with the public. Whether this is so, it is at any rate clear enough from American as well as from English experience, that the zeal of administrative agencies to achieve the immediate end they see before them leads them to see their function out of focus and to assume that constitutional limitations and guaranteed individual rights must give way before their zealous efforts to achieve what they see as a paramount purpose of government. The writer on administrative law referred to tells us that "political development represents a picture of increasing reliance by our society upon the administrative process." Hence, he argues, we must look on arbitrary and unfair bureau action "against a background of what we now expect government to do." It is not, however, wholly a question of what we expect government to do, but also one of how we expect government to do it. We must look at the methods of administrative agencies also in the light of their tendency to see the particular, relatively narrow task of each particular agency out of proportion.

This tendency, to take an example which is no longer controversial, was manifest under the regime of national prohibition. Those who were in charge of enforcement of the National Prohibition Act felt strongly, and no doubt conscientiously, that the objects of that act were of such paramount importance as to justify extra-legal measures and overriding of individual rights and constitutional guarantees. They looked only to what they considered we expected the government to do. Zeal in carrying out policies of service which are felt by bureaus which implement and administer them to be of paramount importance, justifying the means by the end, is demonstrating that our American constitutional polity is by no means something outgrown. The fundamental features of government which our constitutions were set up to deal with are as much in need of restraint today as they ever were. All exercise of power by politically organized society calls for checks. That checks are particularly needed with respect to administrative regulation of business and industry is made clear by consideration of certain tendencies which may be seen in administrative agencies, federal and state, in America, and no less in such agencies in Great Britain and in the British dominions generally.

Most serious among these tendencies is one going counter to what has always been the first principle of judicial justice, namely, to hear the other side. In all administrative adjudication there is an obstinate tendency to decide without a hearing, or without hearing one of the parties, or after conference with one of the parties in the absence of the other whose interests are injuriously affected. Another is to make determinations on the basis of consultations had in private or of reports not divulged, giving the party affected no opportunity to refute or explain. A very serious tendency is to make hearings prescribed by law a mere form, reaching conclusions from one-sided investigations not made public and using the hearings merely to give color of fairness to pronouncement of the predetermined result. In doing this, decisions are reached without evidence, or without evidence of probative force, or even in spite of evidence. In the last published volume of decisions of the United States Court of Appeals there are repeated cases where the courts have pointed out that the administrative agency systematically gave full credence to all witnesses on one side and systematically refused to believe anything testified to by any witness on the other side. One court said that cases of this sort had become a common experience of the federal courts of review. In a service state, regulating every kind of calling and activity by committing control of them to bureaus which conduct propaganda against subjecting them to effective checks, the burden upon business and industry may go so far as to end by turning them from private functions to functions of an omnicompetent state.

The result is to put our constitutional system out of balance. It tends to put the executive in control of agencies with power of life and death over business and industry and in control of a vast political patronage of officials, petty officials, experts, investigators, and employees, which a strong personality at the head can use to maintain himself in power.

In the last century we considered as postulates, as presuppositions of life in civilized society, that everyone was entitled to assume that others would commit no intentional aggressions upon him and that no one would subject him to unreasonable risk of injury. One who committed injurious aggressions or caused injury by unreasonable subjection of others to risk was bound to repair the injury. But where injury resulted without anyone's fault we considered that each of us must bear the risk of such accidents which, after all, are inevitable in human existence. What is called the insurance doctrine, the theory that injuries which are the lot of human existence should be insured against by some form of general social sharing of the burden, is a humanitarian addition to the teachings of the past. But the service of providing such insurance seems to be growing by analogy to a postulate that every loss to anyone is to be shifted to someone else who is better able to bear it. Thus we get a new risk of life in civilized society, added to those imposed by the nature of things, namely, a risk of having to be involuntary Good Samaritans when any of our fellow men suffer loss in case we are convenient to reach as such at the time. There is nothing conducive to thrift or to productive exertion in such a social program. It suggests what Epicurus proposed in the era of absolute military monarchies after the death of Alexander the Great. Epicurus said the wise man would keep as inconspicuous as possible and thus escape the notice of the tyrant.

Another circumstance that needs to be considered enters into the putting in practice of the insurance theory as to injuries in the course of operation of public utilities. Many now propose that all injuries to all persons through the operation of public utilities be committed by the service state to a regime analogous to workmen's compensation to be administered by an appropriate bureau. The theory is that these utilities are in a position to absorb the cost of making good the loss to the luckless victims of loss by accidents without fault (or even through their own fault where no one else is at fault) because they can pass the loss on to the public in their charges for services. But in the bureau state of today this is becoming fallacious in practice. One bureau or commission fixes rates. Another has control of wages and hours. A jury or another administrative agency fixes responsibility and assesses the amount of loss. Also the federal government, state, and municipality may be imposing taxes and license fees. Thus with each of these agencies acting independently the burden cannot be adjusted either by the utility or by any one agency. The result as things are is that the burden is shifted arbitrarily to the most conveniently reached victim. This sort of thing has begun to reach into every side of our law in the service state.

Also another side of employer's liability requires considera-

229

tion from the standpoint of justice which it is not likely to receive under the reign of the idea of the involuntary Good Samaritan. As the law has been and is, an employer is liable to repair injuries due to what is done by his employee in the course of and within the scope of his employment. The reason given for this is that as the employer chooses the employee and has power of discharging him, if he employs a person and keeps that person in his employment he is at fault in choosing and employing one who proves capable of wrongdoing and should be liable for injuries resulting from that fault. Today, under a regime of collective bargaining, administrative constraint to retain or reinstate employees, vested rights of employees in their jobs, closed shops, limitation of the power to choose and abrogation of the power to discharge employees, the reason fails. But the liability of the employer for injury to third persons by the fault of the employee remains and is likely to remain under the doctrine that someone must answer for all loss to anyone, no matter how caused, and employers are the involuntary Good Samaritan most convenient to reach.

In cases against railroad companies in which there was much occasion for sympathy and but little basis for finding the company at fault, Lord Bramwell used to tell the jury a story of the pickpocket at the charity sermon who was so moved by the preacher's eloquence that he picked the pockets of everyone in the pew and put the contents in the plate. Much in the practical application of the humanitarian principle of the service state suggests the charitable activity of the pickpocket. One cannot quarrel with the high humanitarian purposes. But multiplication of charitable services, entailing great expense to be met by taxation and imposition of increasing heavy liabilities for what an enterprise cannot control or avoid, puts a heavy burden upon enterprise and productive activity. It will be much easier to break down the economic order in that way than to rebuild when the mischief has been done.

Nor should we omit to consider the effect of extreme extensions of services rendered by the state on the morale of the people. On the one hand, administrative attempts to impose moral policies of bureaus upon business and industry and, on the other hand, attempts to relieve pressure groups of liabilities which are imposed upon the rest of us confuse the whole relation of law and morals. One notable relaxation of morale is the breakdown of the feeling of duty to perform promises. A manifestation of this in high places may be seen in what is called the prediction theory of obligation. Consider what a promissory note would look like on this theory: Ninety days after date, for value received, I predict that I shall be willing and able to pay John Doe on order five hundred dollars. But this is not confined to juristic theory. Legislation impairing or doing away with the practical legal means of enforcing promises is upheld in a doctrine that a power of the legislature to relieve promissors of liability is implied in the sovereignty of the state. Such relief is one of the services it may render. After experience of revocation of franchises at every turn of political fortune in seventeenth-century England and of colonial legislation interfering with enforcement of contracts and revoking charters, we put in our federal constitution a prohibition of state legislation impairing the obligation of contracts. This has in large part at least become a mere preaching, and the spirit that has substituted that preachment for an enforceable constitutional provision has been affecting regard for the upholding of promises on every side. There is no longer a feeling of moral duty to perform, and impairment of the legal duty as well undermines a main pillar of the economic order. The long-time end result of undermining the security of business transactions may yet show that the service done to a large body of voting debtors by the service state in going to the extreme in relieving them may not prove a service to the public.

That the quest of certainty and uniformity and stability in nineteenth-century law carried what might be called a hardboiled attitude too far is clear enough. We ought, however, to have learned from the history of law that that hardboiled attitude was a reaction from extreme individualized justice in a prior stage of legal development, and should have been able to avoid an extreme of counter-reaction in our zeal to be more humane today.

Again, old age pensions are certainly a great improvement over the parish relief Dickens describes and the poorhouse and poor farm and poor relief we used to provide. But in some states extension of this service is carried to the verge of putting a premium upon inactivity and a burden upon productive activity. It looks as if voters over the age of sixty voted themselves liberal aid beyond reach of creditors, with no obligation of doing anything for themselves and while holding property to transmit to their heirs. One state, at least, by its constitution assures everyone over sixty a pleasant, parasitic life. Older requirements making relief payments a lien on the property of the recipient are abrogated, all such securities given in the past are released and cancelled, and old age pensions are given priority over all other claims upon public revenues. When the state sets out to secure individual conditions of life, the question arises at once what life is it that shall be secured? Is it a minimum life by the standards of the time and place, or a reasonable life by those standards, or an equal life, and if an equal life, equal to the community average or to the highest community level? If government is to undertake to satisfy all the desires and demands of everybody and bring about universal contentment, something more than human energy and productive exertion must be found to provide the goods of existence out of which the desires and demands are to be satisfied.

In the same direction, we may note extensions of bankruptcy relief so as to make escape from debts as easy as incurring them if not easier. For a generation legislation has increasingly limited the power of creditors to collect and created more and larger exemptions. I will not say that the service state is the cause of such things, but the state of mind that is behind extreme manifestations of the service idea must be held accountable. Nothing in the phenomena we have to investigate in the social sciences has a single cause. But current stress upon the high humanitarian designs of the service state and praise of its moral quality as compared with the supposed brutality of the legal order of the last century need to be weighed with the practical disappearance of the strict individual adherence to contracts and performance of promises which was believed in in the formative era of our institutions. What is needed here, as everywhere else, is balance. If letting people of full age and sound mind contract freely and holding them rigidly to the contracts they freely made was carried to an extreme in the last century, a system of restricting individual free contract and relaxing the obligation of contract may be carried quite as much too far in reaction. The man of high moral sense who after bankruptcy worked hard and in time voluntarily paid off his barred debts, used to be pointed out as an example of the just and upright man to whom his neighbors looked up. Today, I suppose, he would be set down a fool.

Now that the state builds great housing units with all conveniences, will not the next generation say, why require payment of rent? Why not furnish free comfortable housing up to at least the middle standard of the community for all who can't provide for themselves and at the same time enjoy the advantages of leisure and entertainment and good living of the middle standard? If men need not pay debts, why should they pay rent? Does not the ideal of absolute equality of economic condition and advantages of life call for this? So men may next be arguing. The service state may easily shade into communism.

There are those who seem to teach people to expect government to furnish them employment for which they are not qualified. Would-be artists, would-be musicians, would-be writers, and would-be actors are to be employed with public money to execute and exhibit what no one wants to buy, to perform or compose what no one wants to hear, to write what no one wants to read, or to act what no one wants to see. Thus no one's ambitions will be frustrated. A secure place in the calling one aspires to pursue is to be made for him by the state. We saw something of this in the era of WPA. It is the logical carrying out of the doctrine that medical treatment and legal advice and advocacy are to be so brought to everyone's back door that no one shall have better medical treatment or better advocacy or forensic talent at his disposal than anyone else. Even then, however, all frustration will not be eliminated. How about those whose energy and productive exertions will be required for the material basis of this Utopia if only to pay the taxes?

But, as I said at the outset, the trouble is not with the idea of a service state in itself. The mere maintenance of order and keeping the peace is a service. What is required in government as in everything else is balance. He that believeth, says Isaiah, shall not make haste. Ultimate perfection of mankind can no more be achieved through government than through the other universal agencies of improving mankind men have believed in in the past. Additional services through the state, where they can be performed by the state without waste of what we are doing and have learned how to do by other institutions, and without reducing the individual to passive obedience or to parasitism, is a reasonable program which need not carry us to the omnicompetent state.*

---

* Questions and answers following the address have been omitted, but may be obtained from The Economic and Business Foundation, New Wilmington, Pa.—*Ed.*

# ஐ ஐ LIBERALISM, PATERNALISM, SECURITY, AND THE WELFARE STATE*

BY DONALD R. RICHBERG†

THE American University was founded for the service of higher education in the capital of the United States. Its location is ideal for the study of government. It has a rare opportunity to develop teachers and students who, by precept and practice, can advance the science and art of government.

Nowhere in the world are more visible the majesty and meanness of a government, the successes and failures of popular government, and the aspirations and tribulations of un-

* I have compounded this title out of three addresses delivered by Mr. Richberg. The first, "Founders Day Address" at The American University, Washington, D. C., February 24, 1949, is here reproduced in full; a few extracts are included from "The Illusion of Security," Address at Luncheon Meeting of the Boston Conference on Distribution, Hotel Statler, Boston, October 16, 1950; most of the Address at Harvard University's Conference on the Welfare State, Monday, July 24, 1950, "What Private Associations Can Survive in a Welfare State?" is also included.—Ed.

† Donald Richberg, distinguished lawyer and devoted public servant (particularly during the pioneering stages of the New Deal when, among other important posts he held, he was general counsel and chairman of the NRA Board), has long been an exponent of traditional liberalism and is uniquely equipped to tell the genuine article from its modern counterfeit presentment.—Ed.

popular government. Nowhere are there more openings for research into the devious processes and fascinating intrigues of invisible government.

Here is a veritable paradise for higher education in the social sciences and, above all others, in political science. Nature has even provided a climate polite enough to attract visitors and rude enough to send them home. Thus residents are permitted and stimulated to do a day's work at least every other day.

Presumably a major objective of higher education is to develop a leadership of trained and well-informed persons who may guide their fellow men toward a better world. It is not expected that this guidance will be always welcome or frequently followed. The idealized average man, or man-in-the-street, is the politically licensed official guide in a democracy. But now and then even the average man becomes distrustful of his own wisdom in approving a program of getting rich by spending more money, or of making more money by doing less work. In such a moment the beneficiary of higher education may get a hearing. The economist may be permitted to guide editorial writers. In the recent complexity of world-wide economic problems even columnists have now and then followed scientific thinking and occasionally caught up with it.

The political scientist, however, has as yet received little encouragement from the practical world. In this era when the improvement of the processes of government is almost everywhere essential to the survival of a ruling class, it is only the occasional, and usually the unsuccessful, politician who will share the platform with a political scientist, in public meetings or private gatherings. Perhaps scientific aid is rejected because there is such a small quantity of political science available that when it is poured into the seas of political controversy it immediately disappears.

Of course, we have volumes of learned discourse on political movements and programs of the past, present, and immediate future. Students of politics are being crammed with factual food, just as students of political economy have been stuffed with statistical carbohydrates and proteins for many decades. But science does not make its great contribution to human welfare by research into the past and mere accumulation of reliable records. It is research into the unknown, and courageous experimentation, that nourishes the higher education from which may come the honorable, devoted leadership that humanity so needs in this intricate, bewildering world that lies around us.

In government, possibly more than anywhere else, the people need guidance to understand and to settle big issues and to avoid wasting their energies on petty issues. In government, especially, the people need guidance to understand and to use the techniques necessary to achieve their ends.

We can leave it to the chemists, the physicists, and the engineers to improve our physical world and the tools with which we can enjoy and exploit it. The radio is developed; and under our hands is placed an instrument which is utterly beyond our untrained powers of construction or even comprehension. But it is so fabricated that, after brief, simple instruction, a child can use it to produce orchestral music, news of the world, or a bedtime story of horror and crime.

Unhappily, the political scientist must create for us better ideas and a better philosophy of government. He must instruct us regarding the function of government in a modern society, which should develop more and more centripetal force to hold men together against those multiplying centrifugal forces that drive men apart. Then, when this adult education has been accomplished, the political scientist must, by research and bold experimentation, develop new techniques of government and teach a multitude to use them.

Is it not clear why it is so difficult to advance new ideas

and new techniques of government without tyrannical abuses of political power? The political scientist has little authority with which to persuade a people to follow his guidance. He may invent a voting machine and persuade commercial-minded manufacturers and politicians to install it, and persuade the voters to use it because it is not much more difficult to operate than a radio. But how can he sell the idea of voting for a government with a new principle?

Could a political scientist have persuaded the German people to accept the principle of leadership (which has scientific merit) without the aid of organized terror and military control? Could a political scientist have persuaded the Russian people to accept the principles of socialism (which have scientific merit) without the organized terror and ruthless rule of a communist dictatorship?

How, let us ask ourselves, can political scientists persuade the American people to accept new ideas of self-government and experiment with new techniques in order to make self-government effective, without resort to measures of compulsion which themselves would be destructive of self-government?

Perhaps this is an impossible task. If so, it is a challenge to the unorthodox scientist. Indeed, it is a challenge to be picked up first by an amateur, because it is the happy ignorance of the amateur that permits him to spend sleepless nights seeking to achieve the impossible. Thousands of such experiments fail, but now and then the amateur stumbles upon that "clue to the treasure-house" that can be later exploited by more competent men of science and of commerce.

For the reasons indicated, I am venturing on this occasion, as a penitent politician and amateur scientist, to suggest the desirability of research to develop a few new ideas and techniques that might be useful to ambitious statesmen, and might eventually improve the government of the United States.

One idea is that the fundamental division of political thought in our country is not between conservatives, liberals, and radicals. Indeed the word "liberal" has been given so many meanings that we can all be called liberals of one sort or another.

The original liberal was a man who believed above all things in freedom for himself and for others. He believed particularly in individual freedom from all unnecessary government restrictions. The modernized liberal believes above all things in freedom for a strong government to liberalize and to angelicize weak human beings with all necessary restrictions on their personal conduct and activities.

The original liberal wanted to preserve your right to make and spend your own money, and other ancient rights of free enterprise, free speech, and free association. The modernized liberal is most notably liberal in spending your money for you and in giving away your rights to control your own business and social relations.

The original liberal thought that a man should be free to make enough money to provide, for himself and his dependents, insurance against the hazards of accident, disease, unemployment, and old age. The modernized liberal thinks that the government should tax away your surplus earnings, and with this money provide insurance for you and your dependents, and for anyone else who doesn't earn enough to pay for his own insurance.

Please do not think that I am scoffing at these modernized liberals. These humanitarians are far more admirable citizens and better neighbors than those greedy moneymakers who destroyed the freedom of private enterprises by operating them with a ruthless disregard for the welfare of their fellow men.

But I do scoff, as an amateur scientist, at the deception practiced when a humanitarian who is a paternalist calls himself a liberal. These miscalled liberals are promoting a paternal government that is to make sure that all its children are employed and properly housed and fed and have no fear of want, a paternal government that collects a large share of the earnings of its children so that Uncle Sam can provide them with insurance against all hardships, and can pay an army of public employees to watch over them and make them happy and virtuous.

These men are not liberals in any true meaning of the word. They are paternalists who call themselves liberals because they know that the American people are not yet reconciled to a paternal control of their lives. They know that the American people still cherish the illusion that they can remain free men and yet be protected by government from all the burdens and hazards that a free man must assume.

So the politician who is engaged in taking away your freedom disguises his thought and purpose by announcing that he is going to set you free from fear and want and insecurity and injustice. A program to set you free would seem to be a "liberal" program. Yet it might be noted that the best example of such freedom from the burdens and worries of self-support which is provided by government today is found in government prisons, which are not called liberal institutions.

Again I beg of you to understand that I am not arguing that a modern government should not accept some responsibility for the economic welfare of its citizens, in addition to its long-accepted responsibilities for public health and safety. That which is called a "welfare state" is the obvious modern successor to what may be called the "protective state" of past decades. The protection of society now calls for more than protection against foreign oppression and domestic disorder and crime and pestilence. It calls for more than merely laying down the rules of fair play in a free competitive economy. This will be generally conceded.

But there is a fundamental division of thought in our country on two major political issues. First: To what extent and at what speed should government undertake to eliminate social and economic injustices and provide economic security?

Second: Is the national government the most competent or desirable instrument of social and economic progress, or should state and local governments be utilized, wherever possible, to do the job?

There is a natural affiliation between paternalists who believe in extensive and rapid reforms and the federalists who would have all welfare laws enacted and administered by the national government. There can be little doubt that the national government, with its command of huge revenues and its remoteness from the pressures of local interests and prejudices, can enact and enforce regulatory laws against minority opposition with greater speed and often with more efficiency and less partiality than local governments.

On the other hand, those who advocate more gradual reforms know that local government will not usually act except under the pressure of a local majority opinion. Thus there will be the sanction of prevailing opinion for a political experiment, and the opportunity for a prompt revision if the experiment should prove unwise. When we observe the continual adjustment and readjustment of state and municipal laws to meet changing conditions and changing public sentiment, in contrast to the slow and difficult process of revising any major federal law, we can see many strong arguments in favor of local self-government. State government, in regulating the liquor traffic and labor relations, has demonstrated a flexibility in response to public opinion which has been notoriously lacking in the national government.

There is, however, a more profound reason for maintaining the authority of local governments against the constant pressure to extend the authority of the national government. The impossibility of retaining a democratic control of a centralized government of one hundred and fifty million people is being demonstrated not only in America but throughout the world. Particularly, it has been made evident that the regulation of the daily living and working conditions of millions of people is only practical through the issuance of volumes of bureaucratic regulations to be applied by a multitude of petty officials, whose speedy and necessarily arbitrary decisions must be enforced by the hurried prosecution and harsh punishment of offenders. The traditional protections of the individual against abuses of official authority, which we call "due process of law," cannot be maintained. In a word, *a comprehensive welfare state must be a police state.*

It was one of the fundamental principles of our constitutional government that the police power—that general authority to protect and to promote the public health, safety, morals, and welfare—should be reserved to the states. No such power was granted to the federal government. Such paternalistic controls over our citizens as became necessary must be exercised by local governments, which, being close to the people, could be readily restrained from interfering unduly with their individual freedom to pursue happiness according to their individual ambitions and abilities.

There is and always should be a deep-seated conflict of opinion between *liberals,* who believe in maintaining individual freedom by strengthening our powers of local self-government, and *paternalists,* who believe in hastening social reforms by increasing the powers of the centralized, national government. Accordingly, it might be expected that the two major political parties would be in opposition on this great issue. Instead, we find that both the Democratic and Republican parties are internally divided on this issue, and potent segments of each are bitterly opposed to many official policies.

Within the Republican party large numbers of Western liberals, who do not want to be governed and have all their earnings expended in Washington, are at odds with large numbers of Northern paternalists who want to extend the reforms of the Roosevelt era by more and more federal expenditures and controls. Within the Democratic party Southern liberals, clamoring for States Rights, are at odds with Northern paternalists whose aim is a socialized economy which can only be developed by an all-powerful national government.

Historically, the stronghold of local self-government should be in the Democratic party, and the Republican party should be the fortress of Federalism. But changing economic conditions and shifts of population have forced each party to attempt an inner coalition of antagonistic elements. Both party platforms in the 1948 campaign promised a paternalistic expansion of federal powers that left liberal devotees of local self-government no clear choice between Truman and Dewey. The candidacies of Thurmond and Wallace, despite the small votes naturally cast for candidates who could not win, demonstrated the important fact that there was real vitality in the uncompromising demand of one for the democracy of local government and of the other for the autocracy of national socialism. In contrast, how uninteresting were the arguments of the two major parties, both advocating an expedient marriage between a democracy of easy virtue and a socialist seducer!

No one can tell whether the farmers, the small businessmen, the skilled workers, the professionals, and other large groups of essentially independent, self-sufficient men and women in the North and West would join with the overwhelming majority of States Rights advocates in the South to swing a national election against the urban paternalists who are largely concentrated in the industrial centers of the North and West. But it can be figured from election returns that if such a coalition of liberals were effected it might win by a large majority.

The political technique to bring about such a coalition of liberals is not difficult to advise, but it might be difficult to develop against the opposition of the Administration now in power. That Administration owes its power primarily to its strategy of capturing the farm vote by assuring the farmers of immediate benefits from supporting a national paternalism which, eventually, will destroy that independent way of life which is the chief incentive and most satisfying product

243

of farm labor. It may be assumed that the present Administration will do all that it can to retain this farm support.

Furthermore, the international situation compels domestic support of the national administration even by those who may be deeply opposed to its domestic program. The need for a strong national government to stand against any foreign aggression is so great, and may become so much more urgent, that any present effort to revitalize local self-government may be criticized as untimely and impractical. Nevertheless, to anyone with a clear understanding of the trend of recent extensions of federal authority, to anyone with a vision of our future if that trend is not soon checked, it is evident that unless the effort is made soon, it may soon be too late.

This is not the occasion for presenting a detailed program for the salvation of liberalism and the preservation of democratic government. But let me dogmatize briefly, as a surviving factotum of the great insurgent campaigns of Theodore Roosevelt and Robert M. LaFollette, as a retired staff officer of the original New Deal, and as an active participant in every national campaign since 1900. Not as an amateur scientist, but as a weather-beaten politician, I venture to assert that a coalition of Democratic and Republican leaders against paternalism and in support of the liberalism of local self-government *could* be achieved and take over the control of Congress within a hundred days. No man would be required to leave his party, to break a pledge, or to betray his constituency. It would only be necessary for men to vote their convictions regarding the course of action necessary to maintain the constitutional government which every member of Congress is sworn to uphold.

From this beginning, the nation-wide coalition of Democratic and Republican liberals for the national elections of 1950 and 1952 could be easily engineered. Only one thing would make this coalition impractical, the absence of vision, the principles, and the courage that inspire and compel men of great responsibility to do great deeds in times of great emergency.

Surely the American people are entitled to receive from their leadership—and particularly from those who have had the advantages of higher education—a clear presentation of the profound issue between democratic liberalism and undemocratic paternalism. Surely they should be offered a political technique whereby, instead of being asked year after year to vote for incoherent and evasive candidates, running on incoherent and evasive platforms, they would be given a simple choice between two parties, two candidates, and two platforms that represent two distinct philosophies and forms of government that have been, and will be, eternally in conflict.

We have been warned repeatedly in recent years that "America must choose." Isn't it about time that Americans were given a chance to choose?

*EDITOR'S NOTE: The following extracts are from Mr. Richberg's Address at the meeting of the Boston Conference on Distribution, Hotel Statler, October 16, 1950:*

\*\*\* Primitive minds envisioned heaven as a place of eternal rest and peace, where there would be safe enjoyment of all that human beings found desirable, perhaps "nectar and ambrosia" for those who suffered from thirst and hunger, or "nirvana," oblivion, for those wearied of passion and hate and pain (and after-dinner speeches), or "happy hunting grounds" for North American Indians. But as mankind grew older and wiser these visions broadened into aspirations for the deeper happiness that comes from the mental enjoyment of doing more and being more than is possible for a mere eating, drinking, procreating animal.

So in modern striving to make a heaven upon earth, civilized men have become more and more intolerant of wars and economic struggles that hamper and destroy idealistic programs of human cooperation to raise the material and spiritual level of human life. The idealists have turned to government as the embodiment of force to make effective the will of a people. They demand that government *compel* men to live in peace and *compel* them to work together and to share one another's burdens, so that all may be free from the pains and privations that prevent men from using their abilities to the utmost to advance the individual and the general welfare.***

The illusion which I would shatter if I could, the illusion which most possesses us at the present time, is that economic security within our borders can be obtained by a widespread use of government force to compel everyone to work and spend his earnings so as to carry out a political program, to conform to a political morality, and to live according to a political gospel. We do not think of this as the employment of aggressive force, because we are not organizing a huge army of soldiers to impose a military rule upon our people. But we are organizing a huge army of civilian administrators to impose government regulations, which are enforced by a civilian police, who are backed up by the armed forces of the national government. This means, in cold reality, that our socializers are relying on armed force to compel our own people to submit to a political control of their lives. Louis XIV said: "The State, it is I!" To which the socialist dictator adds: "And I am God!"

It is the use of so-called democratic methods to achieve this result which deceives and confuses public opinion. We would resist to the end any effort of a foreign government to impose its political rule upon us. We are aroused today to the menace of a communism propagated and controlled by a foreign government, because we see clearly that here is an aggressive force seeking to destroy our individual liberties, which we still hold dear, seeking to deprive us of our rights and safeguards of self-government.

But when, in the name of self-government, we are called upon to abandon self-reliance, self-support, and self-service, and to trust and empower the government to provide us with economic security, we do not see clearly that we are being asked to rely on the aggressive force of government to rule our lives. The illusion that we can obtain security by organizing aggressive force against ourselves blinds us to the fact that we can, and by this method we will, establish a tyranny just as destructive of liberty, just as destructive of security and peace, as the tyranny of foreign aggressors.

We are being reassured, we are being misled, not by would-be tyrants, but by a large number of our well-meaning fellow citizens, most of them inspired by a sincere desire to end the hardships and inequities of a competitive system in which ruthless, greedy, unscrupulous men too often profit at the expense of less aggressive, less skillful, or less fortunate men, who are nevertheless better human beings.

What we are being deceitfully asked to do is to transfer controls over other men's lives from property owners, and others possessed of private economic power, to men wielding political power. We are told that the misuses of political power by public officials can be corrected by the political power of the people; that, by their power to vote their representatives into and out of office, the people will continue to rule their own lives. And so it is argued that economic power, instead of being concentrated in private hands and used for private gain, will be concentrated in public officials who will be compelled to use it for public benefit.

The truth is, however, that in our present competitive economy there is no concentration of economic power in a few hands, because even our biggest big businesses depend on the free buying power of millions of consumers. They must meet the continuing competition of other enterprises and other industries seeking to entice the consumer's dollar. But a government which can fix prices, regulate quantities and

247

qualities of products, tax away the consumer's purchasing power and exercise it for him, borrow indefinitely and inflate or deflate the currency—such a government, now developing in the United States, is concentrating more economic power in a few hands than has ever been wielded by any ruling class anywhere on earth. The creation of a vast, new, evil, monopoly power—certain to be abused—is what the socializers are really attempting—not the mere transfer of any present power.

It seems futile to repeat threadbare arguments to the effect that a multitude of large and small property owners can make a better choice of business leaders than a multitude of voters. It will probably be conceded that private businessmen can make their enterprises more profitable and productive than public officials selected because of their vote-getting abilities. It will probably be conceded that competition in production and selling and buying by millions of people will regulate the quantity, quality, and prices of goods more fairly and wisely than any bureaucracy. It may even be conceded that private insurance companies can provide better insurance against calamities, misfortune, and inevitable risks than any government agency.

But *** the great public services that have been and are being performed by thousands of business executives and financiers are discredited daily in the noisy attacks of fanatics and demagogues on the inevitable failures of a few to justify the confidence placed in their ability or integrity. Worst of all, our well-justified faith in the ultimate fairness, justice, and safety of a competitive system is being corrupted by intellectual theorists who argue that all competition is a survival of barbarism, and that civilized men should cease wrestling and fighting and racing for the prizes of life, and should work lovingly together for their common gain.

That is the dream of an inanimate heaven which has inspired Utopians for centuries. Civilization has made definite progress toward eliminating brutality and needless cruelty in competition. But the only time when the competitive spirit of a human being is stilled is when the human heart ceases to beat.

One can only wonder why the Creator made human beings competitive, and why human beings, in order to survive, have been compelled to fight, not only all the hostile forces of nature, but all the contentious forces of human nature.

No doubt Utopian politicians would decree the end of fogs, thunderstorms, earthquakes, and even darkness, if they believed there was any way in which a government could try to enforce a law against them. But, strange to say, these reformers do contend that the fundamental competitive nature of man can be transformed by government orders. They also contend that age-old differences of taste and morality can be obliterated by government orders, so that a Babel of races, religions, and languages that has afflicted the earth may be dissolved in a universal harmony, by government orders. To sum it up, they contend that a noncompetitive, selfless breed of human beings (whom God, in monumental error, failed to create) can be created by a government devised and operated by competitive, self-serving humans, as soon as they are properly indoctrinated as super-gods to smash "this sorry scheme of things entire and then remold it nearer to"—a fool desire!

\*\*\* Unhappily, there are millions of people who are being misled by the delusion that they can buy security simply by paying high taxes, and can still retain their liberties. That delusion is what gives the appearance of reality to the great illusion that a government can make its citizens economically secure.

For those possessed of this illusion, there is one possible cure. Portents of disaster and appeals to reason and healthy emotion seem commonly ineffective. Those who lack the vision to see what is ahead of them might now be asked to turn around, to open their eyes and to see what has already happened to them—to open their eyes and look back and see how in thirty-six years the United States, along with other nations, has abandoned the road leading to increasing security and peace for all mankind, and has been moving steadily down the road to perpetual insecurity and endless war. Recently our pace has been so accelerated that every day has seemed to bring the dawn of a new error.

A government which assumes the direct responsibility of assuring to all citizens a decent livelihood and financial security against competitive weakness, or against hardships resulting from unemployment, sickness, or old age, must plan and control our entire economy. Such a government must plan and control the operation of all important enterprises and the distribution of all income and products in conformity with government orders.

We can provide protection for the unfortunate and the incompetent without submitting to a controlled economy. We can alleviate the rigors of competition and prevent unfair competition. We can prevent and destroy or regulate private monopolies. But if we establish a governmental, monopolistic control of industry, we will create a vast, practically indestructible tyranny far more evil than the transient oppressions of a few private monopolies that can be readily destroyed.

There is no security for individuals whose livelihood depends upon political favor and political pressure. The greatest security ever given by government is found in the protection by government of the individual's freedom to work and live as he pleases, to acquire and use private property for his own support and protection, without fear of personal injury or loss of property through violence or fraud. The greatest insecurity threatens the individual when his earnings are taxed away substantially, so as to enable the government to use them for the benefit of others and to provide benefits and services for him as a dependent, regardless of his personal desires and needs.

If only the presently proposed programs of the so-called

Welfare State are put in effect, our government within a few years will, according to official estimates, be taxing away 40 percent of the average income.  Our cost of living has more than doubled since 1914, largely because of a politically promoted inflation and a politically devalued dollar.  What has happened to all the billions of dollars of life insurance and old age protection which we have individually saved and sacrificed to obtain? Year by year they have been eaten away, as prices and taxes have been forced upward and the value of the dollar we saved has been reduced to fifty cents.

Is this security?  Is there security in a government promise to pay pensions in dollars that are now worth fifty cents, and may be worth only twenty-five cents, or a dime, when the young men and women of today are old?  It is only the illusion of security that is offered by a government that organizes aggressive force to compel its own people to live their lives under the moral and economic dictates of a socialistic protectorate.

*EDITOR'S NOTE: The following extracts are from Mr. Richberg's Address at the Conference on The Welfare State, Harvard University, Monday, July 24, 1950:*

The so-called Welfare State is not an assured force for good merely because it proposes to organize a nation for universal service to the general welfare.  These were the proposals of Hitler, Mussolini, and Lenin.  These are the proposals of all socialists and dictators of the modern world.  On the other hand, modern free-enterprisers do not propose to organize a nation merely for the profit and glory of a favored few.  That concept of a "free economy" and the "survival of the fittest" is as dead as the dodo.

We will make more progress in our efforts to develop government in the service of the common good if we assume that this is the aim of both the socializers and the free-enterprisers, and if we then debate the real issue, which is: *What extent or limitation of government regulation of industry will be most effective to advance the general welfare?* In this debate we can assume that the accepted aim of our Society, and our reason for supporting a government, is to advance the general welfare.

What is called the Welfare State may be defined as a government which assumes the direct and unlimited responsibility of assuring to all citizens a decent livelihood and financial security against the hardships that may result from unemployment, ill-health, disability, or old age. Such a responsibility cannot be met without giving to the government power to plan and control the operation of all productive enterprises and the distribution of all income and products in conformity with government requirements. In such a Welfare State the function of all private associations which are engaged in, or affect, production or distribution must be to act as instruments or agencies of the government in meeting its assumed responsibility.

Even those who oppose the development of such a Welfare State ought to concede that it *is* the responsibility of our government to establish an adequate legal structure for a Society of men and women who are living and working together for mutual protection and correlative gains. But this legal structure should be an authentic House of Voluntary Cooperation in which citizens can organize and operate voluntary associations through which the opportunity to earn a decent livelihood and to gain financial security against hardships will be assured. The opponents of the compulsory Welfare State (a few million surviving "libertarians"!) believe that when political force is used to *compel* men to associate, and to operate their associations, in conformity with political programs, then the inherent vigor of a free people and a free economy is destroyed. They believe that our material progress will be retarded by this loss of vigor far more than it can be advanced by the disciplinary efficiency of compulsory cooperation. They are sure that our spiritual progress will become a spiritual retreat.

A good example of the two opposing concepts of government is found in the choice between government *protection* and government *control* of labor organizations. It has been our governmental policy for many years to protect labor unions from destruction by, or subservience to, the economic power of large employers. In order to promote an equality of bargaining power labor unions have been aided by law to organize wage-earners in such numbers that they could confront employers with a choice between paying good wages or being unable to operate their properties.

The economic powers of employers and of organized employees have been abused by both, but so long as neither could dominate the other the principle of voluntary cooperation has been maintained. The government has always had and should exercise a police power to correct these abuses—and even to require both parties to break deadlocks when their inability to agree becomes seriously harmful to the national welfare. But the use of police power to restrain and to punish wrongdoers is utterly different from the use of police power to conscript and to reward right-doers.

If, however, the government should assume an unlimited and direct responsibility for the wage earner's livelihood and security, government wage-fixing would become a continuing and imperative duty. Then the fixing of a wage for any important group of workers would require the equalization of wages for all other groups and, inevitably, the determination of reasonable prices for consumers and of reasonable compensation for the owners of properties which are used to provide employment or shelter or services for the workers.

We cannot forget that an underlying factor in the cost of living is the cost of products of the soil, the food, the fuel, and the raw materials of industry that are the products of agriculture, forestry, and mining. The largest factor in all costs is labor cost. How could a government assure a decent livelihood and employment to industrial wage earners without controlling all the other labor upon which the welfare of industrial workers depends? It should be evident to industrial labor that a Welfare State cannot meet its responsibilities to all the people without subjecting all the people to detailed regulation of the working and living conditions of all.

Indeed, the inevitable march of political control is now clearly forecast in the recent official proposal of our nascent Welfare State to guarantee an income to farmers. But what value would a guaranteed income have for farmers if there were no accompanying guarantee of the purchasing power of that income? How can a farmer's buying power be guaranteed unless there is a control of the prices which a farmer must pay for what he buys? How can industrial prices be controlled without a control of industrial labor?

The difficulty of persuading labor unions to support a Welfare State, which would enslave them, was met by the Socialist leaders of the Labor Party in Great Britain by promising a miracle. Sir Stafford Cripps (Chancellor of the Exchequer) said in February 1946: "No country in the world, as far as I know, has yet succeeded in carrying through a planned economy without the direction of labor. Our objective is to carry through a planned economy without the direction of labor . . ." Three years later, despite all its good intentions, the Labor Government had to announce the issuance of directions *compelling* men to remain in mining and in agriculture.

Of course there is no fair comparison between the cruelly enslaved labor of Russia and gently "directed" labor of Britain. It would be silly to prophesy that an American Welfare State would promptly enslave the industrial workers and the farmers who voted it into power. That would be as silly as calling the Taft-Hartley Act a "slave law." But it is even more silly to contend that a Welfare State can fulfill its promises, and guarantee a decent livelihood and financial security against hardship to all able-bodied citizens, without exercising a supreme authority to plan and direct the operation of all major industries and to determine the proper compensation and working conditions for all essential workers.

Advocates of the Welfare State insist that political programs backed by the coercive power of government force are necessary to advance the general welfare. Then why are they so anxious to pretend that there will be no use of force to regiment the workers into the service of a police state? Why do they not admit the truism that the promise of economic security through a politically planned and directed economy is a promise to use force to compel obedience to government directions? Why do they not offer their bribe to wage earners and farmers in plain terms which would be: "Give us your votes and, as the political representatives of your organizations, we will run the Welfare State so that your members will be left free from compulsory service and yet have economic security provided by taxing and coercing the rest of the people"?

The reason that there is no such candor, no such fundamental honesty, in the Welfare State program is that, when clearly explained, it becomes evident that the nascent Welfare State must become eventually a State of National Socialism, or else engulf us in the most calamitous depression of our history. It is no defense of National Socialism to assert that a complete socialization of our political economy might at least make it financially possible to maintain an orderly society under rigid control of a national police. But the attempt of a government to eliminate the incentives and profits of private enterprise, while relying on the taxes and capital produced by private enterprise to sustain its operations, is foredoomed to failure.

To make it plain why a Welfare State must become totalitarian or become insolvent, it is only necessary to reveal exactly how our government has been able to carry the enormous load of its present expenditures. The man-in-the-street is unwilling or unable to analyze this fiscal problem. But no student or teacher of political science can shun the tiresome task.***

1. We have devalued the dollar, borrowed over $200 billion,

255

and in various other ways have inflated our national income in *dollars* to 2½ times what it was twenty years ago.

2. We have increased taxes and federal expenditures from $31.60 per person in 1929 to $268.23 per person in 1948.

3. In addition to payments for national defense and interest on debt the national government is expending about $25 billion per year for the general welfare of ourselves and other people. There will be a serious question of our ability to finance the illimitable costs of another great war, if we continue thus to exhaust our financial resources.

4. The *introductory* program for a Welfare State which the President brought forward this year will add another $25 billion to annual national expenditures. This calculation was made by the staff of the Senate Committee on Expenditures in the Executive Departments, and was reported to the Senate by the committee chairman, Senator McClellan. He estimated that the *increase* in the tax burden to pay for this initial program would be $166 annually for every man, woman, and child in the United States, and that *total* federal taxes would then amount to 30 percent of present national income.

5. If we add state and local taxes to the federal, this would "make the annual tax obligation of the American people more that 40 cents out of every dollar they earn."

6. The major part of all taxes are, and must be, paid by persons of small or moderate incomes.

7. As the voters become too much exhausted or exasperated by increased direct taxation of incomes, political spenders resort more and more to indirect taxes, concerning which millions of people are either ignorant or strangely indifferent. The indirect taxes paid today by the average family have been carefully computed to exceed $700 per year. When direct taxes on small incomes are added, it becomes a proven fact that the average wage earner's family is already paying over $1000 a year for the support of an infant Welfare State that has only just begun to bite!

Any competent student of the fiscal and operating problems of the infant Welfare State must see that with the development of its vast public projects, taxation will become so confiscatory, the regulation of management and labor so detailed, private property rights so reduced, and private enterprise so smothered by political controls, that the emergence of the mature Welfare State as a State of National Socialism is inevitable.

Apparently the concealed justification for taxing people so that the government may spend their individual earnings to advance their individual welfare is that the masses of the people are morons who should not be trusted to spend their own money. It is assumed that they should be glad to have their money spent for them by professional politicians trained and experienced in the art of spending other people's money. Of course this argument isn't made openly because even humble people resent being treated like children. So they are told that they are made more secure by investing their money with politicians than with businessmen. Businessmen are pictured as cold, greedy, fat exploiters, while politicians are those genial backslappers who call you by your first name and work day and night to find ways to buy things for you with your money which you wouldn't buy for yourself.

There are many things of common use which may wisely be paid for through government, such as roads and parks and common school facilities. But the Welfare State proposes to take more and more of a man's earnings to buy things for his *individual* use which he ought to be free to buy less or more of according to his individual need or desire. It proposes to substitute a common standard of living and a common, compulsory pursuit of happiness for the individual rewards and the individual pursuit of happiness which have inspired the American people to raise themselves through voluntary cooperative enterprises to the highest standard of living, coupled with the greatest individual liberty, ever enjoyed by 150 million human beings.

But why shouldn't you buy your own health insurance, or

any other insurance against misfortune, from your own selected insurance organization? Millions upon millions of people have done it. Why shouldn't you organize voluntary cooperatives to buy and sell things for you? Millions of people all over the world have done it. Why shouldn't you use your own labor organizations to provide unemployment insurance either alone or in cooperation with employers? Labor unions can pay strike benefits when men refuse to work; why should they not pay unemployment benefits when men are unable to find work?

The point which I am trying to make briefly is that the *major offerings of a Welfare State are simply offerings to do for you what you can do better, more cheaply, and with greater satisfaction, for yourself.* In so doing you can save yourself from dependency on political favor, political integrity, and political wisdom, those three weak reeds upon which no man who has common sense and a knowledge of history will ever wish to become dependent—three weak reeds upon which no man who has a backbone of self-reliance will be willing to lean.

If, on the other hand, we were resolved to preserve the proven vigor and productiveness of a system of private enterprise, we have ample evidence that we could meet our social responsibilities without accepting a compulsory socialism. We could go forward patiently to expand the cooperative powers of our present private, voluntary associations. The government would lend its aid in legalizing such collective projects as the organization of corporations, cooperatives, trade unions, and trade associations, and the government would impose such restraints as are necessary to prevent private monopolistic controls of commerce, and to preserve competition and a free purchasing power as the natural and impartial regulators of prices and production.***

There are two major excuses for substituting political support for self-support, and political discipline for self-discipline, which merit brief discussion.

One is the excuse that because some men make too much

money out of others, they should be compelled by taxation to share their gains with those whom they exploit; or, because some localities are more prosperous, their gains should be shared with poorer localities. Let us disregard the counter-argument that the forced service of the more competent to the less competent and the leveling down of humanity to a common standard of living is not a democratic but a communistic doctrine. Nevertheless, we may well agree that the exceptional profits of fortunate individuals or favored communities should be taxed away to maintain the common defense and to promote the general welfare. But it is a proven fact that if every dollar of income in excess of a fair compensation for personal services, or for the use of private properties, were siphoned into the United States Treasury, this would provide only part of the federal revenue needed to pay for national defense, national administration of justice, and national expenditures for public works of general value. A major part of all essential public revenues must be obtained by a direct or indirect tax deduction from the earnings of the great mass of workers of small or moderate incomes. So the revenues of the expanding Welfare State will necessarily come from increased deductions from the earnings of those who are the proclaimed beneficiaries of this additional government spending.

The second excuse for a paternal collection and spending of a worker's earnings is that voluntary cooperation will fail to advance the welfare of the cooperators as far as compulsory cooperation would. It is argued that the thriftless or unfortunate, who most need protection, will not or cannot insure themselves. It is also argued that in any industry a chiseling minority will break down the best devised programs for preserving an ideal balance between producing and consuming power. As one of the administrators of the notable NRA experiment, I am familiar with these arguments and believe that I can appraise their merits with the aid of an unusual amount of experience and with, perhaps, an unusual impartiality of judgment. I still believe in the voluntary self-government of industry, which was the announced objective of the NRA. I never believed in the compulsory political government of industry which NRA dabbled in, while floundering down the road to Limbo.\*\*\*

Once upon a time it was the supreme law of our land that there was no "due process of law" by which our national government could deprive a man of the liberty to support and protect himself and his dependents by his free labor and his free use of his own earnings. The government could only tax him to support the strictly limited powers of the government to provide for the common defense and the *general* welfare. It could not tax him to enable the government to take care of his *individual* welfare or the *individual* welfare of his neighbors. It could not deprive him of his "unalienable right" to take care of himself, or to make a fool of himself.

But, today, following the socialist dogma that the individual citizen should be made the bond servant of the general welfare, the courts have invented a new "due process of law" with which the national government can deprive a farmer of the right to raise grain on his own land for his own consumption, unless he obeys government orders limiting the amount of grain he can raise and fixing the prices at which he can sell it. Today, the national government, by using this new "due process of law," can deprive a worker of the right to spend, to save, and to invest his own earnings as he wishes, for the economic support and protection of himself and his family. He can now be compelled to pay taxes which transfer a substantial part of his earnings to the government so that it can then provide such economic protection for him and for others as the government decides to be in the interest of the general welfare.

If ten to twenty percent of a man's subsistence earnings can be taken from him today, there is no legal barrier against taking from him thirty to forty percent tomorrow, which, according to British precedents, will be required to support a young Welfare State. In such a political economy, of what use will be private, voluntary associations, except to serve as pressure groups to try to elect and control public officials so that, in the political distribution of a worker's earnings, he may get back as much as possible after paying a few million political employees for spending his money for him?

For such lowly and limited functions private associations may survive in the Welfare State. They may also serve to maintain the illusion that we are a free people, free to organize, to debate, and to petition the government for the redress of grievances, subject, of course, to laws restricting and controlling lobbying and propaganda, so that a dominant political party will not be unduly hampered by a too vigorous opposition.

It would not be accurate to define associations as "private" or "voluntary" which are, and will be, organized and maintained by political aid to make effective government regulations. Such associations might well be compared to "company unions," which national trade unions have always denounced as mockeries of voluntary organization.

Here is a summary answer to the question presented for this discussion: *Private, voluntary associations, as an influential factor in our political economy, will not and cannot survive in a compulsory Welfare State.* Their powerful influence in the expansion and enrichment of our American way of life will disappear in the politically planned and directed economy of National Socialism.[1]

---

[1] I would like to refer to the stimulating and comprehensive exposition of our capacity and willingness to meet these responsibilities, which is presented by a representative group of industrial leaders in a book entitled *The New Outlook in Business,* published by Harper & Brothers in 1940. When I list, among the twenty-two authors, Paul G. Hoffman, Richard R. Deupree, Robert E. Wood, Walter D. Fuller, and Wallace Brett Donham, you will understand why I think that a reading of this book would be more enlightening than any further argument by me. Also, I believe that the plans and programs of these practicing economists offer more trustworthy guidance than those of the theorizing economists who are befuddling the American people today with roseate visions of a make-believe Welfare State.

# ECONOMIC CONSEQUENCES OF GOVERNMENT SPENDING*

BY WALTER E. SPAHR†

CONCERNED citizens, who wish to do what they can to arrest the unsound and possibly dangerous practices in government spending and fiscal management and the relatively rapid decline in the purchasing power of our dollar, need to understand the significant elements in this disturbing state of affairs in which we find ourselves today. Proper corrective measures presuppose such understanding.

The following analysis is offered for such value as it may have in our collective consideration of our present unfortunate situation.

Although the huge spending by our Federal government has both its peace- and wartime phases, each with many facets, there has been throughout the period, particularly since 1932, the basic issue of the wisdom of government economy versus lavish government spending.

---

* Lecture under the auspices of the New Jersey State Bar Association, "The National Economy in Time of Crisis; Its Meaning to Lawyers and Their Clients," 1951, pp. 17-30; the original title was "Economic Implications of Government Spending." Because of the further light they throw on the subject, the selected questions and answers have been retained.—*Ed.*

† Professor Spahr has been Chairman of the Department of Economics, New York University, since 1927. Since 1946, he has served as Executive Director of the Economists' National Committee on Monetary Policy. A distinguished economist, Dr. Spahr is the author of many articles and books on economic and monetary subjects.

The Roosevelt Administration was elected to office in 1932 on a political platform which committed the Democratic Party to a program of economy in government. The 1932 Democratic Platform, in respect to the issue of economy, pledged the Administration to the following:

"An immediate and drastic reduction of governmental expenditures by abolishing useless commissions and offices, consolidating departments and bureaus and eliminating extravagance, to accomplish a saving of not less than 25 percent in the cost of Federal Government . . . Maintenance of the national credit by a Federal budget annually balanced on the basis of accurate Executive estimates within revenues, raised by a system of taxation levied on the principle of ability to pay . . . A sound currency to be preserved at all hazards . . ."

In giving his enthusiastic endorsement to these and other planks of that platform, in his radio address from Albany, July 30, 1932, Mr. Roosevelt said, among other things: "Any government, like any family, can for a year spend a little more than it earns. But you and I know that a continuation of that habit means the poorhouse."

One week after assuming office, President Roosevelt sent a message to Congress in which he called for drastic economies in government expenditures. Among other things he said: "Too often in recent history liberal governments have been wrecked on rocks of loose fiscal policy. We must avoid this danger."

On April 1, 1933, he sent a message to war veterans asking them to share in the spirit of sacrifice since he had issued an order on March 31, which, he said, "reduced materially all benefits of war veterans." On May 25 and June 10, executive orders were issued providing for the consolidation and abolition of some government agencies.

These steps seem to have marked the end of the program of government economy. By that time a general reversal of policy in respect to economy versus lavish Federal expenditures was under way. Symptomatic of the change, which was soon to be pronounced, was the announcement of President Roosevelt on May 10 that he would restore some of the contemplated cuts in veterans' benefits.

By early July, 1933, the spending program was definitely in the saddle in the manifold form of provisions for relief, aid to various industries and groups, the creation of a great variety of government lending institutions, public works programs, and a multitude of similar enterprises.

## VALIDITY OF THE ROOSEVELT ECONOMY PLATFORM OF 1932

Past experience provided good evidence in support of government economy as a means of aiding economic recovery, although Mr. Roosevelt made insufficient allowance in his campaign for the need for a central government to do what it properly can to aid in providing relief and in stimulating recovery in time of a severe economic recession, and for the fact that such efforts may involve a temporarily unbalanced budget as was the case under the Hoover Administration during the recession of 1929-1932.

For example, the business recovery of 1921-1923, following the sharp drop in prices and production in 1920-1921, took place without there being a program of pump-priming or deficit financing by the government. Indeed, that sharp recovery occurred under government policies which were almost the exact reverse, on practically all major features, of the government spending program asserted by its advocates, particularly after mid-1933, to be necessary to induce or to maintain business recovery. In the years 1920-1923 ordinary expenditures declined each year, ordinary receipts exceeded expenditures each year and, furthermore, public debt retirement exceeded $400 million per year. Nor did the Federal government manipulate or depreciate the currency in any way. There was then

264

no important acceptance of the doctrine that currency devalu-ation or depreciation in some other form was a proper means of aiding a business recovery.

Furthermore, in the first four months of the Roosevelt Administration in 1933, during which period the officially an-nounced policy was that of government economy, the index of industrial production showed, apparently, the sharpest recovery of any four months on record.

These two recoveries, under programs that were almost di-rectly the opposite of those of the advocates of Federal spending, seem to be passed over in silence by the defenders of lavish spending. The omission of this and similar pertinent evidence by those economists who have supported the spenders raises the question of the scientific quality of their methodology.

Further examples of "similar pertinent evidence" which seems generally to be passed over in silence by the advocates of lavish Federal spending include: the persistence of heavy un-employment from mid-1933 up to our entrance into World War II; the persistently low level of the flow of new capital into busi-ness enterprise for the years 1933-1941—a level below that of the years 1920 and 1921; and the persistent fall in the velocity of bank deposits which by 1940 had reached a level much below that of the depth of the depression in 1932.

## STATISTICAL HIGHLIGHTS OF FEDERAL FINANCE SINCE 1933

Federal expenditures started on an upward course from the $3,983 million for the calendar year 1933 until they reached $95,594 million for the peak war year of 1944. Thereafter, they fell to $31,113 million for 1947 after which they rose to $41,370 million for 1949 (all calendar years).

Any attempt to classify Federal expenditures even for one year would involve us without profit in a mass of detail. The nature of these expenditures has been a matter under general discussion in recent years. The evidence of profligate waste of our national patrimony has been painfully apparent every day since this spending orgy began.

Every fiscal year from 1933 to 1950, inclusive, except the years 1947 and 1948, produced a deficit in the Federal budget. These deficits ranged from a low of $1,177 million in 1938 to a high of $57,420 million in 1943. The surpluses were $754 million in 1947 and $8,419 million in 1948.

The Federal debt (including guaranteed obligations) started from $22,539 million for the fiscal year 1933 and reached its peak of $269,898 million in 1946. At the end of the fiscal year 1950 it stood at $257,377 million. The Oklahoma Public Expenditures Council has estimated that at the end of 1929, the Federal debt of $16.6 billion amounted to $571 per family. At the start of World War II in 1939, the debt of $39.9 billion amounted to $1,165 per family. At the end of the year 1950 the debt of $257.1 billion amounted to $6,710 per family.

## MONETIZATION OF THE FEDERAL DEBT

The Federal Reserve System and commercial banks became closely linked with Federal financing and absorbed a large volume of Federal securities. Much of this debt became a basis for the expansion of our currency—money and deposits.

The Federal Reserve authorities tied the activities of the Federal Reserve banks closely into the fiscal affairs of the Federal government chiefly by cooperation with the United States Treasury in the maintenance of the prices of government securities bearing low interest rates. This involved a relatively heavy purchase of government securities. Commercial banks followed along in the shadow of Federal Reserve and Treasury policies.

The Federal Reserve banks held $1,998 million of U. S. Government securities on June 30, 1933. By December 31, 1945, they held $24,262 million. On November 22, 1950, they held $19,296 million. On this last date, total Reserve bank credit outstanding was $20,162 million, of which the $19,296 million represented by U. S. Government securities constituted 95 percent.

Of the $24,018,017,000 of Federal Reserve notes outstanding on November 22, 1950, $10,900,000,000 were covered by United States Government securities deposited by the Federal Reserve banks with their respective Federal Reserve agents.

All commercial banks held $10,307,000,000 of U. S. Government securities on June 30, 1934. By December 31, 1945, they held $90,606,000,000. As of October 25, 1950, their holdings were $62,530,000,000. On this last date, their total credit outstanding was $124,490,000,000 which meant that 50 percent was composed of U. S. Government securities. These represented over 5 times their capital accounts of $11,580,000,000. The time deposits of these banks ($36,370,000,000) and their capital accounts of $11,580,000,000 equaled, on October 25, 1950, $47,-950,000,000 as compared with the $62,530,000,000 of U. S. securities held. If we assume that capital accounts and time deposits can properly be represented by government securities, these banks are overloaded, on this basis, in the amount of $14,580,-000,000—that is, by more than their capital accounts.

The dangers in this picture lie also in the small ratio of capital to this volume of government securities, in the non-self-liquidating character of the securities, in the fact that three-fourths of them have a maturity of one to over ten years, and in the ease with which they can be turned into reserves at the Federal Reserve banks, on which reserves a multiple expansion of deposit credit can be built.

Corporations and credit agencies of the Federal government, now too numerous to list here, have expanded until their assets as of June 30, 1950, were $24,118,000,000.

## THE IMPLICATIONS OF FEDERAL SPENDING

The Tax Foundation, in its *Facts and Figures on Government Finance* (for 1950-1951), lists total Federal, state, and local expenditures for 1949 as $59,661,000,000. Of this amount, Federal expenditures were given as $41,370,000,000—approximately 70 percent of total government expenditures for that year. Total government spending is then related to that statistical estimate called "gross national product" which, for 1949, was given as $255,578,000,000. For that year, Federal expenditures amounted to 16.2 percent of gross national product. For the war years 1942-1945 the percentages ranged from 34.8 to 44.7.

Possibly those figures bring us information as reliable as any we can obtain as to the proportion of government to total expenditures. But there are many questions that may be raised as to the value of those data.

If, say, 40 percent of total spending during a year is by the Federal government, does the latter have a proportionate effect on prices? That does not necessarily follow. We generally measure prices by means of the index of wholesale prices. It is merely a mathematical abstraction of the sample prices of the commodities which comprise that index. In this fairly large list of commodities, it probably is not possible for one to determine with any high degree of accuracy what the government is buying or the relative influence of Federal spending on prices in general. Sometimes, in respect to certain commodities, a fairly accurate determination of government influence can be made.

Government expenditures for war are primarily for destructive purposes, and much unnecessary waste seems invariably to accompany such expenditures. Then we have other large Federal expenditures for subsidies, agricultural parity and control programs, foreign aid programs such as those of the Marshall Plan and military aid, the various welfare programs of the government, and so on.

As this money flows into circulation, people's incomes in

general are increased, and we regard the expansion in national income as evidence of prosperity despite the fact that much of the money income represents goods that are destroyed or not produced (as in cases of payments for nonproduction), and, consequently, are not available for use as part of our real wealth.

We seem to forget that money incomes, in the aggregate, can be raised to any height by pumping a depreciated currency into circulation. We seem to forget to analyze what is happening to our real wealth when a government destroys it, or gives it away, or prevents the type of production that adds to our real wealth.

Our government in recent years, particularly since 1939, has been in the business of destroying and giving away our national wealth to an extent never before seen by the people of this nation and never before seen or practiced by any other nation in the world. The dissipation of our national patrimony is a phenomenon in the history of human profligacy. It is unmatched in world history.

In general, the government has been a factor of importance in both stimulating and obstructing productive activity. The influence of the government during World War II stands out clearly; and any adult person, with only modest insight into such matters, should be able to understand that those high indexes of industrial production represented production for destruction and loss, not the type of production that adds to a nation's real wealth.

Following that war and the attendant constriction in production for civilian use, efforts were made to catch up with our pressing needs in the civilian field. This kept the index at a fairly high level, though much below the indexes of war years. Yet no one could properly say that the lower postwar indexes did not represent more production of goods for civilian use than did the higher indexes of the war years. Now we are shifting again to production of the instruments of destruction and are restricting and creating new maladjustments and scarcities in the field of civilian activities.

## PRODUCTION, PRICES, AND THE
## MANAGED CURRENCY

A summary picture of the behavior of the index of industrial production for selected years may be of some value. This index, based upon the average for the years 1935-1939 as 100, and adjusted for seasonal variation, shows an increase from 54 in March, 1933 (the low was 53 in July, 1932), to 86 in July, 1933. This was during the period in which the official policy was supposed to be that of reduction in Federal expenditures. By November, 1933, the index had fallen back to 69. By May, 1937, the peak before the recession beginning in that year, the index had reached 121. By May, 1938, it was down to 80. In December, 1941, when we became directly involved in World War II, the index stood at 168. The peak of 247 was reached in October and November, 1943. By February, 1946, it was down to 152. In October, 1950, it was at 215.

Perhaps the most important questions for us to ask ourselves as we consult the index of industrial production are these: What does this industrial activity involve? Does it add to or destroy our real wealth? Are there waste and destruction involved that can be eliminated?

For general purposes, the common practice is to use the index of wholesale prices to determine the price level, since it is our most comprehensive index of prices. Taking 1926 as the base year at which the average of prices at the wholesale level is fixed at 100, we find that on January 23, 1951, the wholesale price index stood at 179.9. This gave the purchasing power of the dollar on that date, as compared with the 100 percent of 1926, a value of 55.5 percent. That was the lowest purchasing power on record, up to that time, since the Federal Reserve System was established in 1914.

This unprecedented record of a depreciated dollar since 1914 has been made under a system of what is commonly called a managed currency—meaning a managed irredeemable currency.

When this nation was led into an irredeemable money system in March, 1933, the theory soon developed to justify it was that, if the money managers were freed from the restrictions imposed upon them by a redeemable currency, they could provide the people of the United States with a currency having a more stable purchasing power than would otherwise be possible. To use President Roosevelt's words of October 22, 1933: "When we have restored the price level, we shall seek to establish and maintain a dollar which will not change its purchasing and debt-paying power during the succeeding generation."

The proof that the intended and promised purpose has not been attained now confronts these money managers, but they apparently have made no admission of their error in offering their contentions.

The fact should be recognized that an index of a price level is a mathematical abstraction of the prices that enter that index. Each commodity has its own forces of supply and demand which determine its price. There are millions of prices, of which those in the index number are but samples. The forces that determine all the prices of all commodities at any time are beyond human knowledge or power to measure. The influence of government spending on the price level cannot be isolated from all other forces that are operating. Consequently, it cannot be estimated in any precise manner.

Lying beneath the index of the price level is the very important question of the harmony or lack of harmony in price relationships which comprise that mathematical abstraction. For instance, a fairly steady price average may obscure severe maladjustments. The unusually steady price level of 1923-1929 ended in a severe economic collapse. Furthermore, while a stable price level indicates an unchanging purchasing power of the dollar in general, the purchasing power of the dollar for

271

civilians may be zero in respect to goods taken by the government and denied to civilians.

It is always necessary, therefore, to look behind these indexes and aggregates to determine what the facts are. For example, an increase in the national product figure is supposed to measure an increase in our economic well-being despite the fact that a government can force such a figure to any level by depreciating a nation's currency.

## TOTALITARIAN NATURE OF KEYNESIAN THEORY

The advocates of a governmentally managed economy, particularly the economists of the Keynesian school, have since 1933 been stressing the virtues of what is commonly known among economists as the compensatory principle of fiscal and monetary management.

In general, the contention is that stability and prosperity can be had only if the government through fiscal and monetary management compensates for what such economists regard as the failures of private enterprise. One feature of this theory is that in times of prosperity and full employment the government's budgetary program should yield a surplus, taxes should be relatively high, government spending should be reduced, there should be pressures against an expansion of the currency. Conversely, if there is a recession in business activity and something less than full employment, government spending should be increased, the Federal budget should show a deficit, the currency in circulation should be expanded.

This theory has two chief characteristics: (1) It would require a centralized planning agency with the power to act—and this would mean government dictatorship. Congress would be compelled to abdicate and to place its constitutional duties and prerogatives in the hands of this central planning and enforcement agency with practically absolute power over the nation's fiscal and monetary affairs. (2) The theory is essentially academic in nature, for in practice it has proved to be a drive in one direction—that of persistently heavy Federal spending, an unbalanced Federal budget year after year, heavy taxes, persistent monetization of much of the Federal debt, a persistent and serious depreciation of the dollar.

Nevertheless, the principles of compensatory government planning are still discussed with the utmost seriousness by a large proportion of our economists just as though they are working, or can be made to work. Furthermore, the fact that such a theory involves a totalitarian form of execution is a matter that they apparently assume need not be discussed. Presumably, such planning, control, and management are supposed to be acceptable and accepted without question as to their wisdom.

## WHERE WE NOW STAND—AND WHAT TO DO ABOUT IT

The situation in which we now find ourselves includes these chief features: We are involved in another war—the second within a decade. Our Federal government is still spending the people's money at a frightful rate. The practice of running Federal deficits continues. Taxes are dangerously high. The government is still using irredeemable currency and is still monetizing the Federal debt through the improper use of the banking structure. Our non-gold currency circulates abroad only with diminished honor. Artificially low interest rates are still maintained in order to make government borrowing and spending easy. The purchasing power of the dollar of the people of the United States is now at the lowest level on record since 1914.

All correctives I am about to suggest are directed at dangerous or undesirable practices other than war.

(1) It is supposed to be a fundamental truth that next to war mankind has never devised a more injurious instrumental-

ity than an irredeemable currency. Since this belief seems to rest upon fact, our government should institute a redeemable currency promptly.

(2) The monetization of the Federal debt through the banks should be terminated. The independence of the Federal Reserve System from government fiscal and debt-management policies should be established.

(3) The government should go to the open markets for its funds and pay the interest rates required to obtain the needed funds. These interest rates are one of the devices by which a people help to regulate government spending.

(4) Since money in the hands of those who earned it has a greater value than in the hands of a government which did not earn it and which pays no penalties for wastefulness and bad judgment, government expenditures and taxes should be kept at the lowest possible level at all times, and the Federal budget should be balanced as regularly as possible.

(5) The monetized Federal debt should be driven from the banks and into the hands of savers by being funded at a rate of interest sufficiently high to induce savers to purchase such securities. The commercial banks should then return to their proper functions of financing agriculture, commerce, and industry.

(6) The practice of the government in giving away the people's wealth should be ended. Where matters of charity arise, those who wish to give should be provided with the opportunity to do so, but compulsion is not defensible.

(7) Similarly, direct lending by the government should be ended except in those instances in which national security is involved. The business of our government lending institutions should be shifted to private enterprise and the government lending institutions should be liquidated except in those cases in which such liquidation would endanger our national security.

(8) Our Congress and Administration should return to Constitutional government. They should respect and adhere to the basic principle that our Federal government is one of

delegated powers and that all powers not specified or clearly implied are reserved by the people to the states and to themselves. This applies to our international as well as our domestic activities.

(9) We should make clear to ourselves what dictatorship means and then fight it in all its forms to the best of our respective abilities.

## THE FREE MARKET VERSUS STATE CONTROLS

We are revealing in this country that we do not know the difference between the objective standards of right and wrong provided by the free and fair operation of the forces of competition and the subjective standards of dictatorship.

If all buyers and sellers determine a price under conditions of free and fair competition, that price is proper because it is determined by all who give up money or goods in exchange. It is objective for the reason that no individual could control it. If some outsider insists that the price is too high or too low, he is employing a subjective or arbitrary standard. That is the standard employed by the dictator. It is simply a question of his wish or will and of his power to enforce his will. There is a classical expression for that law which rests upon the will of the dictator. It is: *"Hoc volo; sic jubeo; sit pro ratione voluntas"* which means, *"This I will; thus I order; let my will be in place of reason."* That is the practice of tyranny. There is no standard of right binding alike on the ruler and ruled when the will of the ruler becomes the basis of law. Under such a system "states are," said Mr. Justice Dore, "what St. Augustine called them, 'great bands of robbers.'" That is what happens when the subjective is substituted for objective standards of justice.

The science of economics exists only insofar as it rests upon the objective standards provided by the operation of the forces of free and fair competition. Every other type of appraisal in the economic world is subjective in nature and, therefore, merely a case of wishing or of enforcing one's will when one has the power to do so.

Our confusion between the subjective and objective in the field of economics is a national tragedy. Our economic literature and discussions are chiefly subjective in nature. Personal opinion and desires, and efforts to force one's arbitrary will on others, have practically replaced science in the field of economics. The subjective has crowded out the objective. Dictatorship and would-be dictatorship are booted and spurred and are riding the people of the United States into areas in which much of their proper freedom is lost and in which their future appears, increasingly, to be that of wards of the state.

Our only hope would appear to be that we may yet have the good luck to obtain effective leadership in statesmen who know the difference between the subjective and the objective, and between responsible and intelligent government and dictatorship.

## SELECTED QUESTIONS AND ANSWERS

*Question:* If the government were to re-establish a redeemable currency, such as a gold coin or bullion standard, how can the hoarding of gold be prevented, particularly in the light of present inflationary pressures?

*Answer:* The importance of that question is that it reflects the psychology that prevails among people when they have an irredeemable currency. When a redeemable currency is instituted, the psychology is changed. If one can get gold, one does not ordinarily desire it. It is inconvenient to handle; one loses the interest on it; what one wishes to know is that he can get it if he desires it.

When John Sherman was preparing to bring this country back to a redeemable currency in 1879, there were all sorts of fears expressed and threats made regarding it. One banker said that he would give $50,000 to stand first in line in New York City on the day of resumption, January 2, 1879. They started resumption on January 2, and there was $135,000 of gold demanded, and over $400,000 of gold turned in for paper. We have no record of any action on the part of that banker who offered $50,000 to stand first in line.

The normal hoarding of gold in this country, insofar as our statistics go, has been, roughly, nine percent of the gold stock. We have approximately 22.5 billions of dollars of gold today, and if, say, $2 billion were drawn into circulation, that, I should think, would be beneficial.

There is no record, insofar as I know, of a resumption of specie payments in this or any other country that has given rise to a run on banks for gold.

Let me call to your attention the fact that when the banks were failing in 1929, 1930, and 1931, people were not running for gold; they were running for cash. There was no run for gold of any importance until late in January and in February, 1933, and that was nearly all done by foreign banks in anticipation of devaluation which they understood was coming.

In 1932, from August on, and into January, 1933, we had a net importation of gold into this country every month; and when the banks closed on March 6, 1933, our gold stock was only a little below the highest level on record—the $4,708,-000,000 of August 31, 1931.

There is nothing on record except people's fears of redeemable currency that holds people back when it comes to advocacy of resumption.

*Question:* Exactly how does the purchase by commercial banks of government bonds increase the currency in circulation six- or seven-fold?

*Answer:* The average reserve ratio required by the typical bank—a member bank of the Federal Reserve System—is between one-sixth and one-seventh of its deposits. Therefore, for every dollar of reserve, these banks can have deposits six or seven times the amount of reserves insofar as the system as a whole is concerned.

To be more specific, we classify our commercial banks into three groups as to basic reserve requirements against demand deposits: those requiring seven percent, ten percent, and thirteen percent against such deposits. And against time deposits the minimum required is three percent. Today, we have double those reserve requirements: fourteen percent, twenty percent, and twenty-six percent, and the reserve against time deposits is six percent.

If one takes an average of those out, one will get roughly just about sixteen percent as the ratio required on the average, considering a six percent reserve against time deposits. So we commonly say today that one can multiply every dollar of reserve six or seven times and get the possible expansion of deposits in the banking system.

*Question:* Please explain in A-B-C language how the sale of government bonds to commercial banks promotes inflation.

*Answer:* When bonds are sold to commercial banks by the government, the bank does not turn cash over to the government; it gives the government a deposit on its books, just as it does if one of us should take government securities to the bank and sell them to the bank or borrow against them. One's account would be increased by the amount of securities sold to the bank. Therefore the deposits in the banks expand as the Federal Government sells bonds to the banks. Commercial banks can expand deposits in this manner because they hold fractional reserves against their deposits.

*Question:* What is your suggestion as to the best method for arousing the people as to the necessity for returning to those principles which were departed from in 1933, and a return to which is essential to the national welfare?

*Answer:* In my judgment there are several things one can do about the issues involved. One can write letters to his newspaper and perhaps they may be published; perhaps not.

Another thing is to write one's congressman and senators. One can ask each whether he intends to be a politician or a statesman. He can be surrounded with leading citizens and perhaps be turned into a statesman.

I do not know of anything else to suggest. One can talk about popular education to the end of time, but the mass of people do not understand the issues discussed here. The mass of the people generally seem to want the very thing that hurts them in the fields of money and fiscal affairs. They generally want irredeemable currency. They want more money as expenses increase. They are conscious chiefly of one thing under such conditions: they need more money and, therefore, they will almost invariably advocate the very thing that will hurt them.

There is not a case in history of which I am aware in which the mass of people have demanded a sound currency. The role of the people in general is to get hurt. The correction of a bad currency comes when statesmen emerge and provide the people with a sound money. Some of us are seeking another John Sherman or another Carter Glass, and we are getting our answers slowly, one by one. We are learning this lesson: Those who have replied seem reluctant to say "no," but they also fail to say "yes." Perhaps in due time a John Sherman may appear.

## ॐ ॐ RELIANCE ON NONGOVERN-
## MENTAL SELF-HELP

BY THE EDITORS OF *Life*

### THE MONSTER CALLED "BUDGET" *

*To Regain Control of It, Congress Must Vote Itself the Tools*

T HE President's budget, a 5-3/4-pound, 1316-page volume, asks for $85.4 billion of new appropriations,
about a billion dollars an ounce.   But even more oppressive
than its size is this fact: nobody, except a few of the experts who
prepared it, will comprehend this budget before it is translated
into law.   It will not be subjected to intelligent over-all analysis
by Congress or by anybody else.   Would-be critics read it and
throw up their hands.   *The Wall Street Journal* found "no way
to get hold of it.   So monstrous as to defy reasoned comment."
In any sense congenial to U. S. political principles, our national
budget is out of control.

This alarming fact antedates the rearmament program.
The budget is out of control not because the Pentagon wants
$52 billion, but because a vast executive bureaucracy—that
"giant power wielded by pygmies," as Balzac called its French
counterpart—has become an autonomous and self-perpetuating
feature of our national life.   The budget is out of control
because, as *Fortune* says in a special February issue devoted

---

* Editorial, *Life* Magazine, February 4, 1952.

entirely to the U. S. Government, the executive machinery has grown "too complicated for the human mind to follow."

Of the budget's $85.4 billion, less than $100 million is for Congress and the judiciary; the rest is for the executive branch. Of the 2.5 million civilians employed by the government, 2,490,-000 work for the executive. And these are the people who prepare the budget. Thousands of budgeteers in scores of executive departments and agencies work the year round, each concentrating on a tiny segment of the whole. Like spring freshets into the Father of Waters, their little estimates flow wider and deeper into the great pool of 500 experts called the Bureau of the Budget, where the figures are vetted, cut somewhat, and made to look simpler and more inevitable than they are. The bureau is the last area of over-all comprehension in the budget process. In January the dam is raised and Congress, to which the U. S. Constitution gives the power of the purse, begins its annual folk rite of pretending to command the waters. Command them it does not.

Take the military budget. The Pentagon put millions of manhours into its preparation; its chief auditors are a subcommittee of seven overworked congressmen with a few clerks. A serious inquisition is simply beyond their capacity. Platoons of brass with stacks of charts can make even the vaguest justification sound like the national interest. Said one Representative last year, "The Congress is at the mercy of the executive."

In this plight economy-minded congressmen have taken to demanding across-the-board percentage cuts. Last year they brandished a 10% ax; Senator Ferguson now talks about 17%. Truman calls this method of economy unconstitutional. It is better termed a blind congressional groping for its lost constitutional pursestrings. What offends every basic principle of the Constitution is Congress' impotence before the fiscal monster which predecides everything.

Taking just one of the President's nine Cabinet departments, Interior, *Fortune's* special issue shows how it has grown too vast even for its present secretary to control. (See also *Life,* March 24, 1947.) Interior's budget over the years shows the steady, relentless growth of all bureaucracies, punctuated by occasional leaps, as under the Ickes regime when it increased by 347%; since then it has nearly doubled again (to more than $600 million). But Interior is actually just a name for 19 semi-autonomous and self-expanding bureaus, some of which conduct imperial rivalries with each other (Parks *vs.* Power over dam sites, *e.g.*) and have their own lines to Congress, where they set up echoing rivalries. The Bureau of Reclamation aggressively politicks for more dams whether Congress wants them or not. Such a bureau is not daunted by lack of demand for its services; it goes out and creates one. Among its other functions Interior controls one-third of all the land in 11 Western states, including 82% of Nevada and 59% of Utah. It openly aspires to control the power facilities of 97% of all the running water in the U. S. No extant force seems capable of stopping it.

In setting up our tripartite federal system of checks and balances, founding fathers like James Madison feared that Congress, with its enormous paper sovereignty, might swallow our liberties in an "impetuous vortex" of legislative power. What has happened instead is that Congress has got lost in the executive vortex. Says *Fortune* flatly, "The legislative machinery, which is the heart of democracy, is breaking down. The American Congress is foundering."

Congress is still very good at conducting investigations and its theoretical powers are intact. (As Senator Fulbright said last week, "We have the power to do any damn fool thing we want.") But if Congress is to regain real power of the purse, it must radically change its behavior toward the budget. It must learn to make a budget itself.

The Congressional Reorganization Act of 1946 made a stab at this, setting up a joint committee to fix a ceiling on expenditures. After three unsuccessful attempts at this "legislative budget," Congress backslid into partial and emergency appropriations which deny it an over-all fiscal view. Now Senator McClellan has a bill to revive the joint committee and give it the kind of staff which would enable it to operate the year round. These staffers would sit in on all major phases of executive budget-making, check expenditures at their source, and come out knowing as much as the President's Bureau of the Budget about the appropriations requested. This would at least give Congress some real weapons against the monstrous power of executive bureaucracy, instead of mere incantations.

And Congress had damn well better pass some self-reforming acts and give itself these powers. Otherwise the federal budget will remain the incomprehensible sign of America's creeping retreat from political self-control to tyranny through ignorance.*

## THERE IS ANOTHER WAY!†

*Americans Can Achieve "Security" Without Relying on the State*

The idea of the Welfare State is becoming part of the air we breathe. Individuals may denounce it in the abstract,

---

* When Harry Truman was a senator investigating military expenditures during World War II, he remarked that in the armed services "tremendous sums of money are thrown away with a scoop shovel." Occasionally Congress still catches the Pentagon with scoop in hand. Sample discoveries by Senator Lyndon Johnson's preparedness subcommittee:

In a four-month period 153 staff officers and men of the Submarine Force got hazardous-duty pay (about a third extra) for 18,000 man-days, whereas all but 525 man-days were spent ashore.

The mess at Carswell Air Force Base had a 5-year supply of leaf oregano (a "little-used" spice). The coffee issue also backed up so fast that the sergeant used 200 pounds of it "as sweeping compound for the floor."

Thanks to senatorial needling like this, the Army has set up a "cost-consciousness" program, putting price tags on tanks at training camps, etc. Each little bit helps. But when confronted with a military budget like this year's $52 billion, Congress cannot possibly see where the waste is.

† Editorial, *Life* Magazine, March 27, 1950.

but when it comes down to specific cases—a crop support, a postal subsidy, a pension, a grant-in-aid for a scholarship— practically everyone finds a personal rationalization for taking from the State when and where he can. Since the drift of history is in the direction of the Welfare State, it may appear utterly quixotic to stand in the way of a seemingly ineluctable fate.

Nevertheless, we persist in taking the risks of quixotry. We recognize all of the seemingly inevitable compulsions that have caused people to think they can get an absolute guarantee of security from government. Any guarantee of security that pretends to be absolute is, of course, a delusion. But insofar as security can be had, we insist there is a practical alternative to the Welfare State that is worth wide popular discussion. We insist that history might go off on a new and creative tangent if people were only minded to pause and think the alternative over for a bit.

The practical alternative to the Welfare State is not something called *laissez faire,* or Rugged Individualism, or any of the other pejorative phrases for capitalism. We would be tempted to call the alternative the Welfare Society if we didn't distrust the obsessive connotations which the word "welfare" has come to have. Insofar as security must be one objective of the good society (other and more important objectives are productivity, excellence, creativeness, adventure, honor, and the chance to take a chance), our practical alternative to the Welfare State would concern itself with many welfare devices. In our preferred type of society the means to security would be reliance, not on government, but on organizations promoted by the people themselves. In our society people would predominantly prefer to experiment with their own forms of association for mutual aid.

Seeking health, the people would not run to government for medical aid. Instead, they would turn to Blue Shield and Blue Cross and similar medical insurance societies. In the interests of freedom, the well-to-do would willingly pay a higher Blue Cross rate than those in the low income brackets. Doctors would practice "group medicine," pooling their mechanical facilities for diagnosis (always an expensive item for the individual) and working out fee schedules that would allow low income families to join Blue Cross societies for a nominal sum.

Our society would encourage cheap housing. It would not, however, put its reliance on government to get it. In a self-reliant society, labor unions, for example, would use their treasury surpluses to enable their members to get housing money at low interest rates. Unions would buy tracts of unimproved land and pass individual plots along to members without charging a subdivider's fee. Middle-class people who want homes would enroll in building and loan societies. They would save their money and lend it back to themselves at a low interest rate. They would study the history of housing in Great Britain, where the Building Societies staged a terrific housing boom in the 1930's without government help.

In our society monopolistic prices would cease to exist. They would be progressively undercut and eliminated by consumer cooperatives, of which there would be a steadily increasing number. The potentialities of such a movement have already been demonstrated in the Scandinavian countries, where the cooperatives not only sell to their members at prices close to cost but also go into manufacturing many articles for themselves.

Social Security must be one objective of any society in which the aged are expected to retire. In our society people would get security by establishing either industry-wide or regional nongovernmental public corporations, with public-spirited citizens of wide business experience and proven competence functioning as directors. The public social security corporation would invest its capital in industry on a "balanced fund" basis—one-third of the money in bonds, one-third in preferred stocks, one-third in high-grade common stocks. By following this method, the social security corporation would plow the people's funds back into production—and the production, in turn, would provide for real security.

We are not suggesting here that government has no role to play in helping people. Such things as education, road-building, flood control, and soil conservation, since they involve a general welfare that cannot always be promoted on a large and efficient scale by voluntary private organizations, must involve some measure of governmental action. But even in these areas there could be more, rather than less, reliance on voluntary organization. People in rural areas have been helping themselves for years by establishing voluntary Conservation Districts. There are even instances of nongovernmental river control projects—the Muskingum (Ohio) Watershed Conservancy District is one such instance.

In following us on our little voyage to an imaginary country it will have occurred to readers that we have not been projecting a series of utopian hopes; we have merely been describing what some people are doing already. We have merely been listing a number of specific voluntary welfare mechanisms that have already proved themselves in practice. Private pension plans, Blue Cross and Blue Shield medical insurance, housing societies, consumer cooperatives, public corporations, and voluntary soil conservation districts are old stories. They are success stories, too. And that is precisely our point: welfare on a self-reliant basis is not a vague utopian hope but a very practicable possibility. People can have it if they want it. We are sure that they would want it in increasing numbers if they stopped to think it over.

*EDITOR'S NOTE: In the issue of September 26, 1949, the Editors of* Life *stressed the opportunities offered by "Welfare Capitalism," in the light of the President's Steel Industry Board's report. The ideas here included deserve serious con-*

*sideration by management and labor in the interest of both
and of the general public.*

The report of the President's Steel Industry Board is a
great event.   It is a great event because it shows U. S. enterprise the way toward a true Welfare Capitalism which can
anticipate and fend off the authoritarian solutions of the Welfare State.   In rejecting a fourth-round wage increase and
placing the emphasis on individual security through insurance and pensions, the fact-finding board significantly altered
the patterns of union-management bargaining and has opened
a promising new chapter in industrial relations.   Therefore
it is regrettable that the first result of the report should be a
threat of a huge strike throughout the steel industry.   Philip
Murray of the steel union does his cause a disservice when
he tries to make the report the basis for a squeeze play, and
Mr. Fairless of Big Steel is within his rights when he insists
that bargaining and coercion are two different matters.   The
opportunity presented by the report is so large, the actual
issues are so capable of settlement, that the Messrs. Murray
and Fairless owe themselves and the country a reasonable
attempt to reach reasonable agreement without a strike.

Heretofore the bargaining—and fighting—between workers
and management in the major industries has been mainly over
such things as wages and hours.   With the emphasis put on
insurance and pensions, the problem of where a man stands
in long-time relation to his employer and to his industrial
society has been brought to the fore.   The results are bound
to have a powerful catalytic effect on the reshaping of U. S.
industry—and of U. S. society as a whole.   The trend is already apparent: since the early '30's, when there were only a
few hundred, more than 12,000 pension or profit-sharing plans
have been submitted to the U. S. Treasury.   These plans
cover upward of four million workers.   Such pioneering ad-
ventures in Welfare Capitalism are in the American tradition,

and they reflect the chief hope of escaping the illusory promises of the Welfare State. But it was not until this past summer that there was much reason to hope that a big basic industry like steel could see its way toward incorporating some
really significant Welfare Capitalist features.

Let it be said as strongly as possible that the widespread
introduction of security programs in industry will require
tremendous changes, tremendous adjustments to new costs and
new problems. It cannot be done with a union bulldozer,
and any attempt to bulldoze at the start may wreck the whole
prospect. What is practicable for U. S. Steel, for example,
may not be practicable at all for smaller producers like Alle-
gheny Ludlum or Inland Steel, and Mr. Murray must know
as much. The whole process must be bargained out company
by company. And the issue of worker contribution *vs.* total
financing by the employer must be seriously considered. From
every standpoint—bearable costs, the self-reliance of the individual worker, the values of direct participation in enterprise—the presumption should be in favor of some contribution by the worker.

Management may feel that insurance and pension schemes
are ransom devices to buy off the Welfare State. Nobody likes
to pay ransom, for once you have paid it you may be called
upon to pay over and over again. However the case for
Welfare Capitalism has nothing to do with ransom—it has
its own positive justification. Without conceding that the
20th Century individual is either helpless or irresponsible,
we recognize with the President's board that the business of
exercising prudence *** is a complicated matter. Lacking
a base on productive land, lacking the tools and often the
opportunity needed to engage in small business, the 20th Century worker needs the help of his group, his employer, his
society in establishing security for himself. Management has
people who are used to dealing with the statistical aggregates
involved in the modern practice of prudence, and the indus-

trial worker is entitled to their help in calculation. True, he might get the same type of help from a private insurance agent, but the very demand for other means of security is sufficient evidence that a larger approach is needed.

Perhaps Mr. Fairless should take it as a compliment that the burden of prudence is put up to his administrative force. That amounts to a vote of confidence in steel management. What remains to be seen is whether unions will in fact leave the administration of prudence to management, and whether its assumption by management will result in a notable increase of worker efficiency. Human nature is admittedly perverse, but we think it's a pretty good gamble. If a person's old-age pension is tied up with the prosperity of the Widget Manufacturing Company, it is fairly safe to assume that he will work a little harder for his company's success. The positive case for Welfare Capitalism is that it could add up to a more efficient, more successful productive system all around. It challenges the worker to make himself part of a richer, more meaningful adventure than anything that might come to him through any political channel.

With one aspect of the board's report we take sharp exception: its statement that the worker is a "machine" to be depreciated like any other. Men are manifestly not machines, and the value of worker security to management is in what it does to stimulate day-to-day production during the worker's effective life. Who can calculate the net gain in efficiency that might accrue from a widespread Welfare Capitalism? All that can now be said with any assurance is that the steel industry, in common with other basic industry, has a major opportunity for exploration ahead of it. We hope the steel companies will put their best brains to work on both the actuarial and the efficiency realities involved in pension and insurance programs. We hope also that Philip Murray's steel union will realize that patience is needed while a start is being made toward a great objective.